JOURNAL FOR THE STUDY OF THE OLD TESTAMENT
SUPPLEMENT SERIES

96

Editors
David J A Clines
Philip R Davies

JSOT Press
Sheffield

ANNOUNCEMENTS OF PLOT IN GENESIS

Laurence A. Turner

Journal for the Study of the Old Testament
Supplement Series 96

For my parents Allan and Winifred
who first taught me the Scriptures

Copyright © 1990 Sheffield Academic Press

Published by JSOT Press
JSOT Press is an imprint of
Sheffield Academic Press Ltd
The University of Sheffield
343 Fulwood Road
Sheffield S10 3BP
England

Typeset by Sheffield Academic Press
and printed on acid-free paper in Great Britain
by Billing & Sons Ltd
Worcester

British Library Cataloguing in Publication Data

Turner, Laurence B.
    Announcements of plot in Genesis
    1. Bible. O.T. Genesis—Critical Studies
    I. Title   II. Series
    222.1106

ISSN 0309-0787
ISBN 1-85075-260-5

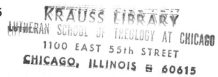

CONTENTS

ACKNOWLEDGMENTS

This present volume is a slightly revised and shortened version of a Ph.D. thesis submitted to the University of Sheffield in November 1988 and I would like to take this opportunity to acknowledge the assistance given to me during its preparation. My supervisor, Professor David J.A. Clines, gave liberally of his time, advice and encouragement, and patiently endured my improbable suggestions over a period of three years, as well as giving a careful scrutiny to the final proofs of this book. In addition, other members of staff and numerous post-graduate students in the Department of Biblical Studies helped me to clarify my thinking. I would also like to thank Avondale College, Cooranbong, New South Wales for granting me study leave, to my colleagues in the Theology department of that institution for the confidence they placed in me, and to the South Pacific Division of the Seventh-day Adventist Church for giving me generous financial support for the entire period of my research. The chagrin I felt at being considered an alien in my native land was offset by being given an ORS award by the Committee of Vice-Chancellors and Principals and my thanks goes to that body as well. Last, but not least, I would like to acknowledge the love and support given to me by my wife Anne, and children Jonathan and Lisa, without whom this book would not have been completed.

ABBREVIATIONS

AB	Anchor Bible
AnglThR	*Anglican Theological Review*
BangThF	*Bangalore Theological Forum*
BibKir	*Bibel und Kirche*
BibLeb	*Bibel und Leben*
BibThBull	*Biblical Theology Bulletin*
BN	*Biblische Notizen*
BR	*Biblical Research*
BZ	*Biblische Zeitschrift*
BZAW	Beiheft zur *Zeitschrift für die alttestamentliche Wissenschaft*
CBQ	*Catholic Biblical Quarterly*
CBQMS	Catholic Biblical Quarterly Monograph Series
CTM	*Concordia Theological Monthly*
CurrThM	*Currents in Theology and Mission*
EglTh	*Eglise et Théologie*
EThR	*Etudes Théologiques et Religieuses*
EvTh	*Evangelische Theologie*
ExpT	*Expository Times*
GThJ	*Grace Theology Journal*
Hexateuch	Gerhard von Rad, *The Problem of the Hexateuch and Other Essays*, trans. E.W. Trueman Dicken (Edinburgh and London: Oliver and Boyd, 1966).
HorBibTh	*Horizons in Biblical Theology*
HUCA	*Hebrew Union College Annual*
ICC	International Critical Commentary
IDB	George Arthur Buttrick (ed.), *The Interpreter's Dictionary of the Bible*, Nashville: Abingdon Press, 1962.

IDBS	Keith Crim et al. (eds.), *The Interpreter's Dictionary of the Bible*, Supplementary Volume, Nashville: Abingdon Press, 1976.
ISBE	Geoffrey W. Bromiley et al. (eds.), *The International Standard Bible Encyclopedia*, Grand Rapids: Eerdmans, 1979–88.
JBL	*Journal of Biblical Literature*
JETS	*Journal of the Evangelical Theological Society*
JJS	*Journal of Jewish Studies*
JNES	*Journal of Near Eastern Studies*
JQR	*Jewish Quarterly Review*
JSOT	*Journal for the Study of the Old Testament*
JSOTS	Journal for the Study of the Old Testament Supplement Series
JTS	*Journal of Theological Studies*
KD	*Kerygma und Dogma*
LexThQ	*Lexington Theological Quarterly*
LIBN 1	Kenneth R.R. Gros Louis et al. (eds.), *Literary Interpretations of Biblical Narratives*, Nashville: Abingdon Press, 1974.
LIBN 2	Kenneth R.R. Gros Louis and James S. Ackerman (eds.), *Literary Interpretations of Biblical Narratives*, Nashville: Abingdon Press, 1982.
NRTh	*Nouvelle Revue Théologique*
NotDEngJ	*Notre Dame English Journal*
OTS	*Oudtestamentische Studiën*
PerRelSt	*Perspectives in Religious Studies*
PTh	*Le Point Théologique*
PTMS	Pittsburgh Theological Monograph Series
RB	*Revue Biblique*
RefThR	*Reformed Theological Review*
RelEd	*Religious Education*
RestQ	*Restoration Quarterly*
RevTh	*Revue Thomiste*
RevThPh	*Revue de Théologie et de Philosophie*
SBL	Society of Biblical Literature
SBTh	*Studia Biblica et Theologica*
SémBib	*Sémiotique et Bible*
StRel	*Studies in Religion / Sciences Religieuses*
StTh	*Studia Theologica*

TaiwJTh	*Taiwan Journal of Theology*
TDOT	Johannes Botterweck and Helmer Ringgren (eds.), *Theological Dictionary of the Old Testament*, trans. John T. Willis, Grand Rapids, Michigan: Eerdmans, 1974–.
ThD	*Theology Digest*
ThZ	*Theologische Zeitschrift*
VC	*Verbum Caro*
VT	*Vetus Testamentum*
VTS	Supplements to *Vetus Testamentum*
WBC	Word Biblical Commentary
WestThJ	*Westminster Theological Journal*
ZAW	*Zeitschrift für die alttestamentliche Wissenschaft*

INTRODUCTION

The aim of this book is to investigate the plot of the Genesis stories. Narratives in general have several ways of alerting readers to what is likely to transpire in the story as it unfolds, or how to make sense out of what they have just read, and Genesis itself uses several such conventions. For example, it prefaces some individual stories with headlines which give advance warning about the significance or meaning of the ensuing narrative, as in 22.1: 'After these things God tested Abraham'. This headline does not tell us *why* God wanted to test Abraham, but it informs us that if we are to read 22.2ff. correctly, we must view it from this perspective. Another technique is to reveal only at the end of a story the information that will help give coherence to the preceding narrative, or perhaps allow the reader to perceive coherence at a deeper level than has been possible up to that point. An example of this is 45.8, where despite Yahweh's apparent absence from the previous episodes in the story of Jacob's family, Joseph reveals that Yahweh had indeed been present and active: 'It was not you who sent me here, but God'. It must be conceded, however, that on the whole the Genesis stories lack such 'notes to the reader' and that in the perception of coherence and plot, the reader is left on his or her own with the text. There are important exceptions to this, however, for Genesis does employ what might be termed Announcements of plot. Each of the four major narrative blocks which comprise the book (i.e. the primaeval history and the stories of Abraham, Jacob and Jacob's family) is prefaced by statements which either explicitly state what will happen, or which suggest to the reader what the major elements of the plot are likely to be. Thus the initial divine command to humans in 1.28 sets out in a brief compass what human beings are supposed to do, and it is a natural question for the reader to ask whether in fact what is expected to happen actually does happen. Similarly, 12.1-3 outlines the basic form of the promise which will sustain the entire Abraham story, and subsequent repetitions, ratifications, refinements and additions underline the importance of this introductory statement. In the Jacob story (chs. 25–36), the divine oracle to Rebekah in Gen. 25.23, and Isaac's blessings which later reiterate and expand it (Gen. 27.27-29, 39-40), serve to define the relationships between Isaac's sons, which maintain the reader's interest for much of the subsequent narrative. In the concluding story, that of Jacob's family, Joseph's dreams (Gen. 37.5-11), and the possibility of their fulfilment, set the scene for the story as a whole and provide much of its dramatic tension. While passages which drop clues concerning plot development are interspersed throughout the Genesis stories, it is significant that statements which have an explicitly programmatic purpose are set right at the beginning of narrative cycles.

My purpose is, therefore, to explore the relationship between these Announcements and the subsequent plot. Because the Announcements cause the reader to expect the plot to develop in certain ways, one key consideration will be the fate of the individual Announcements. Does the plot in fact develop as the Announcement leads us to believe? If so, in what way, and if not, in what way not and why not? Thus the question concerning the fulfilment or non-fulfilment of the expectations aroused by any given Announcement will be to the fore in this study.

It is not to be expected that everything following the initial Announcement of plot will be, or *can* be, directly related to it. Some narrative elements will obviously be more important than others when the reader is reading from *any* perspective, and we will undoubtedly classify narrative events hierarchically according to the strength of their connection with the Announcement. Thus, as far as discerning plot is concerned, some elements can be deleted without disturbing the logic of the plot (although it might well diminish the narrative aesthetically).[1] However, there may be occasions where a certain section is deemed to be of little value, or even irrele-

---

[1] Scholes and Kellogg, *Narrative*, p. 211.

vant, on a first-time reading, only to be elevated to a position of some importance when, retrospectively, the plot is viewed in its final shape. Additionally, we should not be surprised if the unfolding of the plots in the Genesis stories does not flow smoothly from the Announcements. In fact, if these truly are *plotted* narratives, we must allow for the possibility of surprise, mystery and complication, which are essential elements in any plot worthy of the name.[1]

Initially, my purpose is to investigate the plot of the individual narrative blocks rather than attempting to discover *the* plot of Genesis. Whether there is such a thing as *the* plot of Genesis we shall have to wait to discover until the whole book has been canvassed. Another aspect I will address at the end of this study is whether the plots of individual narrative cycles share any common features. Is there a pattern of plot development common to all Genesis stories or is each distinct?

There has been some debate in literary theory over what constitutes a 'plot', and without attempting to enter this debate it would be appropriate for me to set out here the concept of plot I shall be employing. In a much cited illustration Forster distinguished between a story (probably better defined as a chronicle), and a plot thus: '"The king died and then the queen died" is a story [chronicle]. "The king died and then the queen died of grief" is a plot.'[2] The reason Forster gives for this distinction is that although both statements present events in their chronological sequence, only the latter provides the *cause* of the queen's death, thus linking the two events at a level deeper than that of mere chronology. It has been pointed out by several scholars, however, that even the first of Forster's statements can be construed by the 'causally-minded reader' to contain an 'implicit plot'[3] and that

---

[1] Forster, *Novel*, p. 88; cf. Scholes and Kellogg, *Narrative*, p. 212.

[2] Forster, *Novel*, p. 87.

[3] Rimmon-Kenan, *Narrative Fiction*, p. 17; cf. Chatman, *Story and Discourse*, pp. 45-46:

> The interesting thing is that our minds inveterately seek structure, and they will provide it if necessary. Unless otherwise instructed, readers will tend to assume that even 'The king died and then the queen died' presents a causal link, that the king's death has something to do with the queen's.

'temporal succession is sufficient as a *minimal* requirement'[1]
for a plot. Seen from this perspective, it may even be argued
that 'a narrative without a plot is a logical impossibility'.[2]

The events within Genesis are presented, generally speaking, in chronological order, and as such the narratives carry
an 'implicit plot' for the causally-minded reader. In addition,
however, the Announcements of plot which preface the narrative cycles prejudice the reader to look for specific elements
and causal links in the reading of the narrative, i.e. the reader
is not left to his or her own devices to manufacture a plot, but is
guided by the Announcement as to how the narrative should
be read, even where connections between the narrative elements are not stated explicitly. Aristotle observed that a plot
requires a beginning, a middle, and an end.[3] The Announcements which will be the focus of my study may be seen as the
beginning of the plot (or, at least, the single most important
element in that beginning). The *middle* and *end* of the plot
flow from that beginning and will be read in the light of that
beginning.

It is not one of my aims to discover the original intention of
the author(s). No author can be fully aware of the 'meaning'
of his or her work or of the effect it will have on its audience.
This is especially true when, as seems likely in the case of
Genesis, much of the material utilized in the creation of the
final form of the literary work has had prior independent existence.[4] While granting that such a history lies behind our present text, I will adopt an agnostic stance toward such questions
as authorship, date and composition of the book. I am concerned entirely with the final form of the text. As such, source-

---

[1] Rimmon-Kenan, *Narrative Fiction*, p. 18. Cf. Scholes and Kellogg,
Narrative, p. 207:

> Plot can be defined as the dynamic sequential element in narra-
> tive literature... Spatial art, which presents its materials simul-
> taneously, or in a random order, has no plot; but a succession of
> similar pictures which can be arranged in a meaningful order
> (like Hogarth's Rake's Progress) begins to have a plot because it
> begins to have a dynamic sequential existence.

[2] Chatman, *Story and Discourse*, p. 47.
[3] Chatman, *Story and Discourse*, pp. 53-54.
[4] Cf. the comments of Webb, *Judges*, p. 39.

critical and traditio-historical considerations are largely irrelevant for and counter-productive to my present interests. It will become apparent in the following chapters that passages usually assigned to disparate sources can often yield coherent meaning when read together rather than being contrasted and read in isolation. Thus, a particular passage can yield a significantly different meaning when read within the final form of the book than when it is read only within the context of other exemplars of its own hypothetical source. I do not consider it worthwhile entering into debate with those who believe that because a book may ultimately be composed of disparate sources 'we cannot be satisfied simply with interpreting the biblical books in their present shape'.[1] I simply disagree, if for no other reason than the fact that there *is* such a thing as the book of Genesis, while the sources which went into its composition, and the reconstructed history of the book's redaction are hypothetical and are once again the centre of intense debate.[2] That is to say, we do know what the book of Genesis is; whether we will ever know how it came into being is another matter.

In addition, I will attempt to read Genesis as a first-time reader, unaware at any point of what the next development in the plot may be and ignorant of the way in which subsequent narratives both inside and outside the book may utilize material from Genesis. I will have occasion to point out passages where commentators have read certain elements of the narrative solely in terms of later developments. This is a perspective, I would suggest, only possible and legitimate when one has read the whole book. Constantly to be looking ahead of the point one has reached in the text is to do a disservice to the book. There can be a significant difference between the meaning of an element 'in the story so far', and its meaning when read retrospectively, having finished the book.

I do not approach Genesis with any rigid methodological

---

[1] Fretheim, 'Jacob Traditions', p. 436.
[2] For an indication of the diversity of views in modern scholarship see generally the following: van Seters, *Abraham*; Schmid, *Der sogenannte Jahwist*; Rendtorff, *Das überlieferungsgeschichtliche Problem*; idem, *Das Alte Testament*; Whybray, *The Making of the Pentateuch*.

presuppositions other than those outlined here. My focus is upon interpretation and not methodological theory. This is done, not to spurn the literary theory to which I am indebted, but to lay emphasis on the simplicity of the task I have set myself. I find myself in sympathy with recent authors who provide a reading which draws its inspiration from contemporary literary discussion, but who do not set out to advance discussion of the theoretical base of the methodology.[1] I will attempt to read the Genesis stories as a simple naive reader, trying to discern their plots, and assuming that the final form of the text, and this text alone, is the only legitimate source for my investigation. While the task I have set myself is a simple one, I make no apologies for this, as it does address crucial questions which have been largely ignored by more methodologically sophisticated studies.

A number of works have been devoted to explicating the final form of the individual narrative blocks[2] and indeed of the book as a whole.[3] However, none to my knowledge has undertaken a comprehensive study of the whole book from the perspective I am advocating here. Some have seen the significance of what I have termed 'Announcements of plot'[4] but have either followed up this insight on source-critical

---

[1] Cf. Long (ed.), *Images*, especially the editorial comments on p. 4; Webb, *Judges*, passim. The comments of Gunn, *King Saul*, p. 16, are particularly germane:

> I am not persuaded that every scholar needs to be a philosopher of method. That is a valuable role for some to assume, but there is a danger that when the commonality of critics (in which I include myself) is absorbed by the deep puzzlements of 'methodology' all too little actual criticism (interpretation, exegesis, or what you will) of the text gets done.

[2] E.g. Seybold, 'Paradox and Symmetry', pp. 159-74; Fishbane, 'Composition and Structure', pp. 15-38; Miscall, 'Jacob and Joseph Stories', pp. 28-40; McGuire, 'Joseph Story', pp. 9-25; Ackerman, 'Joseph, Judah, and Jacob', pp. 85-113; Greenstein, 'Equivocal Reading', pp. 114-25.
[3] E.g. Dahlberg, 'Unity of Genesis', pp. 360-67; Cohn, 'Narrative Structure', pp. 3-16.
[4] E.g. Brueggemann, 'Kerygma of Priestly Writers', p. 400; *idem*, *Genesis*, pp. 290, 296; Gibson, *Genesis*, 2.12; von Rad, *Genesis*, p. 265.

grounds,[1] or because of the nature of their work have not developed the insight in any depth.[2]

The English translations of the Hebrew text which occur in this volume are usually taken from the RSV, except in those cases where my interpretation depends upon a particular nuance of a term or construction. In these cases I have provided my own translation.

---

[1] Cf. Brueggemann, 'Kerygma of Priestly Writers', p. 400; von Rad, *Genesis*, p. 265.
[2] E.g. Gibson, *Genesis, passim.*

Chapter 1

THE PRIMAEVAL HISTORY

Introduction

The purpose of this chapter is to investigate the relationship
between the divine Announcement to humans in Gen. 1.28
and the subsequent plot of Genesis 1–11.[1] While the exact
meanings of certain terms need to be clarified before they can
be investigated fully, the Announcement prefacing the
primaeval history is less opaque than certain elements of the
other Announcements we will investigate:

> And God blessed them,
> And God said to them,
> > 'Be fruitful and multiply,
> > and fill the earth
> > and subdue it;
> > and have dominion

---

[1] The significance of Gen. 1.28 has been seen by Brueggemann,
'Kerygma of Priestly Writers', pp. 397-414. However, he views it from a
source-critical perspective and treats it in relation to the 'P' narratives
only:

> We suggest that the formidable blessing declaration of Gen 1 28
> provides a focus for understanding the kerygma of the entire
> tradition...

> These five verbs [be fruitful; multiply; fill; subdue; have domin-
> ion], I suggest, are the central thrust of the faith of the priestly
> circle.

Westermann, *Genesis 1–11*, p. 143, sees the programmatic nature of
Gen. 1.26-28, but does not expand on this observation. Smith, 'Structure and Purpose', p. 311, posits a two-fold structure for the primaeval
history, within which the phrase 'be fruitful and multiply and fill the
earth', 'has an overpowering theological emphasis... It is the key
theological focal point in the two parallel sections of Genesis 1-11.'

over the fish of the sea
and over the birds of the air
and over every living thing that moves
upon the earth'.

This Announcement divides easily into three main imperatives:

(i)   Be fruitful and multiply and fill the earth;
(ii)   Subdue the earth;
(iii) Have dominion over the animals.

I shall take each of these elements in turn and see how successful human beings are in turning divine expectations into
reality. I acknowledge that these are not independent units
and that there are degrees of interrelationship between them,
but they do form distinct concepts within the divine
Announcement. Initially, the exact connotations of all of these
imperatives may not be clear. However, the story so far does
enable the reader to view these statements within the context
of the Creation account, in which God has 'filled' the earth
with 'fruitful' creatures, and in his effortless creative act has
demonstrated his 'dominion'. Initially, therefore, the human
task must be seen as somewhat analogous to God's actions in
the days of creation, especially when we remember that
humans were created in the image of God (1.26-27). The
reader, at this stage, must be optimistic that these divine
imperatives will be obeyed, in the light of creation's immediate
and obedient response to God's previous commands in ch. 1.
However, an investigation of their fate in chs. 1–11 reveals a
much more complex picture.

Be Fruitful and Multiply and Fill

This injunction is not one unique to the human species. The
formula 'be fruitful and multiply and fill...' has been delivered
to the sea creatures (1.22b) and the creatures of the air have
been told simply to 'multiply' (1.22c). While this command is
not given to the land animals (1.24-25), it is clear that fertility
and multiplication are not blessings and imperatives[1] reserved

---

[1] Lohfink, '"Seid fruchtbar"', p. 80, insists that 1.28 functions not as a

for humans alone. Yet their importance for humans in particular is underlined by the *tôlᵉdōt* formulas which punctuate
the book as a whole[1] and give it a 'reproductive' framework.
(See below.)

Apart from the brief statement in 2.18 that it was not good
for the Man to be alone (one implication of this being that in
his single state he cannot reproduce), the multiplication motif
does not surface again until the divine curses of 3.14-19,
where the entire Announcement of 1.28 is complicated by
Yahweh Elohim's response to the human offence. I will give
details of the relationship between 1.28 and 3.14-19 in my
treatment of the individual motifs below, but a summary here
will help to show the main lines of relationship. Each of the
three main concepts of 1.28 is modified in 3.14-19 to show that
their fulfilment will be far more troublesome than originally
expected. The dominion which humans should have exercised
over the whole animal creation is now qualified by the ongoing
struggle between the seed of the serpent and the Woman
(3.14-15). The command to humans to subdue the earth is
made much more difficult to fulfil through the cursing of the
ground, its producing thorns and thistles, which will result in
toil and sweat for humans engaged in agriculture (3.17-19).
In a similar manner, my present concern, the imperative to
'be fruitful and multiply and fill the earth', is taken up by
Yahweh Elohim's words to the Woman:

> I will greatly multiply your pain in childbirth [pregnancy];
> in pain you shall bear children,
> yet your desire shall be for your husband
> and he shall rule over you. (3.16)

Childbirth is the means by which the imperative to multiply
will be fulfilled, but here it is made into a painful and troublesome affair—at first sight a disincentive to human procre-

---

command but as a blessing. (Cf. Gilbert, '"Soyez féconds"', p. 741).
While it is true that 1.28a states *wayᵉbārek 'ōtām ᵉlōhîm*, the
'blessing' God delivers contains five imperatives. The Announcement
is both blessing and command: the capacity to be able to perform these
functions is indeed a blessing, but the imperative form underlines the
necessity of so doing. Cf. Kautzsch, *Gesenius' Grammar*, p. 324.

[1] See Gen. 2.4; 5.1; 6.9; 10.1, 32; 11.10, 27; 25.12, 19; 36.1, 9; 37.2.

ation. Also note the irony in the curse. In 1.28 humans had
been commanded to 'multiply' ($r^eb\hat{u}$); in 3.16 what actually
multiplies (*harbâ 'arbeh*) is 'your pain in childbirth'.[1] In other
words, 'In multiplying your pain will be multiplied by me'.
However, what Yahweh Elohim takes away with one hand he
gives back with the other. Having seemingly discouraged
women from giving birth he adds a complexity to the curse[2] by
announcing that the Woman's sexual appetite will continue
unabated—'your desire shall be for your husband'.[3] Thus the
future of the imperative to multiply is guaranteed although it
will become a painful experience for the women who carry it
out.

With the curse delivered in the Garden complicating the
Announcement of 1.28, the first episode outside of the Garden
illustrates how humans cope with the responsibility of fulfill-

---

[1] 'I will greatly multiply your pain *and* your childbearing' is probably
an example of hendiadys. See Westermann, *Genesis 1–11*, p. 262;
Wenham, *Genesis 1–15*, p. 81.

[2] Ogden, '"Curses" of Genesis 3.14-19', pp. 131-32, argues on form-
critical grounds that 3.16 is not a curse. According to Ogden, 3.14-15
and 3.17-19 'are the most expanded curse forms in the OT', while 3.16
lacks both an *'ārûr* formula and an object of the curse, which for him
are the bare minimum requirements for identifying a curse. While
3.16 may not be a *formal* curse, I would hold that it is at the very least
curse-like. Further, it cannot be denied that it modifies in a negative
way the Announcement of 1.28.

[3] Foh, 'What is the Woman's Desire?', pp. 376-83, argues that $t^e\check{s}\hat{u}q\hat{a}$
(desire) should not be translated as *sexual* desire. On the basis that
$t^e\check{s}\hat{u}q\hat{a}$ in 4.7b carries no sexual overtones, she believes that 'the
woman has the same sort of desire for her husband that sin has for
Cain, a desire to possess or control him'. Thus she interprets 3.16b as
having two antithetical parts:

    (i)   You (Woman) shall attempt to control your husband.
    (ii)   But he will master you.

However, it seems to me that Foh argues from the context of 4.7b,
while ignoring the context of 3.16b. *Sexual* desire would be out of place
in the context of ch. 4, but entirely appropriate in 3.16 where the curse
is concerned with childbearing. Also, it may not be irrelevant to point
out that the subsequent narrative shows little evidence of women
trying to control their husbands (the obvious exception being Rebekah
in 27.5ff.), but with the multiplying of the human race there is plenty
of evidence for the survival of sexual desire.

ing its demands under this new regime. Surprisingly, 4.1-2
shows humans working assiduously to obey all three of its
dictates. On the matter of multiplying, 'Adam knew Eve his
wife, and she conceived and bore Cain'—the pain of childbirth
notwithstanding. Human dominion over (some of) the animals is realized with Abel being 'a keeper of sheep', while Cain
does his best to subdue the earth as 'a tiller of the ground'. I
will return to these last two points, but for the moment will
concentrate on the multiplication motif.

The general connection between 4.1 and 3.16[1] is made more
explicit by the verbal links between the two verses: 'and she
conceived' (*wattahar*) and 'and she bore' (*watteled*) [4.1] echoing 'your pregnancy' (*hērōnēk*) and 'you shall bear children'
(*tēleḏî*) [3.16][2] respectively. Whatever meaning Eve's strange
cry may have[3]—*qānîtî 'îš 'et-yhwh*—the birth of Cain confirms the strength of the command 'be fruitful and multiply',
despite the inherent pain in obeying it.

Human reproduction becomes a trend. The genealogies of
4.17-26 and 5.1-32 confirm the relentless march of the generations.[4] Their monotonous repetition stands as a witness to
the success with which humans are fulfilling the command[5]

---

[1] Seen by e.g. Fishbane, 'Genesis 2.4b–11.32', p. 24.
[2] Cf. Cassuto, *Genesis*, 1.197.
[3] There have been many attempts to interpret the troublesome *'et*. The
catalogue of suggestions compiled by Westermann, *Genesis 1–11*,
p. 291, which either interpret *'et* in a way which cannot be demonstrated from any other OT context, or propose hypothetical emenda-
tions, suggests to me that the problem is beyond resolution. As Westermann points out, the usual translation, 'with the help of Yahweh',
has no parallels to support it. Cf. Skinner, *Genesis*, p. 102.
[4] Cf. Fishbane, 'Genesis 2.4b–11.32', pp. 27-28; Westermann, *Genesis
1–11*, p. 6; Wenham, *Genesis 1–15*, p. 126.
[5] Cf. Driver, *Genesis*, p. 75; Cassuto, *Genesis*, 1.275; Wilson, *Genealogy and History*, p. 164; Fretheim, *Creation*, p. 103; von Rad, *Genesis*,
p. 69; Childs, *Old Testament as Scripture*, p. 153; Westermann,
Genesis 1–11, p. 17:

> P relates the genealogies very clearly to the work of God in the
> blessing and its commission: 'Be fruitful and multiply', 1.28. The
> effect of the blessing is described in the genealogies... this god-
> given dynamism is effective in the succession of new births
> which the genealogies report.

The imperative, 'be fruitful and multiply and fill the earth' is

despite the rigours enforced by 3.16. Gen. 5.1-2 makes this connection explicit by prefacing the genealogy of Adam with a direct reference to 1.26-28 and the blessing/imperative given to the human pair. There is a dark side to this success story however. The genealogy of 4.17-26 links the two murderers Cain and Lamech.

> Cain's and Lamech's acts subvert the very nature of genealogical succession, which rests on the command to be fruitful and multiply in Genesis 1.28.[1]

Lurking in the background, therefore, there is the threat that human lust for murder could make the ultimate goal of filling the earth a more difficult task than it should be.[2] Also, the genealogy of ch. 5 includes the refrain 'and he died'. Death comes to all (with the exception of Enoch, 5.24), regardless of whether they are murdered or not. Thus, repeated acts of procreation are balanced by deaths, which makes the task of filling the earth problematic.

Gen. 6.1-4 is notoriously difficult to penetrate, but despite its opacity has some bearing on this theme as the following elements show:

  (a) Humankind began to multiply (*lārōb*) [6.1].
  (b) Daughters were born (*yull*ᵉ*dû*) to them [6.1].
  (c) The 'sons of God' took as wives (*wayyiq*ᵉ*ḥû lāhem nāšîm*) the 'daughters of men' [6.2].
  (d) The 'sons of God' came in (*yābō'û*) to the 'daughters of men' [6.4].
  (e) They bore (*w*ᵉ*yāl*ᵉ*dû*) children to them [6.4].

A detailed study of the problems of this pericope lies outside the scope of this chapter. While a great deal of study has been

being carried out in Gen 5. (p. 348)

Cf. also Smith, 'Structure and Purpose', pp. 311-12; Coats, *Genesis*, p. 71.
[1] Robinson, 'Genealogies of Genesis', p. 600 n. 8.
[2] In this connection it is interesting that Lewis, *Noah and the Flood*, p. 124, notes the rabbinic observation that Noah neglected the command to be fruitful and multiply until he was five hundred (5.32), because he did not want to produce children in such a wicked world.

given to the identification of the 'sons of God' (*bᵉnê hā'ᵉlōhîm*),[1] and the exact nature of their offence, if any, and the identity of their offspring which result from their cohabitation with the 'daughters of men' (*bᵉnôt hā'ādām*),[2] these offspring are not

[1] Some have taken them to be heavenly/divine beings, an interpretation which goes back at least as far as the Greek versions, where LXX and Theodotion translate as οἱ ἄγγελοι τοῦ θεοῦ. Similar positions have been taken by modern critical scholarship, e.g. Driver, *Genesis*, p. 82; Skinner, *Genesis*, pp. 141-42; Kraeling, 'Gen. 6.1-4', pp. 193-208; Knight, *A Christian Theology*, p. 128; Cassuto, *Genesis* 1.291-94; Childs, *Myth and Reality*, pp. 50-51; Kidner, *Genesis*, p. 84; Fretheim, *Creation*, p. 104; von Rad, *Genesis*, p. 114; Cassuto, 'Sons of God and Daughters of Man', pp. 17-28; Wifall, 'Gen 6.1-4', p. 295; Porter, 'Daughters of Lot', p. 138; Petersen, 'Genesis 6.1-4', pp. 57-59; Marrs, 'The Sons of God', pp. 219-20; Van Gemeren, 'The Sons of God', pp. 320-48; Brueggemann, *Genesis*, p. 71; Newman, 'Genesis 6.2, 4', pp. 31-36.
  Most support such an argument on the basis that similar designations elsewhere in the OT carry this connotation. Cf. Job 1.6; 2.1 (*bᵉnê hā'ᵉlōhîm*); 38.7 (*bᵉnê 'ᵉlōhîm*); Pss. 29.1; 89.7 (*bᵉnê 'ēlîm*); Dan. 3.25 (*bar 'ᵉlāhîn*). These terms are usually taken to be the equivalent of *mal'ᵃkê 'ᵉlōhîm*, attested in e.g. Gen. 28.12. In these contexts *bēn* is read as an idiom which places the individuals mentioned in the same class as *'ᵉlōhîm*, in the same way in which the *bᵉnê hannᵉbî'îm* (2 Kgs 2.3, 5, 7) are a group belonging to the same class as *hannᵉbî'îm*. Later traditions are also cited as supporting this interpretation, e.g. *1 Enoch* 6.2ff.; 1 Pet. 3.19, 20; 2 Pet. 2.4-5; Jude 6; Josephus, *Antiquities* 1.73. Thus the pericope describes the cohabitation of angels/gods with human females (as *bᵉnôt hā'ādām* is taken to mean).
  Others have taken the *bᵉnê hā'ᵉlōhîm* to be humans, usually seen as the descendants of Seth. This line of interpretation also boasts an ancient lineage, being attested in the targumim: see Aberbach and Grossfeld (eds.), *Targum Onkelos*, p. 50; Calvin, *Genesis*, 1.238; Kline, 'Divine Kingship', pp. 187-204; Westermann, *Genesis 1–11*, pp. 371-72 (though Westermann's position is ambiguous); Eslinger, 'Contextual Identification', pp. 65-73.
  In this interpretation, the *bᵉnôt hā'ādām* are usually seen as the descendants of Cain. However, Eslinger, 'Contextual Identification', reverses these correlations.
[2] It is argued by some that if the *bᵉnê hā'ᵉlōhîm* are angelic/heavenly beings, their offspring mothered by the *bᵉnôt hā'ādām* are heavenly-earthly hybrids. When God announces that he will withdraw his 'spirit' (*rûaḥ*) (6.3a), it is possible that this is done because the hybrids have a super-abundance of it (more than a human measure; cf. Cassuto, *Genesis*, 1.296; von Rad, *Genesis*, p. 114), or because, as some see it, it is the sole preserve of God and the angels and counter to

seen as anything other than '*men* of renown' (*'anšê haššēm*)
(6.4). Thus 6.1-4, despite its difficulties, gives note that the
fruitfulness and multiplication of humans continues apace.
    Just as 6.1-4, which acts as part of the introduction to the
Flood story, is related to the Announcement of 1.28, so too is
8.21–9.7 which forms part of the postlude. It is obvious that
8.21–9.7 is not a simple repetition of 1.28 but contains significant variations of that initial Announcement. Gen. 8.21a 'I will
never again curse the ground (*ᵃdāmâ*)...', regardless of how
one views the curse referred to (see below), bears some relationship to the original command to subdue the earth. Gen. 9.2
'The fear of you and the dread of you shall be upon every beast
of the earth... into your hand they are delivered', relates to the
same subject matter as the command to have dominion over
the animals, but seemingly intensifies the concept of dominion.
I will look at both of these correspondences when I investigate
the remaining motifs of 1.28. However, it can be seen quite
clearly that the multiplication motif of 1.28 is repeated verbatim in 9.1 and paraphrased in 9.7. This two-fold repetition
shows that it has retained its importance and that none of the
events since 1.28 has negated its force. Taken as a whole,
8.21–9.7 confirms the basic importance of 1.28 for the unfolding story of Gen. 1–11, but also confirms that some of its elements are undergoing modification in the light of subsequent
events.

'flesh'—*bāśār* (6.3a)—characteristic of humans (e.g. Skinner,
Genesis, p. 145). This being the case, the imposition of a lifespan of 120
years (6.3b) prevents these hybrids from living '*ôlām* (cf. Van
Gemeren, 'The Sons of God', p. 347; Brueggemann, *Genesis*, p. 72),
and reestablishes the boundaries between humanity and divinity
(Petersen, 'Organization of the Cosmos', p. 59). The Nephilim (6.4) are
generally taken by proponents of this argument to be the gigantic
hybrid offspring of these unions (e.g. Skinner, *Genesis*, p. 139; Childs,
Myth and Reality, p. 55; cf. Cassuto, *Genesis*, 1.298).
    Alternatively, if the *bᵉnê hāᵉlōhîm* are taken to be human beings,
the withdrawal of Yahweh's spirit (6.3a) is simply the divine judgment of withdrawing or limiting the life-force within humans (cf. 6.17)
to a maximum of 120 years—a considerable reduction from that seen
in the preceding genealogies. Read in this way, the pericope is concerned with the breaking down of the division between the 'faithful'
and the 'rebellious' to produce a humanity almost totally alienated
from God.

(Some have argued that it is at this point that the primaeval history ends, rather than at some point in ch. 11 [or ch. 12].[1] As God once started with Adam he now makes a new start with Noah. As these arguments depend largely on the relationship between 8.21 and 3.17-19 and the matter of the curse on the *ʾdāmâ* I will suspend judgment until I deal specifically with the aspect of subduing the earth.)

The ensuing narrative indicates that the human family was faithful to its divine calling. The lapidary statement that 'from these [Noah's three sons] the whole earth was peopled [*nāpʿṣâ*]' (9.19),[2] summarizes the state of affairs expanded on in ch. 10. While ch. 10 is different in form to the preceding genealogies of 4.17-26 and 5.1-32, and is more properly known as the Table of Nations, its function is similar. The spread of the nations from their eponymous ancestors testifies to the power of the renewed imperatives of 9.1, 7, and through them back to the original Announcement of 1.28.[3]

The concluding narrative of the primaeval history, that of the 'Tower of Babel' (11.1-9), can also be drawn within the

---

[1] First proposed by Rendtorff, 'Genesis 8,21', pp. 69-78; followed by Koch, 'Die Hebräer', p. 72.

[2] Cf. Combs, 'Political Teaching', p. 109, who sees this verse as introducing an ominous note to the narrative. He argues that whereas the reader would expect the text to say that they 'were fruitful and multiplied and filled the earth', the text actually introduces the unfamiliar verb *nāpaṣ*, which 'denotes a shattering or breaking or dispersing in a negative sense', suggesting 'that once again a form of violence has expressed itself in man's filling the earth'. However, while *nāpaṣ* can carry this meaning, the context of Gen. 9.19 would support the traditional translation. Cf. the use of *nāpaṣ* in 1 Sam. 13.11; Isa. 33.3.

[3] Cf. von Rad, *Genesis*, p. 144; Sarna, *Understanding Genesis*, pp. 65-66; Smith, 'Structure and Purpose', p. 312; Brueggemann, *Genesis*, p. 93; Mauldin, 'Singularity', p. 48; Clines, *Theme of the Pentateuch*, p. 68; Westermann, *Genesis 1-11*, p. 528; Robinson, 'Genealogies of Genesis', p. 602.

Cassuto, *Genesis*, 2.175, contends that the number seventy (7 × 10) was used in the ANE to indicate the great abundance of offspring. However, his acknowledgment (p. 177) that the number of offspring in ch. 10 comes to 71 rather than 70 makes it unlikely that ch. 10 can be seen as another example, despite Cassuto's plea that 'one more or less is not material'. He suggests omitting Nimrod to get the correct figure. Wenham, *Genesis 1-15*, p. 213, just as unconvincingly suggests omitting the Philistines.

ambit of our present discussion. However, because of its terse construction, we encounter problems when we attempt to understand the focus of this pericope. What is the sin of the people of Babel which induces Yahweh's displeasure? The sin is nowhere explicitly defined.

The history of interpretation has seen two major suggestions: first, that the builders of Babel were motivated by human hubris to storm the heavens and be like God; alternatively, that the humans had the more modest aim of settling down in a centralized location in order to frustrate the divine command to 'fill the earth'.[1]

The view that the sin of Babel is hubris is based on two elements in 11.4. First, the announcement that they will build a city 'and a tower with its top in the heavens (*baššāmayim*)'. Some read *baššāmayim* quite literally to indicate that humans wanted to enter the divine heavenly realm, and their actions were thus an 'effort of the restless, scheming, soaring human mind to transcend its divinely appointed limitations'.[2] Secondly, that (as a result of building the city and tower?) they want 'to make a name (*šēm*)' for themselves. The desire to make a name represents naked human ambition. Fokkelman suggests that the assonance between *šāmayim* and *šēm* emphasizes the hubris of the human endeavour.[3]

Against these points it may be argued that building a tower 'with its top in the heavens' does not necessarily mean that the Babelites wanted to raise humanity to the level of God. The statement in Deut. 1.28 that 'the cities are great and fortified up to heaven (*baššāmayim*)' is obviously an idiom expressing great height and not to be pressed literally.[4] Also, while the

---

[1] Anderson, 'Unity and Diversity', pp. 73-74.

[2] Skinner, *Genesis*, p. 229. Cf. Fokkelman, *Narrative Art in Genesis*, p. 17, 'Implicitly they want to penetrate the strictly divine and become divine themselves. What drives them is hubris.'; Richardson, *Genesis 1-11*, p. 126; Sasson, 'Tower of Babel', pp. 217, 219; Chauvin, 'Une série', p. 224; Couffignal, 'La tour de Babel', pp. 64, 67, 69; Wenham, *Genesis 1-15*, pp. 239-40, 242.

[3] Fokkelman, *Narrative Art in Genesis*, p. 17.

[4] Von Rad, *Genesis*, p. 149; Gowan, *When Man Becomes God*, pp. 27-28. This objection is acknowledged by e.g. Fokkelman, *Narrative Art in Genesis*, p. 19, but he counters that, 'I deliberately choose a maximising reading [of *baššāmayim*], for here the heavens must be retained for the sake of contrast to "the earth, the whole earth"'. However, I

desire 'to make a name' for themselves obviously expresses
human ambition,[1] the ambition to build a city and tower of
note falls far short of wanting to dethrone God. If these objections are conceded, one is left wondering whether a human
building project of this nature, even if partly selfish in motivation, explains the extreme reaction from Yahweh.

The other main alternative interpretation of this pericope
reads it against its larger context as well as taking certain key
elements of its content into account. Since the Deluge the
human race has successfully 'been fruitful' and has 'multiplied' (as ch. 10 indicates). However, the purpose of such multiplication was to 'fill the earth' and 11.1-9 indicates that
humans were not willing to do this, but 'found a plain in the
land of Shinar and settled there' (11.2). Thus the act of building a city and tower and settling down, rather than being an
attempt to dethrone Yahweh (i.e. hubris), has as its object the
more modest but still serious aim of frustrating the divine will
that humans should spread abroad and fill the earth. In fact
the narrative gives a clear statement of the motivation for
building Babel—'lest we be scattered abroad upon the face of
the whole earth' (11.4).[2] (This statement probably expresses as
much a fear of the uncivilized earth itself as it does a desire on

would suggest that the contrast can still be maintained even when
reading *baššāmayim* metaphorically.

[1] Sarna, *Understanding Genesis*, p. 73, argues that 'the desire for
fame is perfectly human and not in itself reprehensible. Indeed, the
granting thereof is part of the divine promise to Abraham.' Westermann, *Genesis 1–11*, p. 548, comments correctly that the narrator
gives no indication of whether making a name for oneself is bad or not.
However, I would see a contrast between the people of Babel wanting to
make a name for themselves, and Abraham's *being given* a name by
Yahweh.

[2] This line of interpretation goes back at least as far as Josephus. See
Antiquities 1.4. Cassuto, *Genesis*, 2.230, paraphrases the narrative in
this way:

> Your intention was to build for yourselves a gigantic city that
> would contain all mankind and you forgot that it was God's will
> to fill the whole earth with human settlements, and that God's
> plan would surely be realized (cf. also p. 243).

See also Gowan, *When Man Becomes God*, p. 27; Wenham, *Genesis 1–
15*, p. 242.

the part of gregarious humanity to live together). If *this* is the sin of the people of Babel then God's judgment fits the crime. The confusion of language (11.9) is not judgment *per se* but merely the means of achieving the end of 'scattering' them over the whole earth (11.9b).[1] While the verb 'to scatter' (*pûṣ*) used in 11.4, 8, 9 can have negative connotations, e.g. Ezek. 11.17; 20.34, 41; 28.25, when used within the context of Gen. 1–11 it expresses the positive aspect of God's command 'to fill' the earth. In fact the verb has been used with these positive connotations in 10.18, 'Afterwards the families of the Canaanites spread abroad (*nāpōṣû*)'. The verb seems to be used synonymously with *pārad* in 10.32, 'and from these the nations spread abroad (*nipreqdû*) on the earth after the flood'.[2]

> This motif of scattering in our story would then fulfil the blessing given in Genesis 1, since the third element of that blessing is, 'Be fruitful and multiply and *fill the earth*', (1.28). Dispersion may be the means of accomplishing this blessing.[3]

I would conclude that this latter view of the story is more satisfying than the former. Not only does it do justice to the stated fear of the people of Babel ('lest we be scattered abroad') but also allows for a greater degree of integration between 11.1-9 and the rest of the primaeval history than the former interpretation. God takes action to ensure the fulfilment of his command that humans should not only 'be fruitful and multiply' but also 'fill the earth'.

It is fitting therefore, that the subsequent section of the primaeval history, which brings this larger block to a conclusion, should be a genealogy.[4] This time, however, the focus is

---

[1] Sarna, *Understanding Genesis*, p. 67; Clines, ' "Sons of God" Episode', p. 38; Brueggemann, *Genesis*, p. 99.

[2] Brueggemann, *Genesis*, p. 98.

[3] Kikawada, 'Genesis 11.1-9', p. 32. Cf. Anderson, 'Unity and Diversity', p. 79, 'there is no basis for the negative view that pluralism is God's judgment upon human sinfulness. Diversity is not a condemnation.'

[4] Driver, *Genesis*, p. 137, comments that 11.10-26 merely 'bridges over an interval, about which there is nothing special to record, by a genealogy'. However, read in the light of 11.1-9 it is this genealogy which is in itself significant.

on the descendants of Shem, and culminates in the family of Terah. It is difficult to determine the exact point at which the primaeval history ends and the ancestral history begins. It may in fact be better to think in terms of a gradual transition than an abrupt shift from one to the other. However, if one sees the primaeval history proper as concluding in 11.26, 'Terah... became the father of Abram, Nahor and Haran', then one could see it as ending on an optimistic note. The command to multiply maintains its force right to the end of the primaeval history. Alternatively, a radically different view could be upheld if 11.30 is taken as the concluding remark, 'Now Sarai was barren; she had no child'. Here, the command to multiply is threatened. The monotony of the genealogies, expressing the inexorable fulfilment of the Announcement, is shattered by this concluding dissonant note.[1] Not only do people die, but some do not procreate. However, regardless of the view taken, with the focus now limited to the family of Terah, and Abram and Sarai in particular, the note concerning Sarai's barrenness, whether it be a conclusion or introduction, announces that the fulfilment of the command to multiply is under threat.

Subdue the Earth

Perhaps some justification is needed for treating the subordination of the earth as a separate category. Our discussion should demonstrate the merits of doing so, but initially I will make two points. First a general observation, that the subjugation of the earth does not necessarily follow from humans being fruitful, multiplying and filling the earth. That is to say, the earth could be filled with humans who live lives of vagabondage, eking out an existence on a hostile earth; in this situation there would be no human overlordship. Secondly, the narrative itself sees the first three elements (be fruitful; multiply; fill the earth) as a self-contained unit. Gen. 9.2 repeats these three imperatives, omitting 'subdue the earth', indicating that human subjugation of the earth, while it may be related, is a separate matter.

---

[1] Brueggemann, *Genesis*, pp. 95-96.

The initial problem confronting the reader on learning that humans are to 'subdue' (*kābaš*) the earth, is to understand exactly what this might entail. This is the only use of *kābaš* in Genesis, so one must look elsewhere for clues as to its precise meaning. While it can carry the connotation of sexual degradation (?Neh. 5.5 [niphal]) or rape (Esth. 7.8) when it has women as its object, its general meaning seems to be that of subjecting or making subservient.[1] It is a verb used to describe the enslavement of people (e.g. Jer. 34.11, 16). What it might mean when it has the earth (*'ereṣ*) as its object may not be absolutely clear initially, but the Announcement obviously grants to humans great power. As to its precise meaning here, the reader must suspend judgment, and wait to see how this particular command takes shape in the ensuing narrative.[2]

The first clue given by the narrative comes in 2.5, 'there was no man to till (*la'ᵃbōd*) the ground (*'et-ha'ᵃdāmâ*)', a state of affairs rectified by the creation of Adam whom Yahweh Elohim put 'in the Garden of Eden to till it (*lᵉ'obdāh*) and keep it (*ûlᵉšomrāh*)' (2.15). (This close connection between the Man and the ground is emphasized by the *'ādām/'ᵃdāmâ* assonance which, starting here, is used to good effect in the rest of the primaeval history.) This 'tilling' and 'keeping' could well be part of the task involved in 'subduing' the earth.[3] By tilling the earth, humans subject it to their will, making it produce what humans desire rather than what it would produce if left to its own devices. They relate to the earth as a suzerain would to a vassal. Thus tilling is a means toward the end of

---

[1] Koehler and Baumgartner, *Lexicon*, p. 423. Cf. Rendtorff, '"Subdue the earth"', p. 215; Westermann, *Genesis 1–11*, p. 161.

[2] Anderson, 'Creation and Ecology', p. 154, agrees that the meaning of *kābaš* must be found within the context of Genesis 1–11 and must not be decided in isolation.

[3] Cf. Gibson, *Genesis*, 1.112, 'The picture is naively simple, but we are not far from the concept of "man's" stewardship over nature...' set out in ch. 1.

I would disagree with the view of Vogels, 'L'être humain', p. 526, who states that the narrative gives no clue as to why God would want to place the Man in the Garden. This is true only if one reads ch. 2 in isolation from ch. 1. Regardless of one's view of the *origin* of these chapters, their proximity in the present form of the text demands that they be read together.

subduing the earth. It might be objected that tilling or keeping the *ground* ('*ᵃdāmâ*) must be differentiated from subduing the earth ('*ereṣ*), because of the difference in vocabulary. However, this objection is minimized, if not excluded altogether, when one considers the great degree of semantic overlap between these two terms. Additionally, the range of each word is so wide as to render both terms ambiguous when used in isolation. For example, '*ereṣ* can be used to convey 'the whole earth' in e.g. Gen. 7.3; 8.9; 11.1, etc., but it can also be used in the sense of a specific territory, e.g. Gen. 13.9, 15; 41.56, etc. As a result, ambiguity occurs in such passages as Isa. 13.5 (will the enemy destroy the whole *land* or the whole *earth*?).[1] Similarly, '*ᵃdāmâ* can also refer to 'the whole earth' in e.g. Gen. 12.3; 28.14—'all the peoples of the earth' (cf. Exod. 33.16; Deut. 7.6; 14.2 etc.), or to the specifically cultivable areas of it, e.g. Gen. 4.2, 12; 9.20, etc. It can also express the idea of specific territory, as in 'all the land of Egypt' (Gen. 47.20, 26), 'the land of Judah' (Isa. 19.17), 'the land of Israel' (confined to Ezekiel [17×], e.g. Ezek. 7.2; 12.19, 22; 13.19).[2] It can readily be seen therefore that '*ereṣ* is frequently interchangeable with '*ᵃdāmâ*,[3] as it is in e.g. Num. 16.30, 32, 'But if the Lord creates something new, and the ground ('*ᵃdāmâ*) opens its mouth... and the earth ('*ereṣ*) opened its mouth'.[4] It is not necessary to press for identity of meaning between '*ereṣ* and *ⁿdāmâ* in 1.28 and 2.5, 15, but the above indicates that I am not doing a disservice to these terms to suggest that a 'tilling' of the *ⁿdāmâ* may legitimately be subsumed under the imperative to 'subdue' the '*ereṣ*.

We are given no clue by the narrative as to how successful the Man might have been in this God-given task, because we are plunged almost immediately into the account of the human offence and Yahweh Elohim's curses which follow (3.14-19). I have already noted above the general relationship between these curses and 1.28. My interest here is to see how

---

[1] Bergman and Ottosson, "*erets*', p. 393.
[2] Plöger, "*ᵃdhāmāh*', pp. 90-93.
[3] Miller, *Genesis 1–11*, p. 37.
[4] Cited by Cassuto, *Genesis*, 1.223; commenting on Gen. 4.12 he concludes, 'The parallelism in our verse is synonymous not antithetic; '*ereṣ* and '*ădhāmā* are identical'.

Yahweh Elohim's words to the Man relate to his subduing the earth. It is important to see that while the Man was the offender, it is the ground which is cursed, 'Cursed is the ground (*hā*ᵃ*dāmâ*) because of you' (3.17). These verses imply that, prior to this, human subduing of the earth through 'tilling' it and 'keeping' it, while not necessarily effortless, would have been achieved with far less 'toil' and 'sweat' and without the complication of 'thorns and thistles'. From now on, the task of subduing the earth will be a *struggle*, because the earth itself has been cursed into becoming a less tameable environment in which the Man may exercise his sovereignty. While the curse of 3.16 indicated that pain would now be associated with human reproduction, it also asserted that humans would still reproduce. However, the curse on the ᵃ*dāmâ* (3.17-19) raises the question as to whether humans will now ever be able to fulfil this aspect of the original Announcement,[1] at least in an absolute sense. The statement that the Man would struggle to sustain himself,

> till you return to the ground (*hā*ᵃ*dāmâ*),
> 　　for out of it you were taken;
> you are dust,
> 　　and to dust you shall return. (3.19)

suggests that, in the final analysis, it is the earth which subdues the Man.[2] It would appear therefore, that the Announcement of 1.28 has been modified, if not reversed, on this particular point. The tilling of the ground outside of Eden (3.23) is qualitatively different from tilling and keeping the Garden itself.[3]

---

[1] Cf. Kidner, *Genesis*, p. 72, who believes that 'man in his own disorder would never now "subdue" the earth'. Naidoff, 'A Man to Work the Soil', p. 10, suggests that 3.17-19 affirms as much as it negates, with the Man being able to sustain himself with food from the earth. This is true, but still does not amount to a complete human subjugation of the earth.

[2] Patte and Parker, 'Structural Exegesis', p. 74, observe that in the curses on the Woman and Man, the curse is to be dominated by that from which they were taken. Thus the Woman is to be dominated by the Man, and the Man by the ᵃ*dāmâ*.

[3] Jobling, 'Myth and its Limits', p. 23. Wyatt, 'When Adam Delved', p. 119, suggests that 3.23 should be translated as, 'Yahweh God

Despite the problems, Adam's son Cain pursues his father's vocation, and attempts to play his part in obeying the command.[1] Like his parents before him he offends Yahweh, and like them he is punished: 'You are cursed from the ground (*hā'dāmâ*)... When you till the ground, it shall no longer yield to you its strength...' (4.11-12). However, his punishment exceeds that of his parents,[2] just as his offence exceeded their offence. In 3.17-19, the ground was cursed, but at least it would yield plants and bread for human food (3.18-19a). However, in ch. 4 the curse falls on Cain himself, who is banished from the *'dāmâ*. While this sentence cannot be taken absolutely[3] (for he will continue to till the ground [4.12]), it strongly suggests that he will be even less successful in subduing it than Adam. The *'ādām/'dāmâ* motif is used to good effect in highlighting Cain's vocation, offence, and punishment,

> den Acker [= *adāmâ*] hat Qain bebaut, des Ackers Früchte dargebracht, dem Acker Bruderblut zu trinken gegeben: aber vom Acker her klagt das Blut wider ihn, darum verweigert der Acker ihm seine Frucht, so wird er vom Acker verbannt.[4]

The likelihood of Cain being able to subdue the earth has been

expelled him from the Garden of Eden (and) from tilling the soil from which he had been taken'. This is based, unconvincingly, on the view that 3.17-19 contains no reference to agriculture, i.e. the curse is for the Man to be deprived of agricultural work. The reference just a few verses later to Cain tilling the soil renders this argument unlikely.
[1] Cassuto, *Genesis*, 1.203, sees Abel's keeping of sheep (4.2), as an example of human dominion over the animals, as enjoined in 1.26-28, but strangely does not link Cain's agriculture to the Announcement, seeing only the connection with Adam's work in 2.5; 3.23. He is followed by Waltke, 'Cain and His Offering', pp. 363-64.
[2] Cf. Driver, *Genesis*, p. 66; Cassuto, *Genesis*, 1.218; von Rad, *Genesis*, p. 106; Hauser, 'Linguistic and Thematic Links', p. 298; Plöger, "*'dhāmāh*', p. 96; Gros Louis, 'Genesis 3–11', p. 43.
[3] There have been several interpretations of what *min hā'dāmâ* might convey: cultivated soil rather than the earth as such, e.g. Driver, *Genesis*, p. 66; Skinner, *Genesis*, p. 108; the earth as such and not simply the cultivated soil, e.g. Cassuto, *Genesis*, 1.223; Eden or possibly the Holy Land, e.g. Richardson, *Genesis 1–11*, p. 83; the geographical area in which Cain was living at that time, e.g. Westermann, *Genesis 1–11*, pp. 309-10.
[4] Gunkel, *Genesis*, p. 45.

rendered well nigh impossible. Whether the rest of humanity
will be able to do so remains to be seen.

The genealogy which follows the Cain narrative (4.17-26)
may suggest that there are more ways of subduing the earth
than by agriculture. Aspects of civilization such as urbaniza-
tion (v. 17) and metal working (v. 22) may indicate ways in
which the earth is used to serve human ends, and is thus
'subdued'. However, with the birth of Noah at the end of the
next genealogy, Lamech reminds the reader that the curse of
3.17-19 is still in force: 'Out of the ground which the Lord has
cursed this one shall bring us relief from our work and from
the toil of our hands' (5.29). In the light of the story so far, the
reader is led to believe that despite the curse of 3.17-19 the
human endeavour of subduing the earth will be made more
tolerable—perhaps even more likely to be achieved. The Flood
postpones this development. How Noah will be able to provide
such relief for toiling humanity, with the saved remnant after
the Deluge, remains to be seen.

If the curses of 3.14-19 complicate the fulfilment of the
creation Announcement concerning human fruitfulness, subjugation of the earth and dominion over animals, the divine
decisions of 6.5-8 amount to a complete negation. If humans
and animals are blotted out, none of these three imperatives
can be obeyed. The relationship between humans and animals
during the Flood will be the focus of my concern in the next
section of this chapter, but for now I will concentrate on the
relation of humans to the earth. The Flood involves the
physical break up of the cosmos and a return to the pre-
creation state of *tōhû wābōhû*, with a mingling once again of
the upper and lower oceans.[1] Physical conditions are such that
human subjugation of the earth is rendered impossible. In fact
the reverse situation prevails, with the earth threatening to
subdue humans. In this it is largely successful; only Noah and
his family escape annihilation. Here we can see an intensification of the alienation of humans from the earth. With the
Man in the Garden, the earth was cursed, resulting in the
frustrations of working with the soil; with Cain, the earth
would not give its strength and he was banished from the

[1] Cf. Skinner, *Genesis*, p. 164; von Rad, *Genesis*, p. 128.

ᵃ*dāmâ*; matters come to a head with Noah's generation, who
are overcome by the cosmos itself—only a remnant survives.
With the turn of events occasioned by God's remembrance
of Noah (8.1a)[1]—the abating of the flood waters and the dis-
embarking of Noah's family and the animals—God issues a
decree (8.21–9.7), which as we saw above takes up again the
original three-fold Announcement (1.28). Here, my interest is
in whether humans will be able to subdue the earth after the
're-creation' of the Deluge. At first sight, 8.21 'I will never
again curse the ground because of man...' offers great hope,
but this depends on how the statement is understood. In a
landmark study,[2] Rendtorff suggested that this usual translation of 8.21a is incorrect. He argues that this rendering has
been influenced by v. 21b, 'I will never again destroy all flesh'.
The true meaning of v. 21a is, he contends, 'I will no longer
curse the earth'. He justifies this by claiming that *qālal* is not
an exact synonym for *'ārar*, because *'ārar* means *to place a
curse* upon someone, while *qālal* (piel) means *to describe as
cursed*.[3] Its use in 8.21, therefore, does not refer to another act
of cursing such as has just been described in the Flood story,
but means that Yahweh will *no longer treat the earth as
cursed*. When this is recognized, the formula must refer back
to 3.17, and to Yahweh's curse pronounced on the earth.[4]
Yahweh will no longer treat the earth as being under *that*
curse; *that* curse is now without power. This marks a decided
shift in Yahweh's dealings with the world. In the (Yahwistic)
primaeval history up to this point, curse has predominated;
from now on, blessing will rule the earth. Gen. 8.21 therefore,
Rendtorff argues, marks the end of the (Yahwistic) primaeval

[1] On the significance of this verse within the structure of the Flood
narrative, see Anderson, 'From Analysis to Synthesis', pp. 36, 38;
Wenham, 'Coherence of Flood Narrative', pp. 338ff.; *idem, Genesis 1–
15*, pp. 156-57, 183.
[2] Rendtorff, 'Genesis 8 21', pp. 69-78. He is followed in his general
conclusions by e.g. Koch, 'Die Hebräer', p. 72; Fretheim, *Creation*,
pp. 112-13; von Rad, *Genesis*, p. 122; Brueggemann, 'Kingship and
Chaos', p. 326; Clark, 'Structure of Pre-Patriarchal History', pp. 205ff.;
Coats, *Genesis*, p. 82; Fishbane, *Text and Texture*, p. 33; Fritz,
' "Solange die Erde steht" ', p. 609.
[3] Rendtorff, 'Genesis 8 21', p. 72.
[4] This point anticipated by Richardson, *Genesis 1–11*, p. 105.

history. The rest of chs. 1–11 serves as a prelude to the ancestral history.[1]
While Rendtorff's suggestion is attractive in some ways, it has come under serious attack.[2] Petersen argues that Rendtorff's subtle distinction between *'ārar* and *qālal* is not supported by OT usage. *Qālal* is used to describe Balaam's cursing in Josh. 24.9, 'And he sent and invited Balaam the son of Beor to curse (*lᵉqallēl*) you'. Deut. 28 contains a number of curse formulas introduced by *'ārûr* (vv. 16-19), and yet they are referred to as *haqqᵉlālôt* (v. 15).[3] Similarly, its use in Gen. 12.3 cannot be declarative.[4] In this light, Rendtorff's view that *qālal* does not refer to a curse as such is not so convincing as it first seemed. This negative assessment is underlined when we look ahead to the rest of the Genesis story. The curse of 3.17-19 brought thorns, thistles and toil. If *these* curses have been lifted, why do they continue after the Flood? I can only conclude that the curse of 3.17-19 remains in force.[5] I would suggest that the verbatim repetition of part of 1.28 in 9.1 recognizes this fact. It is significant not only for what it repeats, but for what it omits. While repeating 'be fruitful and multiply, and fill the earth' and continuing with a statement concerning human relations with animals (9.2), it omits entirely any call to 'subdue the earth'.[6] Wenham is simply wrong when he asserts that 'the commission first given to Adam "to be fruitful and multiply; fill the earth and *subdue it*" (1.28; 9.1) is

[1] Rendtorff, 'Genesis 8 21', pp. 74-75.
[2] E.g. Steck, 'Genesis 12 1-3', pp. 525-54; followed by Westermann, *Genesis 1–11*, pp. 454-56; Wenham, *Genesis 1–15*, p. 190. Cf. Clines, *Theme of the Pentateuch*, pp. 70-72.
[3] Petersen, 'Yahwist on the Flood', p. 442.
[4] Westermann, *Genesis 1–11*, p. 445.
[5] Cassuto, *Genesis*, 2.119-20 suggests that the force of *'ôd* in a position *after* the verb in 8.21a is, '*I will not curse any more*—more than it is already cursed'; i.e. the former curse of 3.17 still holds—but it will not be added to.
[6] As seen also by Gros Louis, 'Genesis 3–11', p. 47. It might be objected that 8.17, relating to land creatures, omits the injunction 'to fill the earth', and thus the omission of 'subdue the earth' in 9.1 may not be significant. Note, however, that *land* creatures, the focus of 8.17, receive no blessing/imperative at all in ch. 1.

reaffirmed afresh'[1] (emphasis mine). As long as the curse of
3.17-19 remains, this task of subjugation will be impossible.
Noah's cultivation of the vine (9.20ff.) does not negate this
point. His employment of viticulture does not make him any
more successful in subduing the earth than the agricultural-
ists Adam or Cain before him.[2] If anything, his drunken
stupor induced by drinking the produce of the earth could
indicate that the earth still has the upper hand. While an abil-
ity to drown one's sorrows in drink was probably what
Lamech had in mind with his prediction 'this one shall bring
us relief from our work and from the toil of our hands' (5.29),
the blessing (?) of wine does not lift the curse from the earth.

We have already seen how the Table of Nations (ch. 10) can
be read as an illustration of how humans were 'fruitful and
multiplied and filled' the earth. At another level, the spread of
these nations into their respective lands sets the scene for
human subjugation of the earth. But the curse of 3.17-19
places a formidable barrier between them and this goal. My
previous analysis of the Babel story concluded that the human
sin was a refusal to 'fill' the earth, i.e. at best they would not
subdue the (whole) earth, but only part of it. However, the
omission of the command to subdue the earth in 8.21-9.7, suggests strongly that this element has now dropped out of the
plot. Yahweh's curse has rendered it an impossible task.

---

[1] Wenham, *Genesis 1–15*, p. 206 (cf. p. li).
[2] Contra Cassuto, *Genesis*, 2.159-60. He argues that the curse of 3.17-
19 was that the earth would bring forth *only* thorns and thistles.
Noah's cultivation of the *vine* then shows that this curse has been set
aside. However, the statement that 'you shall eat the plants (*'ēśeb*) of
the field' (3.18b) can hardly mean a rigorous diet of thorns and thistles
for humans, as the next verse, 'you shall eat bread [*leḥem*]' (3.19a)
indicates. Cain's offering, whatever its imperfections, consisted of the
'fruit of the ground (*mippᵉrî hāᵃdāmâ*)' (4.3). When Noah is commanded to store up 'every sort of food' (6.21), this must surely be more
than thorns and thistles. In this light, Noah's cultivation of grapes is
not a reversal of 3.17-19. Rather than a complete reversal, some see
9.20ff. as an *amelioration* of the curse, e.g. Fretheim, *Creation*, p. 120;
von Rad, *Genesis*, p. 136; Plöger, '*ᵃdhāmāh*', p. 96. However, while the
drinking of wine may make agricultural toil more tolerable, it does not
diminish it.

42 *Announcements of Plot in Genesis*

Dominion over the Animals

And have dominion (*ûrᵉdû*)
> over the fish of the sea
> and over the birds of the air
> and over every living thing that moves upon the earth.

Gen. 1.26-28 contains the only occurrences of the verb *rādâ* in Genesis. Its usual connotation is 'to rule/govern' (e.g. Ps. 72.8) (although on one occasion it carries the meaning of 'to tread' [Joel 4.13]).[1] It is a verb used to describe the relationship of superiors to inferiors, such as kings to subjects, masters to servants, officers to labourers.[2] Read in isolation the command might seem to give unlimited power to humans over the animal creation. However, read within the context of the Creation account this human dominion has one severe limitation. Gen. 1.29-30 indicates a rigorous vegetarian diet not only for animals but also for humans.[3] Despite the dominion required of them, humans may not kill animals for food.[4] Thus, the concept of dominion intended here must be read within its immediate context rather than determined exclusively by its use elsewhere in the OT.[5]

The second chapter relates how the Man gave names to the animals (2.19-20). There is almost universal agreement among commentators that naming is a sovereign act (cf.

---

[1] Brown et al., *Lexicon*, pp. 921-22; Koehler and Baumgartner, *Lexicon*, pp. 874-75. Cf. Lev. 25.43, 46, 53; 26.17; Num. 24.19; 1 Kgs 5.4, 30; 9.23; Isa. 14.2, 6; Ezek. 29.15; 34.4; Pss. 49.15; 68.28; 110.2; Lam. 1.13; Neh. 9.28; 2 Chron. 8.10.
[2] See discussion by Limburg, '"Have Dominion over the Earth"?', p. 222; Coats, 'The God of Death', p. 229; Westermann, *Genesis 1–11*, pp. 158-59.
[3] Contra Dequeker, '"Green Herbage"', pp. 120ff. Dequeker's argument rests partly on the unlikely suggestion that 9.2-3 conveys the idea that previously humans ate animal flesh, but not the *yereq 'ēśeb* (reserved for animal food in 1.29-30); but from now on they may eat both. Cf. Wenham, *Genesis 1–15*, p. 34, who states that Gen. 1 does not forbid the consumption of meat, and that 9.3 ratifies rather than inaugurates the practice. These minority opinions do not convince me.
[4] Anderson, 'Human Dominion over Nature', p. 44; Duncan, 'Adam and the Ark', p. 191; Houston, '"And let them have dominion"', p. 166. Cf. Limburg, '"Have Dominion over the Earth"?', p. 223; Westermann, *Creation*, pp. 50-54.
[5] Anderson, 'Creation and Ecology', p. 154.

God's 'naming' in ch. 1), and thus amounts to the Man
asserting his dominion over the animal creation.[1] However,
the act of naming does not confer unlimited power as the
restraints of vegetarianism are still in force.[2] Just how limited
human dominion over the animals can be is graphically
demonstrated by the next episode. Among the animals named
by the man was the serpent. This naming had, presumably,
confirmed the hierarchical relationship between the two.
With this background, the events of ch. 3 take the reader by
surprise. Despite suggestions by scholars that the serpent of
ch. 3 is more than just an ordinary animal,[3] the personification
of evil desire within Eve,[4] God in disguise,[5] or Satan in disguise,[6] the narrative presents it quite soberly as being 'more

[1] E.g. Richardson, *Genesis 1–11*, p. 67; Asselin, 'The Notion of
Dominion', p. 289; Cassuto, *Genesis* 1.92, 130; Kidner, *Genesis*, p. 65;
Fretheim, *Creation*, p. 78; Naidoff, 'A Man to Work the Soil', p. 5;
Coats, *Genesis*, p. 53; Gibson, *Genesis*, 1.117; Rosenberg, 'The Garden
Story', p. 7; Vogels, 'L'être humain', p. 527. Duncan, 'Adam and the
Ark', p. 192, argues unconvincingly that the naming of the animals
means that they are 'admitted into a sacred circle of communication
and communion'.
[2] The question of whether the Man's naming of the Woman is a
demonstration of his dominion over her is a controverted issue. However, regardless of whether it is (e.g. Trible, 'Eve and Adam', p. 81
[concerning 3.20]; Clines, 'What does Eve do to Help?', pp. 37-40; Wenham, *Genesis 1–15*, pp. 50, 68, 70), or is not (e.g. Trible, 'Eve and
Adam', p. 77 [concerning 2.23]; Boomershine, 'Structure of Narrative
Rhetoric', p. 119; Ramsey, 'Name-Giving', esp. pp. 34-35), no one
argues that naming in itself confers unlimited power to the one who
names.
[3] E.g. Driver, *Genesis*, p. 44; Fretheim, *Creation*, pp. 80-81.
[4] E.g. Richardson, *Genesis 1–11*, p. 71; Cassuto, *Genesis*, 1.143:

> In reality it is not he [the serpent] that thinks and speaks but the
> woman does so in her heart. Thus we need not wonder at the ser-
> pent's knowledge of the prohibition: it is the woman who is aware
> of it. Nor should we be surprised that he knows the purpose of the
> Lord God: it is the woman who imagines that she has plumbed
> the Divine intention—but is quite mistaken.

However, the fact that the serpent is differentiated from the Man and
Woman in the curses of 3.14ff. shows that it is very difficult to support
this argument.
[5] Burns, 'Dream Form in Genesis 2.4b–3.24', p. 9.
[6] See the list of opinions in Westermann, *Genesis 1–11*, p. 237.

subtle (*'ār û m*) than any other wild creature (*ḥayyat hassādeh*) that the Lord God had made' (3.1), i.e. one of the animal creation named by the Man in ch. 2.[1] Yet, through its 'subtlety', it outwits the human pair and thus exercises some form of 'dominion' over them—the very reverse of what the reader was led to expect. This is highlighted by the Woman's words in 3.13 'the serpent *beguiled* me (*hiššî'anî*)...' which stand in stark contrast to the command 'and *have dominion* (*ûrᵉdû*) over [the animals]...' (1.28). This much is clear, despite the fact that the serpent's motivations are nowhere revealed, nor whether he acts individually or as a representative of the animal kingdom as a whole which is attempting to overturn the divinely ordained relationship to humans.[2] The tables have been turned—but not for long.

The curse of 3.14-15 not only includes a curse upon the serpent personally 'upon your belly you shall go...' (v. 14), but also an indication that serpentine outwitting of humans will not continue for ever: 'I will put enmity between you and the woman...' (v. 15). This curse announces a negative development in the relationship between humans and animals. Chs. 1–2 had shown human dominion but with no indication of hostility between the parties. The curse on the serpent not only reinforces the original human dominion but intensifies it by introducing human *hostility* toward serpents.

[1] E.g. Skinner, *Genesis*, p. 71; Sarna, *Understanding Genesis*, p. 26:

> It is not an independent creature; it possesses no occult powers; it is not a demoniacal being; it is not even described as evil, merely as being extraordinarily shrewd.

Von Rad, *Genesis*, p. 87; Coats, *Genesis*, p. 54; Gibson, *Genesis*, 1.124; Westermann, *Genesis 1–11*, p. 239; Vogels, 'L'être humain', p. 529.

Even Calvin, *Genesis*, 1.140, who takes the serpent to be a representation of Satan acknowledges that from the text of Genesis alone one can only conclude that humans were deceived by an animal.
[2] Cf. Walsh, 'Genesis 2.4b–3.24', p. 170. Rosenberg, 'The Garden Story', p. 7, suggests that 2.18-23 demonstrates the Man's mastery of and independence from the animals, 'by his preference for one of his own kind as sexual and social companion'. In this light, the serpent in ch. 3 may be seen as an 'instrument of revenge by the animal kingdom against its defecting kin, man...' Rosenberg's argument, however, rests more on parallels he sees with the Gilgamesh Epic than on a close reading of the Genesis narrative per se.

The final words of the curse need commenting upon:

> he shall bruise (*hû' yᵉšûpᵉkā*) your head
> and [but] you shall bruise (*wᵉ'attâ tᵉšûpennû*) his heel. (3.15b)

The majority of scholars suggest that this statement guarantees a state of mutual hostility between the two parties in which neither gains the upper hand. The distinction between 'head' and 'heel' is seen as nothing more than the natural points of attack by the warring sides and does not suggest any human superiority in the struggle.[1] I would agree with the minority view which sees a distinction between 'head' and 'heel'; 'the former will crush the head of the foe, while the latter can only wound in the heel'.[2] Read in this way, the Woman's seed will achieve dominion over the serpent's seed—though only with a struggle. I would also suggest that 3.14-15, as a curse on the serpent (v. 14a), is a formal statement outlining a change for the worse in the relations between humans and serpents. Up to this point animals have been subservient to humans. If so, a statement that in their struggles with humans serpents will be their *equal* (which is how most scholars read 3.15b), is promotion rather than demotion and can hardly be seen as a curse. However, an acknowledgment that human dominion will now entail superior death-dealing physical authority over the serpent is an intensification of human dominion over it and this amounts to a 'curse' upon the serpent, and a punishment for its attempt to reverse the divine order.[3] Thus, 3.14-15 announces a decisive shift in human-animal relations. Conflict has replaced simple dominion, with the guarantee of victory going to the human side.[4]

---

[1] E.g. Driver, *Genesis*, p. 48; Richardson, *Genesis 1–11*, p. 74; Fretheim, *Creation*, p. 88; Walsh, 'Genesis 2.4b–3.24', pp. 117, 175 n. 35; von Rad, *Genesis*, p. 93; Fishbane, 'Genesis 2.4b–11.32', p. 21; Gibson, *Genesis*, 1.135; Westermann, *Genesis 1–11*, p. 259; Ogden, 'Genesis 3.14-19', p. 134.

[2] Skinner, *Genesis*, p. 80, who does, however, go on to say that neither side will experience outright victory. Cf. Cassuto, *Genesis*, 1.161.

[3] As seen correctly by Wenham, *Genesis 1–15*, pp. 80, 89.

[4] I would disagree therefore, with Anderson, 'Creation and Ecology', p. 163, who maintains that nowhere in the period from Creation to Flood is there any indication of conflict between humans and beasts,

Perhaps an indication of this new relationship can be seen in
Yahweh Elohim's preparation of animal skins for the Man
and the Woman.[1] While these clothes are presented to them,
rather than being made by them, animals are now seen to
serve human needs, even when this means the death of
animals. It confirms the brutalization of the original dominion.[2]

The subsequent narrative of Cain and Abel gives two fleeting glimpses of how animals fare under human control. Abel
was a keeper of sheep (4.2) and while not being told why he did
so (for wool? milk? meat?), he does present the pick of his flock
as an offering (*minḥâ*) to Yahweh. Moreover, we are told that
'Yahweh had regard for Abel and his offering' (4.4b). Here
then, with divine approval, human dominion extends to the
taking of animal life as part of a cultic act. The worship of
Yahweh by one of his creatures requires the death of another.
A further advance in the growing increase of human dominion over animals could be reflected in the information that
Jabal tended 'herds'—*miqneh* (4.20)—if this term is taken to
include sheep, goats, cattle, asses and camels. Abel had limited
his interest to *śō'n*—sheep and goats.[3]

The next occasion on which humans and animals come into
close relationship is the Deluge. It could be argued that Noah
exercises a benign dominion over the animals in his care in
the ark, which becomes a 'floating Eden' providing sanctuary,[4] and in which there are tender touches of intimacy with

but rather that a 'paradisaical peace' exists between the two parties.
Also, Jobling, 'Myth and its Limits', p. 33, states that 2.4b–3.24 does
not take much interest in animals, in contrast to the surrounding
material (1.26-30; 4.1-16). This position is possible only if one narrows
the perspective to the human use of animals—an unwarranted step.
[1] Rosenberg, 'The Garden Story', p. 8, cites Benno Jacob's suggestion
'clothes *for* the skin', which leaves open the question of whether they
are made from animals or not.
[2] Rosenberg, 'The Garden Story', p. 8.
[3] Brown et al., *Lexicon*, pp. 838, 889; Koehler and Baumgartner,
Lexicon, p. 790; Wenham, *Genesis 1-15*, p. 113.
[4] Molina, 'Noé et le déluge', p. 259; Gros Louis, 'Genesis 3–11', p. 259.
A similar view in Philo, *Mos.* 2.62, is cited by Lewis, *Noah and the
Flood*, p. 48.

the birds (8.9).[1] However, Noah's first act after disembarka-
tion is that 'he took of every clean animal and of every clean
bird, and offered burnt offerings (*'ōlōt*) on the altar' (8.20)—
an act of butchery on a scale which makes Abel's offering look
insignificant. These animals were saved from drowning only
to feel the sacrificial knife at their throats. This note struck by
Noah's act is amplified by the divine statement of 9.2 that 'the
fear of you (*ûmôra'ᵃkem*) and the dread of you (*wᵉḥittᵉkem*)
shall be upon every beast of the earth...'[2] After the carnage of
8.20 it is not difficult to see why. But worse is to follow: 'Every
moving thing that lives shall be food for you' (9.3a).[3] Animals
will not only be used for sacrifices to God, but for everyday food
for humans as well. The restriction on eating blood with the
flesh (v. 4) is no comfort to those creatures whose life-blood will
be drained. 'Dominion' has now become despotic.[4] The parenthetical statement regarding Nimrod, 'he was a mighty
hunter (*gibbōr-ṣayid*) before the Lord' (10.9), indicates that
humans successfully pursued the licence given to them
against animals.

Conclusion

As we review the role of the Announcement of 1.28 within the
primaeval history we can see that the reader's intuition that
its imperatives would be prominent in the ensuing narrative
has been justified. All three major elements congregate in
crucial passages which determine future developments (e.g.

---

[1] Westermann, *Genesis 1–11*, p. 448; Wenham, *Genesis 1–15*, p. 186.
[2] The force of this statement is diluted by the translation of Fishbane,
'Genesis 2.4b-11.32', p. 34, '... may your lordship and power rule the
creatures of the earth...'
[3] Cf. Calvin, *Genesis*, 1.291; Kidner, *Genesis*, p. 101, who both maintain, surprisingly, that permission to eat meat might not be an innova-
tion here. Similarly, Dequeker, 'Green Herbage', p. 127.
[4] Cf. Driver, *Genesis*, pp. 95-96; Skinner, *Genesis*, pp. 169-70;
Richardson, *Genesis 1–11*, p. 107; Fretheim, *Creation*, p. 113; Clines,
'Theology of the Flood Narrative', p. 138; Westermann, *Genesis 1–11*,
p. 462. Cf. *Genesis Rabbah* 34.12, where it is stated that 'fear and dread
returned, but dominion did not return'. (This assumes 'fear' and
'dread' were part of the original ordinance in 1.28.)

3.14-19; 8.21–9.7) and also incidentally in other pericopes (e.g. 4.1ff.). On the other hand, chs. 1–11 tend to be more fragmented than chs. 12–50, and as a result the plot Announcement appears to be less well integrated than is the case with the respective Announcements in chs. 12–50. Nevertheless, while there may not be so many smooth transitions in the plot of the primaeval history, every episode can be related to the Announcement of 1.28 in one way or another, without any special pleading. As we investigate the fate of the three-fold Announcement of 1.28, we can see that none of the imperatives remains untouched by the turn of events recounted in chs. 1–11. Matters are far more complex than originally seemed likely. There is modification, intensification, negation. The first ('be fruitful, multiply and fill') is executed throughout the narrative, but is threatened by several factors: the pain of childbirth (cf. 3.16); murder (ch. 4); death (cf. chs. 5, 10); human desire to settle in one place (11.1-9); infertility (11.30). The second ('subdue the earth'), is largely negated; it cannot be fulfilled absolutely. Even more significant than the Deluge demonstrating the earth subduing humans, the curse on the ground, and the Man's eventual return to it, together indicate why 8.21–9.7 excludes the possibility of humans subduing the earth. The third (dominion over the animals) degenerates into a relationship of hostility and fear between the two parties. The limited dominion humans enjoy in chs. 1–2 becomes increasingly despotic, beginning with the divine curse on the serpent (3.14-15) and gathering pace as we learn of animal sacrifices by Abel and Noah, and the acknowledgment that animals stand in 'fear and dread' of humans and may be eaten as food (9.2-3). The mighty hunter Nimrod (10.9) stands in stark relief to vegetarian Adam in the Garden. He is a symbol of the transformation the Announcement has undergone.

Thus, two of the imperatives in particular (subjugation of the earth and dominion over the animals) undergo significant modification. Although humans increasingly dominate the animal creation and eventually rule despotically (an *intensification* of the original command), there is an ironic sense in which animals, through the serpent, exercise an ongoing dominion over the humans (a *reversal* of the original command); i.e. the serpent's tempting of the first humans to commit the offence affects the rest of their lives and, indeed, human history. Also, the earth becomes increasingly difficult to dominate. It overwhelms most of humanity in the Flood, and all of humanity in death. Interestingly, God seems more willing to modify these second and third elements of the Announcement than he is the first—'be fruitful, multiply and fill the earth'. Not only are humans reasonably successful in obeying this, but when they give notice of disobedience (e.g. at Babel), God intervenes to ensure it is obeyed, willingly or not. The curse on the Woman (3.16) may have made it more *difficult*, but it still remains *necessary* to procreate. As we shall see, this strong focus on multiplication is maintained in the ancestral history. By the end of ch. 11 it has become clear that the failure of the Announcement of 1.28 to translate itself into fulfilment on all points is not entirely the fault of humans, although they bear primary responsibility. God also orders events in such a way that makes obedience to his original commands increasingly difficult.

A careful reading of Gen. 1–11 leads to the following conclusion regarding the divine blessings/imperatives. They are not to be taken as absolutes. They are malleable, subject to change or negation by various outside forces. The primaeval history provides enough evidence for us to treat with great suspicion statements such as Wenham's, that

> the word of blessing, whether pronounced by God or man, guarantees and effects the hoped-for success... Once uttered, the word [of command or promise] carries its own life-giving power and cannot be revoked by man (cf. 27.27-40). Genesis may be described as the story of the fulfillment of the divine promises of blessing.[1]

Just *how* fallacious this point of view is will be demonstrated in the chapters that follow.

---

[1] Wenham, *Genesis 1–15*, p. 24. See Thiselton, 'The Supposed Power of Words', pp. 283-99, for a trenchant criticism of the view that any word, human or divine, has such inherent power. However, I believe that the evidence from Genesis must modify Thiselton's conclusions regarding the power of divine words. See succeeding chapters.

Chapter 2

THE ABRAHAM STORY

Introduction

The purpose of this chapter is to probe the plot of the Abraham story (Gen. 11.26–25.11). I will adopt a similar approach to that employed in the previous chapter, and analyse carefully the divine Announcement of 12.1-3, and trace the fate of the imperatives and promises given there as they unfold in the rest of the narrative.

That there is an essential link between 12.1-3 and the Abraham story as a whole should be obvious to the first-time reader of Genesis, and this connection will be reinforced by the results of this study.

> Everything he does following his call and everything that happens to him are either directly related to them [i.e. the promises of 12.1-3] in the narratives or may be brought into connection with them by the exercise of a little imagination... the working out of the promises supplies both the main element of tension in the plot of the stories and the primary key to their interpretation.[1]

[1] Gibson, *Genesis*, 2.12. This is an almost universally accepted position (though usually confined to the 'Yahwist' strand). Cf. Gunkel, *Genesis*, p. 167; Muilenburg, 'Abraham and the Nations', p. 393; Wolff, 'Kerygma of the Yahwist', p. 137; Clements, *Abraham and David*, p. 15; Müller, 'Imperativ und Verheißung', p. 558; von Rad, *Genesis*, pp. 165-67; Wehmeier, '"Blessing for the Nations"', p. 2; Tsevat, 'Hagar and the Birth of Ishmael', p. 53; Yarchin, 'Imperative and Promise', p. 164; Westermann, *Promises to the Fathers*, p. 156; *idem*, *Genesis 12-36*, p. 146; Martens, *Plot and Purpose*, pp. 26, 32; Goldingay, 'Patriarchs', p. 3.

The influence of 12.1-3 stretches beyond Gen. 12–25, of course. Cf. Bright, *Covenant and Promise*, p. 24, 'The whole story of the exodus, the wilderness experience, and the giving of the land is seen in the ful-

However, I shall have reason for suggesting later in this study that the relationship of the initial divine Announcement to the Abraham story is more complex than in similar Announcements in the primaeval history and in the stories of Jacob and Jacob's family.

While 12.1-3 is essential for understanding chs. 12–25 as a whole, it also has a very important connection with the preceding material in chs. 1–11. A detailed study of this relationship will not be attempted here, but some general observations will be instructive. It is commonly observed that ch. 11 in general, and the Babel story in particular (11.1-9), provides a backdrop for reading the promises of 12.1-3. This observation allows a number of comparisons and contrasts to emerge. For example, Yahweh promises Abraham,[1] 'I will make of you a great nation' (12.2a), almost immediately after we have read, 'Now Sarai was barren; she had no child' (11.30). (Let me note, immediately, that Yahweh does not in ch. 12 promise fertility to Sarah, but the juxtaposition of these two statements engages the reader's interest at the outset.) Abraham is told to set out 'to the land that I will show you' (12.1b)—an enigmatic statement which is only subsequently clarified, but which stands in suggestive relationship to the movement of the citizens of Babel, who like Abraham migrated from the east and 'found a plain in the land of Shinar and settled there' (11.2). Abraham is promised that 'all the families of the earth' will in some way find blessing because of him (12.3b), when by way of contrast these same human groups were dispersed from Babel in utter confusion (11.7-9).[2] When we add to this other possibilities, such as the contrast between the tower-builders' 'let us make a name for ourselves' (11.4) and God's 'I will make your name great' (12.2), enough has been said to show how the call of Abraham recalls the Babel story. Thus when reading the Abraham story in the light of 12.1-3, we must remember that this divine Announcement itself is illuminated by being read against the

filment of the promise made to the fathers'.
[1] I will use this form of the name throughout, retaining the form Abram only in quotations. Similarly with the forms Sarai/Sarah.
[2] Cf. von Rad, 'Form-Critical Problem', pp. 65-66; Dequeker, 'La vocation d'Abraham', p. 9.

background provided by the primaeval history,[1] of which ch. 11 is the climax.[2]

Before investigating the major motifs in 12.1-3, two important problems of translation need to be addressed. These are, first, the meaning of the imperative form *wehyēh* in 12.2d, and secondly, the exact nuance of *nibrᵉkû* in 12.3b. Both of these issues have been the subject of much scholarly attention.

Since it contains an imperative, one would expect 12.2d to be rendered, 'be a blessing'. However, some have taken the lead of Rashi in repointing the 2nd m.s. impv. to provide a 3rd m.s. perf., *wᵉhayâ*.[3] The resultant translation would then be, 'and it [i.e. your name (v. 2c)] shall be a blessing'.[4] Another possibility, if one adopts a 3rd m.s. reading, is to see 12.2d as expressing a *consequence*, rather than a *declaration*, which would give, '...so that it will be a blessing'. The basis for this, in Yarchin's words, is that 'a consecutive-perfect form following an

---

[1] Wehmeier, '"Blessing for the Nations"', pp. 2-3; Lundbom, 'Abraham and David', pp. 203-209; Dumbrell, 'Covenant with Abraham', p. 50, states, 'the new powerful word, which in Gn. 12.1-3 forms the substance of the Abrahamic covenant, is to annul the curse of Gn. 1–11'. In this, he is in agreement with, e.g., Muilenburg, 'Abraham and the Nations', pp. 389-90; de Pury, 'La tour de Babel', pp. 80-97; Gibson, *Genesis*, 2.6-7.

[2] This observation still stands, substantially, even if one accepts the view that the primaeval history as such ends in Gen. 8.21. Cf. Rendtorff, 'Genesis 8,21', pp. 69-78. (For a convincing rebuttal of Rendtorff's argument, see Steck, 'Genesis 12 1-3', pp. 525-54.) Wherever one draws the lines of demarcation, 12.1-3 is preceded by chs. 1–11, and immediately by the Babel narrative and the genealogies; the points of contact outlined above make a comparison mandatory.

[3] Yarchin, 'Imperative and Promise', p. 165.

[4] This has been taken up by, e.g., Skinner, *Genesis*, p. 244; Speiser, *Genesis*, pp. 85, 86. Speiser comments (p. 86) that the second person is syntactically unacceptable. However, he gives no good reason why the second person *imperative* is unacceptable. His problem occurs only if he shifts from imperative to perfect. Coats, *Genesis*, p. 107, argues that the 2nd m.s. impv. disrupts the flow of impfs. with waw. He suggests prefixing a yod to the MT to maintain this flow of impfs., with the resultant, '... so that I may make your name great, so that it may be a blessing'. He does not, however, explain *why* the disruption in the flow of impfs. is a problem. If the passage wished to convey the impv. in this line (v. 2d), which it is perfectly free to do, it could not have done so any better than the present MT.

imperfect, cohortative, imperative, or participle can serve as a continuation or natural outgrowth of the preceding verb'.[1] Another suggestion is to keep the 2nd m.s. impv. form and translate, '... so that you will effect blessing'. This is done on the basis that 'a consecutive clause in the second person, after a cohortative, is formed with the indirect imperative'.[2] Proponents of such arguments display great erudition, but fail to convince me that repointing is necessary, or that the impv., if kept, fails to convey its usual force. Andersen addresses the meaning of 12.2 in his discussion of consecutive commands issued by means of 'imperative verb clauses'.[3] A simple form is found in Gen. 17.1: *hithallēk lᵉpānay wehyēh tāmîm*—'walk before me and be perfect'. He argues that Gen. 12.1-2 presents essentially the same construction: *lek-lᵉkā...wehyēh bᵉrākâ*— 'You go... and be a blessing'. Andersen maintains that the string of two imperatives, even though separated by a three-clause promise, keep their imperative force. There is therefore no need to emend *wehyēh*; 'the MT is by all means to be retained'.[4] Another example of discontinuous imperative coordination cited is Exod. 3.10: *wᵉᶜattâ lᵉkâ wᵉᵉešlāḥᵃkā ᵓel-parᶜô wᵉhôṣēᵓ ᵓet-ᶜammî*—'And now *come*, I will send you to Pharaoh; *bring forth* my people...' While not always arguing from the same basis, many recent studies[5] argue for the

---

[1] Yarchin, 'Imperative and Promise', p. 166.

[2] Wolff, 'Kerygma of the Yahwist', p. 137 n. 28. Unfortunately, the two examples he cites do not prove his point beyond any shadow of doubt. 1 Kgs 1.12 may be rendered in a way which preserves the force of the impv. form, i.e., 'Now therefore come, let me give you counsel: save your own life and the life of your son Solomon...' (cf. RSV, '... *that* you may save...'). 2 Kgs 5.10 is a stronger example, but even here the force of the imperative is still possible; 'Go and wash in the Jordan seven times, and your flesh shall be restored—be clean! (cf. RSV, '... and you shall be clean') (cf. the discussion by Burney, *Notes on Kings*, p. 6). Nevertheless, this line of argument is followed by several, e.g., Driver, *Tenses*, p. 69; Joüon, *Grammaire*, p. 318; Green, *Old Testament Hebrew*, p. 154; Vriezen, 'Bemerkungen zu Genesis 12.1-7', p. 387; Ruprecht, 'Vorgegebene Tradition', p. 180; Westermann, *Genesis 12–36*, p. 144; RSV.

[3] Andersen, *Sentence*, p. 108.

[4] Andersen, *Sentence*, p. 108.

[5] E.g. Mitchell, 'Abram's Understanding', p. 35; Klein, 'Yahwist Looks at Abraham', p. 44; Terrien, *Elusive Presence*, p. 73; Dequeker,

retention of the imperative force of *wehyēh* in 12.2d. As
Terrien states,

> The imperative phrase 'be a blessing!' is indeed unusual,
> but the Masoretic pointing is well established, and there is
> no valid reason to correct it (Gen 12.2c). This is the mission
> of Abraham and of Israel: 'Be a blessing!'[1]

If the form and force of the imperative is maintained, then the
sense is:

> Be a blessing,
> so that I may bless those who bless you,
> and those who curse you I will curse...

Such a translation not only conveys the weight of the command to be a blessing, but also makes the following promises
contingent on Abraham obeying this decree. A cohortative
(*waᵃbārᵃkâ* [12.3a] following an imperative (*wehyēh* [12.2d])
expresses the purpose or result of the imperative.[2]

Another problem confronts the reader in 12.3b, whether
nibrᵉkû should be understood passively, i.e. 'by you shall all the
families of the earth be blessed', or reflexively, 'by you shall all
the families of the earth bless themselves'. Discussion of these
alternatives is no new development—Calvin was aware of a
long-standing debate over the exact nuance of the niphal in
this verse.[3] Because of the programmatic nature of 12.1-3 an
understanding of the precise intention of the term could have

'Noah and Israel', p. 123; Auffret, 'Structure littéraire de Gen 12.1-
4aα', p. 247; Dumbrell, 'Covenant with Abraham', pp. 42-43. Cf. Coats,
Genesis, p. 108; Yarchin, 'Imperative and Promise', p. 171; Chew,
'Blessing for the Nations', p. 167.
[1] Terrien, *Elusive Presence*, p. 74.
[2] Cf. Driver, *Tenses*, p. 64; Joüon, *Grammaire*, pp. 314-15 (who notes
other possibilities); Davidson, *Hebrew Grammar*, p. 197; Lambdin,
Biblical Hebrew, p. 119; Kautzsch, *Gesenius' Grammar*, p. 320;
Greenberg, *Hebrew*, pp. 183-84; Alexander, 'Genesis 22', pp. 19ff.,
demonstrates this convincingly in analysing an identical construction
in Gen. 17.1-2. Such an understanding calls into question the view of
12.1-3 as a *purely* gracious pronouncement, such as that expressed by
Moberly, 'Akedah', p. 318, commenting on ch. 22: 'One of the most
notable features about the divine promises elsewhere in Genesis is
that they always constitute a unilateral and unconditional offer on
God's part'.
[3] Calvin, *Genesis*, pp. 348-49.

repercussions on the reading of the rest of the Abraham narrative; therefore an outline of the major arguments on both sides will be helpful.[1] The 'passive' interpretation appears to have the longest pedigree. This was the LXX understanding: καὶ ἐνευλογηθήσονται ἐν σοὶ πᾶσαι αἱ φυλαὶ τῆς γῆς.[2] The NT (Gal. 3.8) follows a similar line: Ἐνευλογηθήσονται ἐν σοὶ πάντα τὰ ἔθνη.[3] The passive is found also in the ancient versions. In addition to these witnesses it is pointed out by its proponents that the niphal usually represents the passive voice.[4]

On the other hand, those who favour a reflexive translation can claim a tradition going back at least to Rashi.[5] While the niphal is usually passive, it is argued that it is *primarily* reflexive.[6] If the intention of the text were to convey the passive, this could have been done unambiguously by using the pual. This form of *brk* is not found in Genesis, but occurs in the Pentateuch (Num. 22.6; Deut. 33.13) and occasionally elsewhere. In addition, it is pointed out that the essential formula found in the niphal in 12.3b (and 18.18; 28.14), is found in the hithpael in 22.18 and 26.4. As *hitbār°kû* is unambiguously reflexive, the disputed niphal, it is argued, should be explained by the unambiguous hithpael form.[7]

---

[1] I follow here the helpful outline provided by Chew, *'Blessing for the Nations'*, pp. 5-10.

[2] Rahlfs (ed.), *Septuaginta*.

[3] Aland et al. (eds.), *The Greek New Testament*.

[4] See Kautzsch, *Gesenius' Grammar*, p. 138. Modern advocates of a passive translation include, Cassuto, *Genesis*, 2.315 and Kidner, *Genesis*, p. 114. A very similar translation is possible if the niphal is to have a similar force to the Greek middle, as advocated by Schreiner, 'Segen für die Völker', p. 7, and followed by Wolff, 'Kerygma of the Yahwist', p. 137; Vogels, *God's Covenant*, p. 42; Martin-Achard, *Actualité d'Abraham*, p. 68; Wehmeier, '"Blessing for the Nations"', p. 7; Dumbrell, 'Covenant with Abraham', p. 49. In this case, the intention would be, 'in you all the families of the earth shall find blessing'.

[5] Westermann, *Genesis 12–36*, p. 151.

[6] See Kautzsch, *Gesenius' Grammar*, p. 137; Davidson, *Hebrew Grammar*, p. 103; Rowley, *Election*, pp. 65-66; Joüon, *Grammaire*, p. 113; Vogels, *God's Covenant*, p. 42.

[7] As argued by Driver, *Genesis*, p. 145; Rowley, *Election*, pp. 65-66; Speiser, *Genesis*, p. 86; Vriezen, 'Bemerkungen zu Genesis 12.1-7',

To summarize the situation: the pual form of *brk* which is
distinctively passive occurs nowhere in Genesis. The hithpael
of *brk*, distinctively reflexive, does occur and significantly so in
passages which essentially repeat the promise formula of
12.3b (22.18 and 26.4). However, if the niphal of *brk* in 12.3b
(and in 18.18 and 28.14) is intended to have an identical
meaning with the hithpael form, then why was the hithpael
not used here as it is in 22.18 and 26.4? Chew makes the
significant suggestion that as *nibrⁱkû* occurs only in the
ancestral narratives, then the key to its meaning should be
sought there. He suggests that the meaning of *nibrⁱkû* should
not be decided (in fact, cannot be decided) on a purely
grammatical basis. Given the programmatic nature of 12.1-3
as a whole, the meaning of the verb in v. 3b should also be
decided by the context of the passage and by the role played by
Abraham in the narrative.[1] I wish the situation were more
clear cut than this, but grammatical analysis alone does not
allow any dogmatic conclusions at this stage. I will therefore
suspend judgment on this issue until we have surveyed the
Abraham narrative as a whole.

We are now in a position to define in more detail the function of 12.1-3 which is made up of two main elements:
imperatives and promises.[2] We need to answer a basic question: What is the *content* of the imperatives and promises?

The passage commences with an imperative which governs
the whole: 'Go!' (*lek*). Abraham is to go *from*, and to go *to*. It is
likely that the sequence expressing what he is to leave
behind—'country' (*'ereṣ*), 'kindred' (*môledet*), and 'father's
house' (*bêt 'ābî*)—is to be seen as a cumulative list which

p. 388; Westermann, *Genesis 12–36*, p. 151. This approach assumes, of
course, that the formula found in 12.3b has identical meaning regardless of verb form or context, whenever it is used in the subsequent
ancestral history. This assumption needs to be proved. Chew,
'Blessing for the Nations', passim (following Vogels, *God's Covenant*,
p. 42), argues for subtle distinctions in the force of the formulas, in the
light of their contexts. Skinner, *Genesis*, p. 244, arguing from source-
critical grounds, concludes that the usages of the hithpael in 22.18 and
26.4, 'are not necessarily decisive of the sense of 12³'. This concession,
however, does not prevent him from favouring the reflexive.
[1] Chew, *'Blessing for the Nations'*, p. 10.
[2] Cf. Coats, *Genesis*, p. 107.

becomes increasingly specific, personal and demanding.[1] The specificity of this challenge contrasts sharply with the vagueness of his destination—'the land that I will show you'. The second imperative is, as we have seen above, 'Be a blessing!' (v. 2d). These two imperatives thus embrace the negative and the positive. Abraham must, negatively, leave behind the stability of cherished family ties, and, positively, embrace the challenge of being a blessing. As we analyse the plot of the Abraham story, the degree to which Abraham obeys these two commands will be a crucial point to ponder. For, if my understanding of the divine Announcement is correct, the plain meaning of the text is that the fulfilment of the *promises* is contingent upon obedience to the *imperatives*.

There are several promises, flowing from the imperatives, of which five require little explanation, even if at this stage we are unsure how they might work out in practice:

(a)	I will make of you a great nation	v. 2a
(b)	I will bless you	v. 2b
(c)	I will make your name great	v. 2c
(d)	I will bless those who bless you	v. 3a
(e)	I will curse those who curse you	v. 3b.

How these promises might work out in practice, and how much overlap there might be between some of them (e.g. between b and c), need not detain us at this point.

There are two points of uncertainty. The first concerns the reference to land in v. 1e. If the criterion of reading 'the story so far' is applied rigorously, the question to be asked is whether, *at this point*, Abraham has received a promise of land ownership. Yahweh tells Abraham to go 'to the land that I will show you' (*'ar'ekā*). Does this amount to a promise that Abraham will *possess* that land? Jeyeraj has studied this question in great detail.[2] He outlines three approaches to the issue. Some argue that the land promise is present.[3] Those who

---

[1] Cassuto, *Genesis*, 2.311-12; Skinner, *Genesis*, p. 243. However, Speiser, *Genesis*, p. 85 translates as, '...Go forth from *your native land* / And from your father's home...', explaining *m ē'arṣēkā ûmimôladtᵉkā* as 'a clear case of hendiadys' (p. 86).
[2] Jeyeraj, *Land Ownership in the Pentateuch*, pp. 28-31.
[3] E.g. Clements, *Abraham and David*, pp. 15ff., 57.

suggest this point out that 12.1-3 is programmatic for the entire (Yahwistic) ancestral history, in which the land promise features; it follows, therefore, that the introductory divine Announcement contains this important narrative theme. Others see the land promise as lying behind 12.1 only as a secondary feature.[1] Finally, some see no land promise at all in 12.1.[2] Jeyeraj argues convincingly that the hiphil of *rā'â* does not convey the sense of *possession*. '"Causing Abraham to see the land" is different from "giving the land"... Verse 1 is only an assurance that God will make Abraham to see that unknown land during his journey.'[3] In addition, I would add that of the 59 occurrences of the hiphil of *rā'â* found elsewhere in the OT, none carries the connotation of 'give' or 'possess'. In fact, what evidence there is points in the opposite direction. In Deut. 34.1, 4 Moses ascends Mount Nebo 'and Yahweh showed him (*wayyar'ēhû*) all the land... and Yahweh said to him,... I have let you see it (*her'îtîkā*) with your eyes, but you shall not go over there'. This demonstrates that 'showing' the land to Moses does not mean 'giving' the land to Moses. However, 12.1 does arouse the curiosity of the reader (and, presumably of Abraham). Why does Yahweh wish to show Abraham this land, wherever it is? What purpose will be served by Abraham going to it? Will it be merely another land in which he will live as a sojourner? I would argue, therefore, that while the promise of land *possession* is not present in 12.1, the opaqueness of the divine command starts the reader mulling over its specific focus, and the narrative continues to engage such interest with periodic references to land in the subsequent story line. This aspect of the plot will be dealt with later in this chapter. Provisionally, however, it may be stated that no categorical promise of land possession is given in 12.1, but the reader is alerted to the importance of a particular land; whether this will develop into a promise of land possession for

---

[1] E.g. Zimmerli, 'Promise and Fulfillment', p. 92; Wolff, 'Kerygma of the Yahwist', p. 140. Habel, 'Gospel Promise to Abraham', p. 348, sees the land promise 'implied' in the command to move from Ur to Canaan.
[2] E.g. von Rad, 'Promised Land', p. 79; *idem*, *Genesis*, p. 159; Westermann, *Genesis 12–36*, p. 148.
[3] Jeyaraj, *Land Ownership in the Pentateuch*, p. 29.

Abraham, only time will tell.[1]

The second point of uncertainty about 12.1-3 concerns the correct translation of v. 3b, the problems of which I have discussed above. The possibilities are that either the nations will be blessed because of Abraham (which is what a passive translation implies), or that the nations will wish to bless themselves with the name of Abraham (which is what a reflexive translation implies). Either way, the nations will have a positive assessment of Abraham. As far as tracing the fate of this promise in chs. 12-25, which is the aim of this chapter, I do not need to be any more specific at the moment. However, I will return to this issue at the end of the chapter.

My analysis will be based on the following translation:

> v. 1 Now Yahweh said to Abraham:
>   'Go from your country and your kindred and
>   your father's house
>   to the land that I will show you.
>
> v. 2 And I will make of you a great nation
>   and I will bless you and make your name great.
>   Be a blessing,
> v. 3 so that I may bless those who bless you, and
>   those who curse you I will curse;
>   and by you all the families of the earth shall find
>   blessing.'

Before I begin my analysis of the plot, one final observation needs to be made. While I wish to see how the imperatives and promises of 12.1-3 fare in chs. 12–25, the question might arise in the mind of the reader as to whether some promises can be fulfilled within the limits of the Abraham story. For example, Yahweh promises, 'I will make of you a great nation'. Is it intended that this be fulfilled within the lifetime of Abraham, or even within Genesis as a whole? The first-time reader does not know the answer to this and so must suspend judgment until the end of the story has been reached. However, a legiti-

---

[1] Von Rad, 'Promised Land', p. 84:

> the promise of the land is thus to some extent kept apart from the great pronouncement in which God declares His purpose, but by virtue of this special treatment it actually gains in importance.

mate question I will ask is whether its *eventual* fulfilment is being hampered or facilitated by the events occurring within chs. 12–25.[1]

The Promise of Nationhood

Of all the promises, it is the one concerning Abraham becoming a great nation (v. 2a) which implicitly and explicitly dominates the Abraham story and for that reason I start by analysing it.

On hearing that Abraham will become the father of a great nation, the attentive reader is immediately reminded of the stark statement previously made in 11.30, 'Now Sarai was barren; she had no child'. It is commonly assumed that Sarah's barrenness is a major obstacle to Abraham having descendants.[2] However, the promise in 12.2a makes no mention of Sarah as the mother of this promised great nation. All that the reader, and Abraham, are told is that *Abraham* will become a great nation. To hear the promise as Abraham heard it, we must bracket out any later developments we now know will take place. 'I will make of you a great nation' must not be garbled into 'your barren wife will have a child'. Sarah's

---

[1] Childs, *Old Testament as Scripture*, p. 151, is too restrictive in his assessment that 'the promises function *only* as a prelude to the coming exodus, and extend into the distant future' (emphasis mine). That they extend beyond Genesis cannot be denied; that they get a chance to do so depends on the treatment they receive in Genesis.

Westermann, *Promises to the Fathers*, p. 126, comments,

> This is the most important distinction between the various promises: the promises that will be fulfilled for those who receive them or for their families must be distinguished from those that can only be fulfilled after Israel is a nation.

This does of course raise the question as to when, in the mind of the *narrator*, the nation began. From Westermann's source- and traditio-critical perspective, nationhood appears only at the time of the Davidic-Solomonic hegemony (the milieu for the 'Yahwist'). Even granting the correctness of this position, the ancestral narrative shows that the *future* goal ('great nation') depends on the present behaviour of Abraham. Westermann's two categories may be distinguished, but not separated.

[2] Cf. most major commentaries.

barrenness rules out her giving birth; but there are many avenues open to Abraham to get descendants.

Abraham's immediate response to this divine Announcement reveals that this is how he has understood it: 'So Abram went, as the Lord had told him; and Lot went with him' (12.4a). From a rigidly literal point of view, this report of Abraham's response is inherently contradictory. On the one hand we are told that Abraham obeyed the imperative to go— an imperative which demanded that he leave behind his country, kindred and father's house. On the other hand he took Lot (cf. 12.5a). It was impossible for him to have done both; Lot, being the son of his deceased brother Haran, belongs to his kindred—i.e. in taking Lot, Abraham has *not* left behind his kindred, and did not, therefore, go 'as the Lord had told him'.[1] The most reasonable solution to this conundrum is that Abraham did set out obediently, honestly believing that he was going as the Lord had commanded, but that he did not consider Lot to be his 'kindred' or simply part of his 'father's house'. He must have thought Lot was someone far more important—none other than his surrogate son and the one through whom the 'great nation' would come.[2] There is no other logical explanation why Abraham should take Lot. Some have suggested that the premature death of Haran left Lot in need of being adopted and protected by his uncle Abraham.[3] However, the evidence is that Lot was no mere stripling in need of protection. No sooner will he have joined Abraham's trek to Egypt and back—surely occupying no great period of

[1] Coats, *Genesis*, p. 108, fails to see the inherent contradiction in his statement, 'Abram executed the instructions as received and took Lot along'. Cf. Alexander, *Literary Analysis of Abraham Narrative*, p. 34; Gibson, *Genesis*, 2.29; Coats, 'Curse in God's Blessing', p. 31. Chapter 24 reinforces my point. In 24.4 Abraham sends his servant 'to my country and to *my kindred (môledet)*', i.e. the servant is sent to the place and people whom Abraham was earlier commanded to leave (12.1). The 'kindred' in question here are the members of Nahor's family, Nahor like Abraham being Lot's uncle. The three key terms of 12.1, (*'ereṣ; môledet; bêt 'ābî*) recur in 24.4, 7; Lot belongs to this social group. Abraham may have left behind the rest of his kindred—but he took Lot.
[2] Cf. Clines, 'Ancestor in Danger', pp. 69-70.
[3] E.g. Dequeker, 'La vocation d'Abraham', p. 4.

time—than he has control of herdsmen (13.7-8), and his uncle is suggesting that the two of them live separately (13.9)—thus giving the lie to the suggestion that Lot, a mere youth, needed parental protection and guidance. It would appear, therefore, that Abraham was working to another agenda. (While it might be suggested that the narrative portrays Abraham deliberately disobeying the call in one respect when he took Lot, I hope to demonstrate that Lot's function in the Abraham story makes this unlikely.) The closeness Abraham felt for Lot is underlined by the fact that whereas he took Lot with him he left his own father, Terah, in Haran. The simple mathematics of comparing the chronologies of 11.26, 32 and 12.4b show that Terah lived for a good sixty years in Haran after his son abandoned him.[1] Abraham was willing to leave his father, but not Lot. His hopes are clearly invested in his nephew. For these reasons I reject the argument of some who impute base motives to Lot for accompanying Abraham.[2] Abraham *took* Lot (12.5) for his own personal reasons.[3]

Just how crucial Abraham feels Lot to be is seen when Abraham sets off for sanctuary in Egypt clinging to the hope

---

[1] Cassuto, *Genesis*, 2.310, 317, is one of the few to have noticed this obvious fact. Cf. von Rad, *Genesis*, p. 158. Most assume, impossibly, that 11.32 is chronologically prior to 12.1; e.g. Vogels, 'Lot', p. 141. Westermann, *Genesis 12-36*, p. 140, states for no apparent reason that 'Abraham would have left Haran for Canaan only after the death of Terah'. Kidner, *Genesis*, p. 112, notes the difficulty of maintaining (on the basis of the MT), that Abraham left after Terah's death, and follows the LXX which gives Terah's age at death as 145.

[2] E.g. Vogels, 'Lot', p. 142.

[3] Also, I am not persuaded by the arguments of Miscall, *Workings of Old Testament Narrative*, p. 12, who contends that the text tells us *that* Abraham went, but not *why* he went. It is impossible to state categorically, he argues, why Abraham set out. But this is hardly true even if one stares in blinkered fashion only at the letters on the page. If Abraham 'goes' immediately after receiving a command to 'go', I do not believe that the text has to say mechanically, 'by the way, this was in response to God's command'. If it did, we could hardly call it literature, nor would we wish to read it. Miscall argues that 'the particle "as" (Hebrew: *ka'ăšer* [12.4a]) is frequently used to point to a congruence between a course of action and a previous statement without positing a necessary causal relation'. This is arguable: but can it seriously be suggested for Gen. 12.1-4?

that the nation promise will be fulfilled through his nephew.[1]
The narrative of his sojourn there (12.10-20) has been the
object of much scholarly interest. Most of the attention paid to
the pericope has been taken up with comparing and contrasting it with 'parallel' wife-sister stories in chs. 20 and 26, the
usual assumption being that 'these three passages are three
different portrayals of the same narrative'.[2] If one limits one's
interests to uncovering a hypothetical evolution of a narrative
theme, one may be satisfied with this. But my interest is to see
how the incident relates to the unfolding plot of the larger
story, and its significance *at this point* in the story so far. Abraham acts in 12.10-20 unaware of what he will do later in
ch. 20. I will read the story from the same perspective.[3] I agree
with Clines's contention that,

> where that inference about the prehistory of Genesis is
> utterly unsatisfactory is that it cannot explain why the tale is
> told three times in Genesis, nor what the point of each of the
> tellings, at the specific places where they are located, can
> be.[4]

Abraham enters Egypt assuming the cruciality of Lot to the
divine purpose. Once there, he assumes that his own life is in
danger (12.12). These two pieces of data give a perspective on
the story, and a base for ascribing motives to Abraham's
behaviour.

From a purely Machiavellian viewpoint, Sarah, not being
essential to the fulfilment of the divine promise (as Abraham
understands it), is expendable. But it is essential to protect his
heir, Lot, and also himself, because none of the other promises
of 12.1-3 have yet been fulfilled. He must preserve himself if
he is to be 'shown' the promised land, be a blessing, and see his
friends blessed and enemies cursed, etc. In order to effect these

---

[1] While 12.10 does not state explicitly that Lot accompanied Abraham
and Sarah, 13.1 more or less demands this understanding.
[2] Westermann, *Genesis 12–36*, p. 161. Cf. von Rad, *Genesis*, p. 167.
[3] Most studies of 12.10-20; ch. 20; ch. 26, treat the pericopes as isolated
units, and do not relate them to the position they hold in the plot of the
Abraham story. See e.g. Polzin, '"Ancestress in Danger"', pp. 81-98;
Gordis, 'Lies, Wives and Sisters', pp. 344-59.
[4] Clines, 'Ancestor in Danger', p. 68.

ends Abraham tells the lie that Sarah is his sister.[1] This results in Abraham's life being spared and the only cost is that his wife enters the Pharaoh's harem and is forced, as it appears, to commit adultery![2] Actually, the costs were probably higher. One wonders how many ladies worthy of the high calling of joining the Pharaoh's harem would ever leave the palace. All things being equal, when Sarah joined Pharaoh's household, it would be the last time she would see Abraham. But, as far as Abraham was concerned, the divine promise had made clear that his wife was expendable because of her infertility. Those called by the Lord, like Abraham, must be prepared to make a few sacrifices along the way.[3] The important point is that through Abraham's guile and initiative both the patriarch and his 'seed' have been spared, and with them the promise of Abraham's great nation.

Such an interpretation of 12.10-20 is, I believe, entirely consistent with reading the pericope in the context of the story so far and accepting the programmatic nature of 12.1-3. Almost without exception modern scholarship has not read the passage from this perspective, but has read it in the light of later narrative developments. Alexander is typical when he says, '12.10–13.1 recounts how the birth of an heir to Abraham is placed in jeopardy by Pharaoh's abduction of Sarah'.[4] Abra-

---

[1] Some take the position, on the basis of 20.12, that Abraham spoke the truth here—Sarah being his half-sister, e.g. Kidner, *Genesis*, p. 116. (Driver, *Genesis*, p. 149, considers Abraham not to have been telling the whole truth.) However, Gen. 11.29 informs us that Nahor married within the family, his wife Milcah being his brother Haran's daughter. The same verse tells us that Abraham married Sarah. Given what we are told regarding Nahor's marriage, if Sarah, like Milcah, had also been a close relative, we would surely have been told.
[2] Despite the protestations of e.g. Calvin, *Genesis*, 1.362-63, there can be little doubt that Sarah ended up in the Pharaoh's bed. Cf. Koch, *Growth of Biblical Tradition*, p. 125; Bledstein, 'Trials of Sarah', p. 412; Coats, *Genesis*, p. 111; Gordis, 'Lies, Wives and Sisters', p. 355.
[3] Calvin, *Genesis*, 1.359, argues in this vein. It was essential for Abraham's life to be spared, for the purposes of God were centred on him. Cf. Gros Louis, 'Abraham: I', p. 59: 'That faith by itself is not sufficient is indicated in Egypt, when Abram, remembering the Lord's promises and believing in them, must act to ensure that they are not thwarted by Pharaoh'.
[4] Alexander, *Literary Analysis of Abraham Narrative*, p. 21. Cf. von

ham has no intention of jeopardizing the promise of posterity—in fact quite the opposite—and the reader of the *story so
far* has no grounds for drawing such a conclusion. Nor can it
be maintained, with Brueggemann and Coats, for example,
that the incident shows Abraham's active *disbelief* in the
promise[1]—again, the very contrary. Nor is it really possible to
argue that the danger to Sarah is that she might become
pregnant by Pharaoh and thus dash the promise of offspring
to Abraham. Gen. 11.30 must be read with full patriarchal
chauvinism. Infertility is the fault of the woman—Sarah is
barren—and remains so regardless of her sexual partner.
More importantly, of course, the promise of 12.2a does not
demand the biological paternity of Abraham—and Abraham
is acting on this assumption. These other readings of 12.10-20
seek to read it from hindsight. I resolutely refuse to do so—at
least not until I have come to the end of the story and can then
afford the luxury of looking back. The problem of reading
from hindsight is best illustrated by the title given to the story
almost universally—'The Ancestress in Danger'.[2] While
Sarah's *honour* may be in danger, the one who feels himself to
be in real danger at this stage is Abraham. Thus, 'The
Ancestor in Danger' would be more appropriate.[3]

Once the ruse has been discovered, Pharaoh expels the trio
from Egypt, and they return to Canaan—which as far as we
know is still suffering from the famine. The repeated references to Lot (13.1, 5) remind the reader of his importance to
the action. The presence of huge flocks and large numbers of
servants (12.16; 13.1) is a great drain on natural resources,
which causes tension between Abraham's and Lot's workers.
Abraham and Lot come to an amicable agreement and agree
to separate. It should not surprise us that in making his choice

---

Rad, *Genesis*, p. 169; Gibson, *Genesis*, 2.34.
[1] Brueggemann, *Genesis*, p. 129; Coats, *Genesis*, p. 111. Cf. Kidner,
Genesis, p. 116.
[2] E.g. Koch, *Growth of Biblical Tradition*, p. 111; von Rad, *Genesis*,
p. 167; Coats, *Genesis*, p. 109; Westermann, *Genesis 12–36*, p. 159.
[3] As suggested by Clines, 'Ancestor in Danger', p. 68. Baldwin, *Genesis 12–50*, p. 36 entitles the episode, 'Abram in Danger', suggesting a
similar viewpoint. Berg, 'Ein Sündenfall Abrahams', pp. 7-8, likewise
suggests a shift of emphasis from Sarah to Abraham.

of land, Lot appears to be quite selfish. In 12.10-20 we saw Abraham motivated by self-interest (for the best of reasons, of course). We should then be sparing in our condemnation of Lot when he acts with similar motives in ch. 13. (I am tempted to say, 'like *father*... like *son*'.) What is important for us to bear in mind at this point is the exact tract of land chosen by Lot. Lot having chosen all the Jordan plain (13.11) for himself, we are told that 'Abram dwelt in the land of Canaan, while Lot dwelt among the cities of the valley...' (13.12). I will look at the geography of the promised land below when I analyse the land promise in more detail, but I will make this observation now. Abraham probably did not expect Lot to choose the Jordan plain. Helyer argues persuasively that Abraham offered Lot a portion of the land of *Canaan*, but Lot chose the plain of the Jordan—*outside* of Canaan.[1] This can be seen clearly by the distinction made between the two territories in 13.12. (In whatever ways the boundaries of the 'land of Canaan' might change in the succeeding narrative [and wherever we as readers might think their location to be], at *this* stage, and for *this* narrator, the cities of the plain are not Canaanite.) In the story so far, Abraham knows that his descendants will possess the land of *Canaan* (12.5b-6; cf. 12.7); the fact that he offers part of the land to Lot suggests that he sees Lot as his descendant.[2] With Lot having taken up residence in an area distinct from Canaan, Abraham must think that he has returned to his initial situation—he is now, once again, 'childless'. Or, at least, his descendant has taken up residence outside of the area promised to him by Yahweh. However, no sooner has Lot seemingly been removed from the sphere of the promise,[3] than God reveals in 13.14ff. that the land of

---

[1] Helyer, 'Separation of Abram and Lot', p. 79. Cf. Weippert, 'Canaan', p. 126.
[2] Contra Vogels, 'L'offrande de la terre', p. 52, who argues that Abraham's offer of land to Lot meant that he was making an offer outside the terms stipulated in the divine promise, i.e. that the land was his descendants' (12.7).
[3] Cf. Vogels, 'L'offrande de la terre', p. 53:

> Le texte montre aussi que dans cette démarche purement humaine, en se séparant d'Abraham, l'homme de la promesse, Lot se sépare de ces promesses et par conséquent s'éloigne de

Canaan so far promised to Abraham's descendants is only part of the total promised land, which actually includes the Jordan valley. Given the story so far, it must seem to Abraham that Yahweh is reassuring him that Lot retains his status as true descendant and is still important for Yahweh's purposes.

We see, therefore, that far from excluding Lot from contention, ch. 13 shows that he is still central to the promise—as far as Abraham is able to interpret events. The repetition of the promise of many descendants (13.16) thus acts as a fitting epilogue to the episode.[1] In these first two major episodes since Abraham heard Yahweh's Announcement, we see him doggedly pursuing the promise. In 12.10-20 he pushes moral considerations to one side for the sake of preserving himself, his heir, and the promise. In 13.8ff., having been promised that his descendants would possess Canaan, he offers part of that land to Lot—completely in accord with the divine promise as he understood it. This counters the view which sees a stark contrast between the two episodes, with a faithless Abraham in Egypt and a faithful Abraham in Canaan.[2]

This background helps to provide an understandable motivation for Abraham's rescue of Lot in ch. 14. Lot is still Abraham's 'descendant' and his capture by the foreign kings places him in danger of being killed and bringing an end to Abraham's posterity. In addition, Lot is now on his way out of the land of promise as the captive of the Mesopotamian kings (14.1) and needs to be brought back within its boundaries. The reader may wonder why Abraham is placing all his eggs in one basket, when he has 318 'trained men' (*ḥ^anîkîm* [14.14]), any one of whom could have been pressed into service as his

plus en plus de Dieu.

Helyer, 'Separation of Abram and Lot', p. 86: 'after Lot's separation, Abram has no heir; he is thrown back entirely upon Yahweh's promise of an heir'. Coats, 'Lot', p. 127: 'Lot chooses to separate himself from Abraham and thus from the blessing of God'. Cf. Cassuto, *Genesis*, 2.366.

[1] I believe that the assertion by Westermann, *Genesis 12–36*, p. 178, that 13.14-17 is an insertion because 'the content of the promise does not fit the narrative to which it is appended', misses the point entirely.
[2] Cf. Brueggemann, *Genesis*, p. 132, 'The problem for Abraham is to trust only the promise. This he does in 13.1-18, in contrast to 12.10-20.'

heir, though perhaps with a lesser claim and fewer evidences
of Yahweh's leading than his dead brother's son.
I believe that this reading of ch. 14 is more satisfying and
coherent than the usual understanding which takes ch. 13 to
be the final rupture between godly Abraham and his hedonist
nephew, with Abraham's rescue mission in ch. 14 merely
illustrating that he believed in family solidarity. Sarna's
comment is typical:

> Although Lot had quarrelled with his uncle and had chosen
> to live among the Sodomites of his own free will, yet he was
> still a member of the family and clan and the ties of blood
> imposed a sense of solidarity or responsibility upon the
> patriarch so that he could not stand indifferent to Lot's fate.[1]

Such explanations can not be more than partially satisfying.
All that is said of Lot above, regarding kinship, applies equally
well to Sarah. Yet this did not stop Abraham from abandoning
her to her fate in 12.10-20—in fact even instigating the sexual
liaison. We must ask ourselves whether Abraham would risk
his life for Lot, when in Egypt he had been unwilling to risk his
life for Sarah, if the responsibilities of kinship were the only
ruling factor. I can only conclude that in Abraham's eyes his
nephew is of more value to him than his wife. This reinforces
my point that on Abraham's present understanding of the
nation promise, Sarah is expendable, but Lot is crucial.

If this argument is accepted, then 15.1-3 poses a problem.
Abraham complains that he is 'childless' (15.2)—which is
literally (i.e. biologically) true—and his heir is *dammešeq*
ᵉlîʿezer (usually rendered 'Eliezer of Damascus'). What has
happened to Lot? Who is 'Eliezer'? Also in 15.3 Abraham
complains, 'You have given me no offspring (*zeraʿ*)'. In 12.7 he
had been promised, 'to your descendants (*lᵉzarᶜᵃkā*) I will give
this land'. Chapter 13 indicated that Abraham placed Lot in
the category of *zeraʿ* when he offered him part of the land
reserved for his *zeraʿ*. Abraham's complaints in 15.1-3 seem to
indicate that he no longer views Lot in such a way. However,
the narrative provides no indication as to why he should have
changed his mind. A detailed investigation of 15.1-6 is thus

---

[1] Sarna, *Understanding Genesis*, p. 116. Cf. Westermann, *Genesis
12–36*, p. 199.

called for, especially in light of the generally accepted fact that ch. 15 occupies a crucial position in the Abraham narrative as a whole.[1] This is particularly true when looked at from my perspective, because several promises made in the initial Announcement of 12.1-3 are developed further here—most importantly, the promise of posterity (12.2a; cf. 15.2-6) which I will discuss here, and the promise of land (12.1; cf. 15.7ff.), to be discussed below.[2]

My first task is to identify the enigmatic 'Eliezer of Damascus'. There is scholarly consensus that 15.2b is unintelligible. It is sometimes suggested that as 15.3b is parallel to v. 2b, the problem is minimized;[3] but, as Skinner points out, 'there is only a *presumption* that the sense agrees with 3b'[4] (emphasis mine). Additionally, as we shall see, v. 3b itself is open to a wide range of interpretations. In fact the familiar 'Eliezer of Damascus' is merely an attempt to make some sense from *hû' dammeśeq* *li'ezer*, which cannot, of course, be rendered 'this is Eliezer of Damascus', nor even the unintelligible, 'this is Damascus, namely Eliezer'.[5] While Cazelles observes that mention of Damascus in 15.2b comes after the ch. 14 narrative in which Abraham pursued the kings north of Damascus (thus suggesting some link between the two passages and the correctness of the MT), the actual connection remains elusive.[6] The term standing in apposition to this problematic designation (*ûben meśeq bêtî*) does not help matters. *Meśeq* is a hapax legomenon which was not understood by any of the versions.[7] The LXX renders the whole, ὁ δὲ υἱὸς Μασεκ τῆς οἰκογενοῦς μου, οὗτος Δαμασκὸς Ελιεζερ, which when read in context is deemed by Skinner to be 'a meaningless sentence' unless sup-

---

[1] Brueggemann, *Genesis*, p. 140: 'This chapter is pivotal for the Abraham tradition. Theologically, it is probably the most important of this entire collection.' Cf. Gross, 'Glaube und Bund', p. 25; Rendtorff, 'Genesis 15', pp. 74-75; Westermann, *Genesis 12–36*, p. 230; Hunter, 'Father Abraham', p. 8.
[2] Cf. Snijders, 'Genesis XV', p. 265; Clements, *Abraham and David*, p. 16; Anbar, 'Genesis 15', p. 40.
[3] Westermann, *Genesis 12–36*, p. 219.
[4] Skinner, *Genesis*, p. 279.
[5] Skinner, *Genesis*, p. 279.
[6] Cazelles, 'Connexions et structure de Gen., XV', p. 330.
[7] Skinner, *Genesis*, p. 278.

plemented by κληρονομήσει (as in some Philo MSS).[1] Render-
ings such as 'the heir of my house/to my household' (RSV/NEB)
are valiant attempts to provide a smooth translation of a
clause which 'as a whole is generally regarded as hopeless'.[2]
In the absence of any plausible suggestions to the contrary I
will treat the whole of 15.2b as being untranslatable, and resist
the urge to submit it to creative reconstructions.[3] I will, therefore, limit myself exclusively to 15.3b in trying to identify the
person whom Abraham announces to be his heir.

The key term is *ben-bêtî*. The familiar translation, 'a slave
born in my house' (e.g. RSV, NEB), is itself an interpretation.
Taken literally, 'a son of my house' could possibly refer to a
number of individuals, though it may not be without significance that the designation for Abraham's servants in 14.14 is
different (*yᵉlîdê bêtî*). By itself however, the term does not
allow us to be any more specific than seeing *ben-bêtî* as referring to a member of Abraham's household.[4] Who could this
be? There is only one obvious choice. Driver eliminated Lot
from contention here because he believed ch. 13 saw the final
parting from Abraham.[5] However, I have suggested above

[1] Skinner, *Genesis*, p. 278.
[2] Speiser, *Genesis*, p. 111.
[3] E.g. the compounded hypotheses of Seebass, 'Gen 15 2b', p. 139, who
builds on a suggestion by A.B. Ehrlich, *Randglossen zur hebräischen
Bibel* 1 (1908): 58. He conjectures the following evolution:

$$h\hat{u}\ l\hat{\imath}\ zera' \rightarrow h\hat{u}'\ {}^*l\hat{\imath}'ezer$$

He assumes that *ben-mešeq* is an allusion to Damascus. However,
Snijders, 'Genesis XV', p. 270, believes that *mešeq* should be read in
the light of *mašaq* (Isa. 33.4), which describes locusts attacking crops,
and suggests that *ben-mešeq* describes 'the attacker, the man who
forces himself upon a person'. The term would then refer to Abraham's fear that a stranger—Eliezer—would usurp the position of the
promised seed. Unger, 'Text of Genesis 15 2, 3', p. 50 suggests the
coherent (?) translation 'And the "son of my house" is the "son of
Meseq", which is Damascus... and beheld [sic], the "son of my house"
shall be my heir', but even this assumes haplography and the insertion of a later gloss.
[4] Cf. Driver, *Genesis*, p. 175; Skinner, *Genesis*, p. 279; Westermann,
Genesis 12–36, p. 220.
[5] Driver, *Genesis*, p. 175.

that this is not the most likely intention of that episode, and that ch. 14 reveals Lot still to hold primary place in Abraham's hopes. I would suggest, therefore, that Lot fills the bill as a *ben-bêtî*, even though now living separately. I conclude, therefore, that there is nothing in 15.1-3 to indicate that Lot has been displaced as Abraham's heir.

If Lot remains, however, another question is raised: why does Abraham complain if his heir has just been rescued from the foreign kings and maintains his prestigious position? The answer to this question must be sought in the divine words which spark Abraham's response: 'Your reward shall be very great' (15.1c). Despite suggestions that the 'reward' promised here is Yahweh himself,[1] or the land,[2] I would agree with von Rad in seeing it as referring to posterity[3]—this is certainly the main focus of Abraham's riposte, and it allows for greater coherence between divine statement and human response than the other two suggestions. I would suggest that the force of Abraham's protest must be connected with the announcement that his reward (posterity) would be *'very great'* (*harbēh me'ōd*). Abraham's complaint is that it is unlikely that his 'reward' will be *'very great'* when he himself is biologically childless (15.2), and he has only a *single* heir (Lot). We learn later that Lot has only two daughters (until the incestuous conception of sons in ch. 19), so not a great deal can be expected from that quarter. That is to say, his complaint is not that God has given him no reward whatsoever, but concerns the *degree* or *amount* of the reward. It is hardly 'very great'— very small beer in fact. Seen in this light the sign given by Yahweh is particularly germane to Abraham's complaint. Likening Abraham's descendants to the numerous stars of heaven (15.5) underlines the 'very great' aspect of the promise. Immediately after being assured of the *great number* of his descendants, we are told, 'and he believed the Lord' (15.6a), the very point which he had previously questioned.

---

[1] E.g. Calvin, *Genesis* 1.399-400; Luther, cited in von Rad, *Genesis*, p. 183.
[2] E.g. Brueggemann, *Genesis*, pp. 141-42.
[3] Von Rad, *Genesis*, p. 183. Cf. Gaston, 'Abraham and the Righteousness of God', p. 41.

Gen. 15.1-6 does bring about an important shift of focus for
the posterity promise. Regardless of the answer to the problems of translation in vv. 2b, 3b, crucial new information
regarding the promise is provided by v. 4, 'And behold the
word of Yahweh came to him, "This man shall not be your
heir, rather your own son [lit. that which goes out of your
inward parts] he shall be your heir". Abraham will have a son
of his own, and his numerous descendants (the point at issue
in Abraham's complaint) must now be traced through this
son. Abraham must stop trusting in Lot as the source for his
descendants—and if my interpretation of his complaint is
correct he had already started to do just that.

No sooner has Abraham been promised, for the *first* time, a
son of his own, than the reader is reminded of an obstacle to
this. The infertility of Sarah, unmentioned since 11.30, comes
to the fore again in 16.1, 'Now Sarai, Abram's wife, bore him
no children'. Up to 15.4 her barrenness had not been a threat
to the promise—as understood by Abraham—because Lot was
the obvious candidate and Sarah was not needed. But now Lot
has been eliminated. This does not make Sarah essential for
the promise (her maternity has nowhere been promised), but
her continuing infertility means that from the perspective of
the story so far the son of promise will not come from her
womb, though it will come from Abraham's loins.[1] This raises
a serious, though not insurmountable, problem.

It comes as a slight surprise, given Abraham's dominating
role in the plot so far, that the action in ch. 16 is initiated by
Sarah who up to now has been the passive victim of her husband's ambitions. Up to this point there has been no indication
that she has any personal contribution to make to the fulfilment of the posterity promise, and she acts here accordingly.
She says, 'Behold now, the Lord has prevented me from bearing children; go in to my maid; it may be that I shall obtain
children by her' (16.2). Here she makes no claim to being

[1] Reading the development of the plot up to this point gives no justification for stating that Sarah was to be the mother of a great nation and
that her infertility threatened the promise. For this common mistake
cf. von Rad, *Genesis*, pp. 191, 196; Berg, 'Der Sündenfall Abrahams
und Saras', p. 7.

involved in the posterity promise,[1] but is simply concerned to do something about the reproach and curse of her childlessness.[2] However, this ambition of Sarah's introduces yet another subtle twist to the plot. Sarah may well fulfil *her* maternal longings by having a surrogate son by Hagar, but the child itself would be the prime candidate for fulfilment of the promise of a son to *Abraham*. That is to say, Sarah's *motive* may be personal, but the *result* will certainly have ramifications for the promise. This raises a further question: did Abraham slip into Hagar's bed in order to do his wife or himself a favour—or to achieve both ends through the one act? Perhaps we will learn the answer to this from the ensuing story.

Abraham experiences no difficulty in impregnating Hagar. His acquiescence to Sarah in the dispute with Hagar (16.6) presents a number of questions regarding his motives. His action obviously carries the potential for endangering the unborn child (although unlike ch. 21 Hagar's life does not seem to be threatened here). But, at the very least, it would result in the separation of the child from his father. If Abraham views the child as the child of promise then either of these dangers is a very serious matter.[3] Why does he act in such a way? Does he think that regardless of the fate of this child he can always fall back on Lot? After so long has he given up any real hope of getting a son? Does he simply not believe the promise of 15.4 (notwithstanding 15.6)?[4] Or does he see it simply as 'Sarah's child', and is willing to act as cavalierly with it as he was with his wife in 12.10-20? Gen. 16.1-6 does

---

[1] Contra von Rad, *Genesis*, pp. 192, 196; Kidner, *Genesis*, p. 126; Brueggemann, *Genesis*, pp. 150, 153.

[2] As seen by Westermann, *Genesis 12–36*, p. 237; McEvenue, 'Narrative Styles in the Hagar Stories', p. 68; Tsevat, 'Hagar', p. 67; Coats, *Genesis*, p. 130. It is sometimes suggested that Sarah's initiative and Abraham's response is a great sin. But this can only be maintained if one argues that the intention of both from the outset was to force God's hand in the posterity promise. Cf. von Rad, *Genesis*, p. 191; Magonet, 'Die Söhne Abrahams', p. 207; Berg, 'Der Sündenfall Abrahams und Saras', pp. 8ff.

[3] Tsevat, 'Hagar', p. 56.

[4] Mitchell, 'Abram's Understanding', p. 42; Brueggemann, *Genesis*, p. 151.

not provide a clear answer to any of these questions; we will have to wait to see if any is provided.

The narrative of 16.7ff. develops in a similar manner to that of 13.8ff. In this earlier passage I noted that no sooner had Lot seemed to be eliminated from contention than Yahweh acted in such a way as to reinforce Abraham's belief that Lot was essential for the fulfilment of the promise (see above). Similarly, no sooner has Hagar fled from Sarah with Abraham's child in her womb than the angel meets her and makes his pronouncement in 16.8-12. (Abraham must have been told of Hagar's experience because *he* names the child Ishmael, as the angel had commanded Hagar [16.15].) The promise to greatly multiply her descendants reminds the reader of the identical promise just recently made to Abraham that he would have a son and his descendants would be innumerable (15.4-5). The most reasonable interpretation of this incident with Hagar, given our knowledge of the story so far, is that Ishmael is that very son of promise.[1] This is reinforced by the command to return to Sarah (with the child being born in Abraham's house [16.9]). Abraham can certainly be forgiven if this is how he interpreted the incident. This interpretation receives extra weight from 16.15. Despite Sarah's statement

---

[1] This is a position rejected by many. For example, von Rad, *Genesis*, p. 194, states that in the blessing on Ishmael, 'there is not a word about the great promise to Abraham'. However, this rests on making the promise to Hagar (16.10) and the blessing on Ishmael (16.11) mutually exclusive units, which is hardly tenable in the context. The child in Hagar's womb is obviously the first of her many descendants. Westermann, *Genesis 12–36*, p. 245, also misses the mark. He sees the intervention of the angel at the spring 'as the fulfillment of Sarah's original plan; if Hagar goes back, Sarah can have a son by means of her'. However, this ignores the facts that Hagar's descendants [through Ishmael] are described in terms which recall the son promise to *Abraham*, and that 16.15 stresses the paternity of Abraham. No mention at all is made of the adoptive maternity of Sarah. Therefore I agree with the assessment of Alexander, *Literary Analysis of Abraham Narrative*, p. 47:

> In contrast to later episodes, the present pericope makes no suggestion that Ishmael is not the divinely appointed heir... Indeed, the divine intervention in vv 7-14 leaves one with the definite impression that Ishmael must be the promised son.

that this ploy of giving Hagar to Abraham was to allow her (Sarah) to have children (16.2b), Ishmael is described in the following way: 'Hagar bore Abram a son; and Abram called the name of his son whom Hagar bore, Ishmael... Hagar bore Ishmael to Abram.' In the light of the story so far, this must be seen as the fulfilment of the promise given in 15.4.

With this issue settled, ch. 17 introduces several new elements in the unfolding of the promise. The first of these could easily be missed if we fail to notice the force of the construction in 17.1b-2a. When looking at 12.2d-3a above, I had occasion to note that an imperative followed by a cohortative means that the second clause expresses the purpose or result of the first. There I translated,

> Be a blessing (*wehyēh bᵉrākâ*),
>   *so that* I may bless (*waᵃbārᵃkâ*)
>   those who bless you...

Following this line, I would agree with Alexander[1] in translating 17.1b-2, 'I am God Almighty; walk (*hithallēk*) before me, and be (*wehyēh*) blameless, *so that* I may make (*wᵉ'ettᵉnâ*) my covenant... and... multiply you exceedingly'. This is in line with the thrust of the initial Announcement (12.1-3) in which I have already noted the contingency of the promises, although here more rigorous ethical requirements are stipulated. If the requirement to be 'blameless' (*tāmîm*) signifies 'simply the duty of leading generally a righteous and holy life',[2] are we to infer that up to now Abraham had left something to be desired in this area, or simply that Yahweh is making clear for the first time that the fulfilment of the promise depends on Abraham's ethics? In either case, the reader is alerted to keep an eye open for Abraham's behaviour from this point on.

In addition, up to now the main elements of the promise that have been revealed are that Abraham would become a great nation (12.2), and he would have numerous descendants (16.10) like the dust or stars. These categories are now expanded somewhat: he will now be 'the father of a multitude

---

[1] Alexander, 'Genesis 22', p. 19; cf. Yarchin, 'Imperative and Promise', p. 174.
[2] Driver, *Genesis*, p. 185.

of *nations* (pl.)... I will make *nations* (pl.) of you, and *kings* shall come forth from you' (17.5, 6). Yahweh will now 'be God to you and to your descendants after you'. These new elements of (i) nations (pl.); (ii) kings; (iii) divine-human relationship with descendants, must from Abraham's understanding of the 'promise so far' be fulfilled through Ishmael. His birth in 16.15-16 has effectively ended Lot's candidature, as it was theoretically ended in 15.4.

However, the course of the promise takes another turn in 17.16 with Yahweh's announcement that he will bless Sarah. Here we encounter the novelty that *Sarah* will have a son; and the son *she* will bear is the one through whom the nations and kings previously referred to will be traced—17.4-6 (cf. v. 16). Sarah's *maternity* will become as important as Abraham's *paternity*. Strictly speaking, nothing in what Yahweh has said so far in ch. 17 has stated explicitly that Ishmael is to be replaced as 'firstborn son'. But Abraham surmises (17.18) that if he and Sarah produce a child together, it would necessarily supplant Ishmael. Gen. 17.18 confirms that up to this point Abraham has seen Ishmael as the fulfilment of the promise.

With the possibility of Abraham now having two sons, a differentiation between them is made. The basic difference between the two is found in Yahweh's announcement that 'I will establish my covenant with Isaac' (17.19, 21). It is not immediately clear what this means, nor whether it signifies Isaac's superiority to Ishmael, who though not accorded such an honour will be blessed; made fruitful; multiply exceedingly; be father of twelve princes; become a great nation (17.20). Therefore, up to 17.21, Abraham *has* one son who will be greatly blessed, and he *will have* another son with whom Yahweh 'will establish his covenant' (whatever that means; cf. the equally enigmatic 21.12). In 17.9 all of Abraham's descendants are commanded to keep Yahweh's covenant. At that point the only descendant Abraham has is Ishmael, so it must refer to him. Thus, Abraham circumcises Ishmael and other members of his household (17.23), bringing Ishmael and them within the covenant (cf. 17.14). A question arises: What is the essential difference between Ishmael now *within* the covenant, and Isaac with whom God *will establish* (*qûm*) his covenant? The final act of ch. 17, rather than dismissing

Ishmael from consideration, *seems* to bind him closer to Abraham (both are now circumcised) and to Yahweh (he now bears the mark of covenant). So, by the end of ch. 17 Abraham *has* a son who now bears the mark of Yahweh's covenant; and yet Abraham also *will have* a son with whom Yahweh will *establish* his covenant. This future son will apparently supersede Ishmael (cf. 17.18-21), but *how* and *why* is not yet clear.

One could be forgiven for assuming that Abraham must have been extremely confused by all of this. Just when he thought he understood the exact focus of the posterity promise, it went into a blur once again. His laugh of exasperation and disbelief (17.17)[1] and heartfelt plea, 'O that Ishmael might live in thy sight' (17.18), certainly elicit some sympathy from the reader. In fact Gibson paraphrases his words as 'When are you going to stop badgering me and leave me in peace with what I have?'[2]

We enter ch. 18 with Ishmael receding into the background, and the as yet unborn Isaac coming to the fore. The visit of the three strangers centres on Sarah. Chapter 17 had for the first time shown that she was as essential for the fulfilment of the posterity promise as was Abraham. Chapter 17 had shown Abraham's response to this idea; ch. 18 shows Sarah's.[3] She too reacts with a laugh of disbelief.[4] Both parties to the promise simply cannot believe it. Sarah's words are very revealing:

---

[1] Cf. Driver, *Genesis*, p. 188; Neff, 'Birth and Election of Isaac', p. 8; Brueggemann, *Genesis*, p. 156; Gibson, *Genesis*, 2.67; Chertok, 'Abram the Doubter', p. 463. Calvin, *Genesis*, 1.460 suggests that Abraham's laugh shows him to be 'partly exulting with joy, and partly being carried beyond himself in admiration'. If Abraham is so pleased at the news, however, one wonders why he pleads with God for Ishmael in the next verse. Speiser, *Genesis*, p. 123, suggests the translation, 'Abraham threw himself on his face, and he smiled...' The *reader* may smile at the turn of events, but Abraham's violent action of throwing himself on the ground reveals deeper emotions than a mere smile.

[2] Gibson, *Genesis*, 2.67.

[3] Aalders, *Genesis*, 2.1; Westermann, *Genesis 12–36*, pp. 279, 281.

[4] Cf. Speiser, *Genesis*, p. 131. Kidner, *Genesis*, p. 132, states, 'Her derision suggests that either Abraham had not yet told her of the promise (17.16, 19) or he had failed to convince her'. This opinion suggests that Abraham believed the promise—an assumption not borne out by the events of ch. 18, as we shall see.

'After I have grown old, and my husband is old, shall I have *pleasure ('ednâ)*?' (18.12). This term is a hapax legomenon, the most likely meaning of which is *'sexual* pleasure'.[1] Perhaps more than their individual laughs, this statement shows that neither of them believed the promise. If Sarah at this point is experiencing no sexual pleasure it means, presumably, that she and Abraham no longer have sexual relations. Chapter 17 had announced that the promised son would be born of the two of them. Unless they expected an immaculate conception, their sexual abstinence shows that they simply do not believe the promise.[2] When the promise is repeated in ch. 18, it meets with the same response.

This background may help to explain Abraham's behaviour in 18.22ff. Scholars have arrived at no consensus over the function of these verses. Suggestions include that it is merely 'to emphasize the wickedness of the city';[3] an attempt at 'the *reconciling of evil* with the knowledge that God intends *salvation for mankind'*;[4] to emphasize 'the "vicarious preserving function" of the righteous man';[5] a theological critique of 19.1-28;[6] a midrash explicating the theological problems arising out of the fall of Jerusalem[7]—to mention but a few proposals.[8] However, none of these suggestions really ties this pericope into the overarching plot. When one attempts to do this, an obvious question arises. When Abraham argues for the sparing of Sodom, is it purely coincidental that Lot lives there? We have just seen Ishmael dismissed by Yahweh as the son of promise (17.18, 19). Isaac has not yet been born. It is true that Lot has been previously eliminated from contention (15.4), but if he should die it would leave Abraham feeling exposed—especially as he does not yet believe in Isaac. Before the birth of

---

[1] Westermann, *Genesis 12–36*, p. 281.
[2] Cf. Gibson, *Genesis*, 2.78.
[3] Coats, *Genesis*, p. 142.
[4] Crenshaw, 'Popular Questioning', p. 380.
[5] Rodd, '"Judge of all the Earth"', p. 137.
[6] Brueggemann, 'Shape for Old Testament Theology, II', pp. 409-10; *idem, Genesis*, p. 167.
[7] Blenkinsopp, 'Abraham and Righteous of Sodom', p. 129.
[8] See Harrisville, 'God's Mercy', pp. 170-71, for a helpful, though less than exhaustive, brief survey of approaches.

Isaac—should he ever be born—Abraham has two 'half chances' in Ishmael and Lot, and he wishes to preserve them at all costs. This explains why he circumcises Ishmael and pleads for Sodom. I would suggest that Abraham's plea to save the whole city on ethical grounds is motivated largely by a desire to save his nephew and potential heir.[1] The reader may well recall that the last time Abraham came to the aid of Sodom he was likewise motivated by a desire to rescue Lot— 'when Abram heard that his kinsman had been taken captive, he led forth his trained men...' (14.14). Lot is nowhere presented as being righteous[2] (cf. 19.30-38), therefore Abraham does not plead for the escape of the righteous alone, but for the whole city—and with it, Lot. It is possible that Yahweh's preface to the bartering scene shows his awareness of how Abraham's mind might be working. Yahweh asks, 'Shall I hide from Abraham what I am about to do, seeing that Abraham shall become a great and mighty nation...?' (18.17-18). This is a strange statement. At first sight there is no logical link between Abraham's destiny to be a great nation and Yahweh's decision to destroy Sodom. However, the statement makes sense if Abraham is putting his (partial) trust in Lot as his descendant. In Abraham's eyes, with Lot living in Sodom, there is a crucial link between its destruction and his destiny as a great nation.

To understand the significance of ch. 19 we must remember the exact conditions of the bargain struck by Yahweh and Abraham. Yahweh states, 'For the sake of ten [righteous people] I will not destroy it [i.e. Sodom]' (18.32). Lot hardly cuts the figure of the righteous man. His initial act of hospitality (19.2) hardly compensates for his advocacy of rape and fornication on the streets of Sodom (19.8). Nevertheless, many still feel constrained to defend Lot's character. In commenting on ch. 19 Calvin, for example, referred to 'the holy man' and 'the faith and piety of Lot'.[3] Driver accepted the negative aspects of his character ('selfish, weak and worldly'), but still main-

[1] Contra von Rad, *Genesis*, p. 212; Hasel, *The Remnant*, p. 148.
[2] Cf. Coats, *Genesis*, p. 114.
[3] Calvin, *Genesis*, 1.495, 506. However, Calvin saw the limits of such a position: 'They are therefore under a mistake, who so highly extol his faith' (p. 508).

tained, that 'relatively, indeed, he was righteous (2 P. ii 7, 8);
his personal character was without reproach'.[1] That both
judgments could be made of the same man does not seem to
strike Driver as contradictory. According to Skinner, the offer
of his daughters to the mob 'shows him as a courageous
champion of the obligations of hospitality... and is recorded to
his credit'.[2] Aalders believes that 'God did spare *righteous*
Lot'.[3] Recently Alexander has argued similarly, but his
argument is really more of an apologetic for 2 Pet. 2.8-9 than
an exegesis of Gen. 19.[4] However, I would argue that Lot's
treatment of his daughters in Sodom; his unwillingness to flee
the wicked city under the judgment of God; the drunken
seduction of him in the cave[5]—all these factors point in the
opposite direction.

Despite painting such a portrait of Lot, the narrative relates
how he was rescued. It is at this point that the reader notes a
discontinuity between the bargain struck in ch. 18 and the
actual turn of events in ch. 19.[6] Yahweh had agreed to spare
the entire city if ten righteous could be found. But no righteous
could be found—and that included Lot. Accordingly, the city
was destroyed, *but Lot was preserved*. This counters the
agreed conditions—and one wonders if Abraham would have
bothered to use the ethical argument (18.23f.) if he knew this
was how events would turn out. Now of course, the narrative
does not tell us that Abraham knows anything at this point
about Lot's rescue. When he sees Sodom destroyed, he must
assume that Lot is dead. However, if (or when) Abraham gets
to hear about Lot's deliverance, it must make him wonder
again about Lot's candidature. Lot's rescue could only be seen

---

[1] Driver, *Genesis*, p. 205.
[2] Skinner, *Genesis*, p. 307.
[3] Aalders, *Genesis*, 2.22.
[4] Alexander, 'Lot's Hospitality', pp. 289-91.
[5] Porter, 'Daughters of Lot', p. 128, tries to exonerate Lot on the
grounds that he did not know what was happening, and his daughters
on the grounds that they acted out of 'extreme necessity'. This attitude
is difficult to maintain when the passage is read within the context of
the Abraham story as a whole. Coats, 'Lot: A Foil', pp. 122ff., correctly
notes the shortcomings of Lot's character.
[6] Contra Aalders, *Genesis*, 2.22; Martens, *Plot and Purpose*, p. 31;
Alexander, *Literary Analysis of Abraham Narrative*, p. 53.

as a further example of Lot's crucial importance to the fulfilment of the promise—how else could one view the preferential treatment extended to him? This is now the third such
example of Yahweh reinforcing Abraham's regard for an
individual—and the second involving Lot. In ch. 13 I noted
how no sooner had Lot seemingly removed himself from the
land of promise than Yahweh revealed that he was still within
it. Similarly, Yahweh's command to Hagar to return home
and his blessing on her and Ishmael in ch. 15 served to
underline Ishmael's continuing importance to the posterity
promise. From Abraham's perspective, despite occasional
confusing divine announcements to the contrary, Yahweh in
ch. 19 reinforces the cruciality of Lot to the posterity promise.[1]

Developments in ch. 20 confirm my reading of the story so
far. As in ch. 12, Abraham quits the land but this time for no
apparent reason. Once again, in an attempt to save his skin,
Abraham pretends Sarah is his sister.[2] She is no longer as
expendable as Abraham could have argued in 12.10-20. What
therefore does Abraham's lie and Sarah's connivance reveal
about their attitude to the promise? The most reasonable
deduction to make is that Abraham did not believe, or did not
want to believe, the promise of a son through Sarah. Now that
Sarah knows that she is crucial for the fulfilment of the
promise, her actions also need to be questioned. Does her
willingness to tell a lie (20.13) indicate a lack of faith on *her*
part? Has she now come to accept Ishmael as the fulfil-

---

[1] Nevertheless, the reader of the story so far can see that Abraham's
half trust in Lot was misplaced. Lot is not circumcised and is therefore *outside* the covenant (cf. 17.14, 23), even though he is *inside* the
land of promise. For this reason, his fathering of Moab and Ammon
can hardly be a step forward in the fulfilment of the covenant promise
to make Abraham the father of nations (17.5) (contra Clines, 'Ancestor
in Danger', p. 73); these children were begotten by an *uncircumcised*
father in an act of *incest*. (Note that the promise of *nations* was made
in the context of covenant—the sign of which was circumcision [17.4-7,
10-11].)

[2] Cassuto, *Genesis*, 2.276 is one of the few who notes Abraham's
deception here. Many take Abraham's claim at face value, e.g., Koch,
Growth of Biblical Tradition, pp. 123, 130; Petersen, 'Thrice-Told Tale',
pp. 39-40; Alexander, *Literary Analysis of Abraham Narrative*, p. 54.
For discussion of this point see p. 65 n. 1.

ment?—she was, after all, the instigator of the plan which resulted in his birth. A number of scholars have seen an added irony in all of this by suggesting that Sarah was already pregnant and that Abraham's lie endangered not only his wife but also his unborn son.[1] This line of argument depends upon understanding the problematic *kā'ēt ḥayyâ* of 18.10, 14 as referring to a period of nine months of pregnancy.[2] This would mean that Sarah's pregnancy began at the time of those divine disclosures and she is thus necessarily pregnant in ch. 20. This understanding is possible, but the enigmatic terminology makes it difficult to be dogmatic. Others interpret the meaning as 'at this time next year', thus making it identical with *lammô'ēd hazzeh* of 17.21. This would see a twelve month gap between 18.10, 14 and the birth of Isaac in ch. 21.[3] If this is the case, although the intended time scale is difficult to determine, Sarah might not have been pregnant in ch. 20. In fact, this is allowed by 21.1-2 which *suggests* that Sarah's conception was subsequent to her meeting with Abimelech.

I conclude that ch. 20 shows some danger to the fulfilment of the promise, with Sarah, the *mother* of promise, entering Abimelech's household. (Being barren, however, means she is in no danger of becoming pregnant by Abimelech.)[4] However, it also reveals just as clearly, and perhaps even more importantly, that Abraham does not yet believe the promise of Sarah's maternity. Therefore, this chapter presents him as being more culpable than he was in 12.10-20. In that previous episode, he was morally accountable for the maltreatment of his wife, but at least he could argue that he was doing his best to preserve the promise. In ch. 20 he is again morally culpa-

[1] E.g. Gibson, *Genesis*, 2.96; Miscall, *Workings of Old Testament Narrative*, p. 32; Clines, 'Ancestor in Danger', pp. 75-76.
[2] E.g. Skinner, *Genesis*, p. 301; Speiser, *Genesis*, pp. 128-30; Clines, 'Ancestor in Danger', p. 76.
[3] E.g. Kautzsch, *Gesenius' Grammar*, p. 376; Driver, *Genesis*, p. 195; Westermann, *Genesis 12–36*, p. 273. 2 Kgs 4.16 could possibly support this interpretation.
[4] This fact counters the suggestion of Aalders, *Genesis*, 2.31:

> that God had made Abimelech temporarily sterile was a miraculous protection for Sarah. Thus it was also God's protection for the promised child that Sarah was to produce.

ble,[1] but can no longer argue that his actions serve the divine purpose.[2]

In reflecting on ch. 20 we notice that the tactics of Abraham and Sarah could have resulted in Abimelech's sinning against Yahweh (20.6). In the light of 17.1 and 18.19, this is ironic: Abraham was charged to live a blameless life himself (17.1), and to make his children do *righteousness* ($s^e d\bar{a}q\hat{a}$) and *justice* ($mi\check{s}p\bar{a}t$) as a condition ('so that...') for the fulfilment of the promises (18.19). This irony is compounded in the transition to ch. 21 with the announcement of the conception and birth of Isaac (21.1-2), and with it the fulfilment of the promise contained in 17.16a, 19a, *immediately after* Abraham has behaved quite unethically. One wonders, however, about the significance of Abraham's prayer in 20.17. This is the first time we read of Abraham engaging in prayer[3] (although there is some evidence of his worshipping [12.8; 13.4]), and perhaps even more significantly, the first time Abraham does anything for anyone which was not calculated to further his own ends in the fulfilment of the promise. The renewal of fertility to both Abimelech's household and Sarah after Abraham has offered his prayer may well be more than coincidental.[4] 'Then Abraham prayed to God: and God healed... so that they bore children. For the Lord had closed all the wombs... because of Sarah... The Lord visited Sarah... and Sarah conceived and bore Abraham a son' (20.17–21.2). (Note also Isaac's prayer resulting in Rebekah's fertility in 25.21.) Was Abraham's turning away from his own self-interest something for which

---

[1] Contra McEvenue, 'Elohist at Work', pp. 319-21, who makes the following amazing statements: Abraham 'has *no choice* but to expose Sarah to the whims of men in authority wherever he goes' (p. 319); 'Abraham was *forced* to expose Sarah to dishonour because originally there was no fear of God in Gerar (v. 11)' (p. 321 [emphasis mine]).

[2] Cf. Aalders, *Genesis*, 2.30. Brueggemann, *Genesis*, p. 177, states unconvincingly that the incident at Gerar is less damaging to Abraham's reputation than that in 12.10-20.

[3] I can find no justification for the view of Baldwin, *Genesis 12–50*, p. 83, that Abraham 'had been praying over decades for an end to Sarah's barrenness... and Abraham was soon to see the answer to his prayers for a son'.

[4] Coats, *Genesis*, p. 149 notes the general cohesion between the two chapters when 20.18 and 21.1 are read together.

Yahweh had been waiting for some time—in fact the
condition for fulfilling the promise?

Just in case the reader misses the import of Sarah's giving
birth, the narrator states, 'The Lord visited Sarah as he had
said, and the Lord did to Sarah as he had promised' (21.1).
Brueggemann states: 'the birth of the child is the fulfillment of
all of the promises, the resolution of all of the anguish'.[1] While
this is obviously an exaggeration—the promise of land, for
example, not being in view here—the birth of Isaac is obviously of climactic significance for the posterity promise. The
laughter of nonbelief (17.17; 18.12) is converted into the
laughter of rejoicing (21.6).[2] Given the importance of Isaac's
birth it is surprising that it occupies such a small space in the
narrative. It soon becomes clear, however, that the narrator is
much more interested in the relationship between Ishmael
and Isaac. Despite Isaac's birth, Ishmael is still in the household. Whether Ishmael will be able to maintain his position as
heir or not remains to be seen.

With the birth and circumcision of Isaac (21.4), Abraham
has two sons, and both are circumcised. The inevitable clash
between the destinies of the two brothers comes to the fore in
21.8ff. Sarah's demand that Hagar and Ishmael be cast out
(21.10), whatever personal animosity might be involved,[3] is

---

[1] Brueggemann, *Genesis*, p. 180. Cf. the similar exaggeration in
Alexander, *Literary Analysis of Abraham Narrative*, p. 60: 'In ch. 21
the impression is given that God has substantially fulfilled all his
promises to Abraham'.

[2] Kidner, *Genesis*, p. 139; Speiser, *Genesis*, p. 155; Westermann,
Genesis 12–36, p. 334. Cf. Rabinowitz, 'Sarah's Wish', pp. 362-63, who
translates, 'And Sarah said, "God has made a joke of me; whoever
hears will laugh at me"'. This has the advantage of maintaining the
nuance of *ṣḥq* found in 17.17 and 18.12-15, but the disadvantage of
being unlikely within the context of ch. 21.

[3] There is disagreement over the meaning of 21.9. The problem is
twofold. First, the MT states merely that Ishmael was 'playing'
(*mᵉṣaḥēq*). There is no inference that he was playing with Isaac or
with anyone else. The LXX adds, μετὰ Ισαακ τοῦ υἱοῦ αὐτῆς, and most
agree that such an addition is necessary to complete the sense. The
second problem concerns the nuance of *mᵉṣaḥēq*; is it used with a good
or evil connotation? Some, e.g. Calvin, *Genesis*, 1.542; Kidner,
Genesis, p. 140, argue from context, i.e. Sarah's reaction, that it must
be rendered by 'mocking' or something similar: 'It was, therefore, a

based ostensibly on the premise that 'the son of this slave woman shall not be heir with my son Isaac' (which shows that she at least believes Ishmael is equally an heir). The narrator's subsequent comment that 'the thing was very displeasing to Abraham on account of his son' (21.11)[1] shows quite clearly that he is displeased about the fact that Ishmael will no longer be his heir (or at least joint-heir). This understanding is confirmed by Yahweh's announcement in 21.12. Isaac's superiority to Ishmael is because 'through Isaac shall your descendants be named'. This means, presumably, that the promised nation will trace its origin exclusively to Isaac, rather than to Ishmael even though both Isaac (v. 12) and Ishmael (v. 13) are referred to as Abraham's *zera'*.[2] If Ishmael does become the father of a nation (21.13), then this would be partial fulfilment of the expansion of the nationhood promise found in 17.4, where Abraham is promised that he will become 'the father of a multitude of nations', but not of *the* promise of nationhood. It is ironic that in sending away Ishmael, Abraham must do 'whatever Sarah says' (21.12), just as he had once 'hearkened

malignant expression of scorn, by which the forward youth manifested his contempt for his infant brother' (Calvin). Others take it as conveying the simple playfulness of youth with no negative associations whatsoever. Driver, *Genesis*, p. 210; Skinner, *Genesis*, p. 322; Speiser, *Genesis*, p. 155; Westermann, *Genesis 12–36*, p. 339, point out that for the verb to carry a negative connotation, *b^e* would be needed to designate the object. (However, if one follows the LXX this argument falls by the way.) These, together with Gibson, *Genesis*, 2.101, argue that either Ishmael was playing by himself, or if with Isaac, was amusing rather than abusing him. Von Rad, *Genesis*, p. 232, does not believe it is possible to decide between these options. Coats, *Genesis*, p. 153, makes the interesting suggestion that 'Sarah saw Ishmael *mĕṣahēq*, playing the role of Isaac' (i.e. acting as though he were Abraham's heir). Basically, the argument concerns whether Sarah was justified in expelling Hagar and Ishmael, or whether she was acting out of envy and jealousy. For my present purposes it is enough to note that Sarah saw Ishmael as a threat to Isaac as heir. This fact is more important than any more immediate justification she may have felt.

[1] Schwartz, 'Free Will and Character Autonomy', p. 65, commenting on this rare example of a psychological, moral signpost, observes that 'when it does occur, it tends to mark points of confrontation between human judgment and divine will'.

[2] See the discussion in Westermann, *Genesis 12–36*, p. 340.

to the voice of Sarai' (16.2), in her suggestion which resulted in
Ishmael's birth.[1] The first suggestion he eagerly accepted; the
second he resents. It might be significant that not only does
Abraham give provisions to Hagar and Ishmael (not part of
Sarah's instructions), but the verb $y^e\check{s}all^eh\bar{e}h\bar{a}$ which describes
Abraham's action is milder than that demanded by Sarah
$(g\bar{a}r\bar{e}\check{s})$.[2]

By the time ch. 22 begins, with the exception of Isaac all
other candidates for the position of 'promised son' have been
explicitly eliminated by Yahweh (albeit reluctantly by Abraham). Also, with this chapter we come to the climax of the
Abraham narrative as a whole.[3] The story continues in the
next few chapters, but the tension of the plot is resolved here.
The reader is struck by several echoes of that initial
Announcement in 12.1-3. Abraham is commanded to take his
son and 'Go!' $(lek-l^ek\bar{a})$ (22.2). The last time this term was
used was in 12.1. There it was spoken at the beginning of the
enterprise. Its repetition here recalls that former
Announcement and invites the reader to contemplate the
relationship of ch. 22 to the promise theme as a whole.[4]
Stylistic similarities also underline the connection, e.g. the
multiplication of descriptive epithets, 'your country, your
kindred, your father's house' (12.1; cf. 'your son, your
favoured one, Isaac, whom you love' [22.2]).[5] Crenshaw refers
to these passages as: 'A Son Sacrifices His Father (Gen. 12)',

---

[1] Magonet, 'Die Söhne Abrahams', p. 208.
[2] Gordon, 'Hagar', pp. 275-76.
[3] Cf. Sarna, *Understanding Genesis*, p. 160; Yarchin, 'Imperative
and Promise', p. 173; Lawlor, 'Test of Abraham', p. 25; Gros Louis,
'Abraham II', p. 76, 'a kind of coda that epitomizes the themes of the
Abraham narrative'.
[4] Cf. Sarna, *Understanding Genesis*, p. 160; Lawlor, 'Test of Abraham', p. 22; White, 'Initiation Legend of Isaac', p. 14; Brueggemann,
Genesis, p. 185; Westermann, *Genesis 12-36*, p. 357; Mazor, 'Genesis
22', p. 82; Magonet, 'Die Söhne Abrahams', p. 205, cites the midrashic
question regarding which was the hardest $lek-l^ek\bar{a}$—the first or the
second? Yarchin, 'Imperative and Promise', p. 174, believes that this
connection 'underscore[s] the programmatic nature of the chapter 12
text'; Vriezen, 'Bemerkungen zu Genesis 12.1-7', p. 383, notes that the
only other occurrence of the formula (with cohortative) is Song of
Songs 2.10.
[5] Sarna, *Understanding Genesis*, p. 160.

and 'A Father Sacrifices His Beloved Son (Gen. 22)'. Abraham had earlier turned his back on his father in order to obey a divine imperative. That command severed him from his past; this command threatens to sever him from his *future*.[1]

The command to sacrifice Isaac is not only unexpected but also nonsensical. While it is true that Abraham's hopes have been pinned on a succession of individuals, Yahweh's bias toward Isaac as the son of promise has been made quite clear. Yet once Isaac has been born, after a tortuous journey in which Abraham was left to guess at the divine will more often than not, Yahweh acts as if Isaac is expendable. Or is it that *Abraham* is expendable, and all of the repeated promises concerning his future greatness were part of a game played by a sadistic deity who, having sated himself with the view of Abraham fumbling his way through life, now declares that the game is over, and the players can return to their original positions? The divine command certainly does seem to bring the promise, *as defined by Yahweh*, to a crashing halt.

> The *command* of God is that Isaac must be killed. It follows that there will be no descendants, no future. We are back to barrenness. The entire pilgrimage from 11.30 has been for nought. Abraham has trusted the promise fully. Now the promise is to be abrogated. Can the same God who promises life also command death?[2]

Given not only the horror of being told to take the life of his son, but also bearing in mind who Isaac was in the purposes of God, Abraham's reaction to the command is odd in the extreme. This is not the first time that Abraham has seen one of his 'sons' threatened, but his response this time is completely different. On hearing that Isaac will be born to Sarah he remonstrated, 'Oh that Ishmael might live in your sight!' (17.18). When previously faced with the possible death of Lot, Abraham put up a great deal of resistance, even asking, 'Shall not the judge of all the earth do right?' (18.25). Similarly, he

---

[1] Crenshaw, 'Journey into Oblivion', pp. 244-45. Cf. Lawlor, 'Test of Abraham', p. 22.

[2] Brueggemann, *Genesis*, p. 188. Cf. Sarna, *Understanding Genesis*, p. 163; von Rad, *Genesis*, p. 239; White, 'Initiation of Isaac', p. 14; Hopkins, 'Between Promise and Fulfillment', p. 181.

2. *The Abraham Story* 89

showed his objection to Sarah's request that Hagar and Ishmael be expelled—'the thing was very displeasing to Abraham' (21.11). Yet when commissioned now to kill Isaac, he
passively surrenders: 'So Abraham rose... and went to the
place of which God had told him' (22.3). The contrast is strik-
ing; how do we explain it? Given Abraham's lack in the ethical
sphere previously (e.g. 12.10-20; ch. 20), one is perhaps entitled
to be cynical about his motives. One could argue that while
Isaac's death would end *Yahweh's* version of the promise (e.g.
21.12), it could actually confirm Abraham's favoured version,
in which Ishmael filled the role (e.g. 17.18). Actually, at the
beginning of ch. 22 we simply do not know what is going
through Abraham's mind. However, a more charitable version of his motives can be deduced from the words of Yahweh,
'Now I know that you fear God, seeing you have not withheld
your son, your only son from me' (22.12). While one could
argue that Yahweh has been hoodwinked here—if Abraham
has his trust in Ishmael then of course he would be willing to
sacrifice Isaac—such an interpretation is too subtle and
unlikely. Yahweh is not presented here or in some other
episodes as being omniscient, but his assessment of Abraham's
motives, leading to the repetition of the covenant promises
(22.15-18), seems to tip the scales in Abraham's favour. He is
shown to be a God-fearer, not a self-server. We see here a
similar sequence to that observed above in the transition from
ch. 20 to ch. 21. There, Abraham's selfless prayer for Abimelech was followed by the fulfilment of the promise with
Isaac's conception and birth. Here, Abraham's selfless willingness to forfeit the promise results in the ratification of the earlier promises: 'because you have done this, and have not withheld your son, your only son, I will indeed bless you, and I will
multiply your descendants...' (22.16b-17a).

As we investigate the divine command itself in more detail,
we notice that from the outset Yahweh 'tested' (*nissâ*, 22.1)
Abraham. Almost without exception, scholars see this admission as divesting the sacrifice scene of any tension. Thus it is
commonly argued that it is only a test; we know in advance
that God has no intention of going through with it.[1] It seems

---

[1] Cf. Skinner, *Genesis*, p. 328; von Rad, *Genesis*, p. 239; Sarna,

that only White has seen correctly that,

> the reader has no reason to think that because this is a test, God does not intend for Abraham to actually go through with it to the bitter end... The category of the 'test' serves not to lessen the suspense for the reader, but to provide an explanation for the command of God without which it would be totally dissociated from the narrative context.[1]

In addition, I might add that Abraham is not privy to the information given to the reader; he simply receives the divine command, without any explanatory glosses, and the tension is not relieved for him until the angel of Yahweh calls from heaven (22.11).

The actual death of Isaac would have had very important ramifications for the promise. Why, therefore, did Yahweh give such a command?[2] At the outset we should note that although this is the only divine command in the story designated a 'test', it is not unique; other incidents in the Abraham narrative also have the quality of a test.[3] In fact the whole story, beginning in 12.1-3, could be seen as a test of his obedience and perseverance. However, the fact that ch. 22 is the only episode so designated invites the reader to discern its specific focus. Crenshaw has suggested that 'Abraham's excessive love for the son of promise comes dangerously close to idolatry and frustrates the larger mission'.[4] Yahweh, being a jealous God, tolerates no rivals and commands his immediate despatch. However, there are severe problems with this suggestion. First, we have no evidence in the text that Abraham did have an *excessive* love for Isaac. His reluctance to expel Ishmael (21.11) shows that Isaac did not have exclusive

---

Understanding Genesis, p. 161; Speiser, *Genesis*, p. 164; Coats, 'Abraham's Sacrifice', p. 392; *idem*, *Genesis*, p. 158; Lawlor, 'Test of Abraham', p. 27; Starobinski-Safran, 'Sur le sens de l'épreuve', p. 26; McEvenue, 'Elohist at Work', p. 324; Westermann, *Genesis 12–36*, p. 361; Mazor, 'Genesis 22', p. 82.
[1] White, 'Initiation of Isaac', p. 13. Even if the narrator's note relieves the reader's tension, it creates a new tension between the reader's comfort and Abraham's angst.
[2] Cf. Swindell, 'Abraham and Isaac', p. 51.
[3] Cf. Skinner, *Genesis*, p. 327; von Rad, *Genesis*, p. 239.
[4] Crenshaw, 'Journey into Oblivion', p. 249.

claims on his paternal emotions. Secondly, Abraham's attraction to Lot and Ishmael had previously threatened to trip up the fulfilment of the promise as Yahweh envisaged it, yet these candidates were simply pushed to one side, not executed. We must, therefore, look elsewhere for a motivation.

The key to this issue seems to be found in 22.12. The angel of Yahweh says, 'Do not lay your hand on the lad or do anything to him; *for now I know that you fear God* seeing you have not withheld your son, your only son, from me'. In other words, before the test Yahweh did not know whether Abraham was willing to accept his plans without question (i.e. 'fear God') or not[1]—or at least, was suspicious. Abraham had seemed to invest too much in Lot and Ishmael, and was less than enthusiastic when God finally revealed his hand with Isaac (cf. 17.17-18; 18.22ff.; ch. 20; 21.11). Whether Yahweh has treated Abraham fairly in these matters is another issue. But Abraham had not thrown himself wholeheartedly into the divine plan of accepting only Isaac. By the beginning of ch. 22 Lot and Ishmael have been irrevocably dismissed by Yahweh— underlined by the command to 'Take your son, *your only son* ($y^e\hat{h}\hat{i}d^ek\bar{a}$) ...' Strictly—biologically—this is not true; but it is Yahweh's truth, and he is writing the script. If Isaac goes, there are no sons left to go back to—just in case Abraham had that ploy in mind. The test is designed, therefore, to discover the limits of Abraham's faith in God when in a situation where it is impossible for human initiatives to change the outcome in any way. It is a test designed to see whether Abraham will unquestioningly accept and unquestioningly obey, regardless of the consequences.

In trying to understand why Yahweh should want to see

---

[1] Cf. Driver, *Genesis*, p. 216; Speiser, *Genesis*, p. 166; Brueggemann, *Genesis*, p. 187; Lawlor, 'Test of Abraham', p. 27; Gibson, *Genesis*, 2.108. There have always been objectors to such a position. As pointed out by Starobinski-Safran, 'Sur le sens de l'épreuve', p. 27, commentators ask—If God knows the thoughts of human beings, why does he need such concrete experiences to verify what he already knows? (To this one might add that the 'visitors' in ch. 18 knew what Sarah was thinking [18.12].) Cf. the objections of Sarna, *Understanding Genesis*, p. 162; Aalders, *Genesis*, 2.49. Nevertheless, the narrative of ch. 22 gives us no grounds for assuming that Yahweh does know.

Abraham acting like this I am in broad agreement with
Alexander whose basic thesis is that 'Genesis 22 describes the
establishment of the covenant of circumcision first mentioned
in Genesis 17'.[1] One does not have to accept Alexander's whole
argument in order to see the cogency of his key points. I have
already noted the correct translation of 17.1-2, '... walk before
me and be blameless (*tāmîm*) so that I will make my covenant
between me and you, and will multiply you exceedingly'. The
making of the covenant is dependent upon Abraham's
'blameless' behaviour. From this basic premise of Alexander's
we may observe that from Yahweh's perspective, Abraham's
subsequent behaviour is anything but blameless, with a laugh
of derision at Yahweh's promise (17.17), his bias toward
Ishmael (17.18), his refusal to acknowledge Sarah's place in
the plan (ch. 21), etc. Chapter 22 presents the final 'test' (v. 1),
to see whether, despite the evidence to the contrary, Abraham
is prepared to 'fear God' (v. 12), and present himself
'blameless':

> Abraham is tested by God in order to ascertain whether or
> not he truly fulfils the conditions laid upon him in 17.1. Does
> Abraham walk before God? Is he blameless?[2]

Abraham passes the test, and his action is accepted by Yahweh
as being decisive for the continuance of the posterity promise
(the aim of the condition in 17.1-2): 'because you have done

---

[1] Alexander, 'Genesis 22', p. 17.
[2] Alexander, 'Genesis 22', p. 21. Moberly, 'Akedah', pp. 320-21,
suggests the following perspective for understanding 22.15-18:

> Abraham by his obedience has not qualified to be the recipient of
> blessing, because the promise of blessing had been given to him
> already. Rather, the existing promise is reaffirmed but its terms
> of reference are altered. A promise which previously was
> grounded solely in the will and purpose of Yahweh is trans-
> formed so that it is now grounded *both* in the will of Yahweh *and*
> in the obedience of Abraham. It is not that the divine promise has
> been contingent upon Abraham's obedience, but that Abraham's
> obedience has been incorporated into the divine promise. Hence-
> forth Israel owes its existence not just to Yahweh but also to
> Abraham.

This rather forced interpretation is obviated if one accepts the argument I have presented previously, that there was an element of contingency in the promises from the outset (12.1-3).

this... I will indeed bless you, and I will multiply your descendants...' (22.16-17). This is a point chillingly echoed in Yahweh's later speech to Isaac, the possible victim in this set piece: 'I will multiply your descendants... because Abraham obeyed my voice...' (26.4-5). Yet Abraham's obedience threatened Yahweh's entire scheme of promise: the angel and the ram arrived just in the nick of time.[1]

This incident in the land of Moriah reveals the fundamentally paradoxical nature of the ancestral promise. At the moment when the promise was given (12.1-3), it contained the paradox that only in giving up his present land could Abraham be shown another land; only in giving up his present kindred could he become the father of a great nation. That paradox is compounded in 22.16-18: only in being willing to give up *his only son* is he able to become the father of a multitude (22.16-17).

Having been through such a protracted, painful process of first being childless for so long and then of being told to kill his 'only son', Abraham is reminded of how other humans live. Someone, not Yahweh, gives Abraham the news: 'Behold, Milcah also has borne children to your brother Nahor: Uz the first-born, Buz his brother, Kemuel the father of Aram, Chesed, Hazo, Pildash, Jidlaph and Bethuel' (22.20-21). Nahor and Milcah, plus their eight sons, an untold number of daughters and offspring from a concubine (22.24), enjoy their family bliss in Ur of the Chaldees (cf. 11.28-29). Yet the one promised to become the father of a multitude has only one son who counts. Abraham could be forgiven if he were to long for the quiet fulfilment of being the non-chosen.

Within the Abraham story, ch. 22 marks the greatest crisis in the ongoing story of the posterity promise. The promise is not prominent after that point as the story winds down to its conclusion, but it remains in the background. Thus in ch. 24 Abraham has the son through whom his descendants will be

[1] Cf. Peck, 'Murder, Timing and the Ram', p. 24:

> If Abraham had discovered the ram too late, the child would have been dead... or if Abraham had discovered the ram too early, before facing the full meaning of the act... [he] would have depended upon an easy answer, upon cheap grace.

traced, but that line will not continue unless Isaac gets a wife. Hence the mission of Abraham's servant to the homeland and his return with Rebekah. The final episode, 25.1-6, shows Abraham's final resignation to Yahweh's favouritism of Isaac. Although Abraham has many sons by other women, he realizes that only the sole child of himself and Sarah is the crucial one; thus in order to protect Isaac's unique position, 'while he was still living he sent them away from his son Isaac, eastward to the east country' (25.6).

There is one curious footnote. Despite Isaac's role as the son of promise, and Ishmael's previous separation from the family (21.20-21), the two are united again at Abraham's death: 'Isaac and Ishmael *his sons* buried him in the cave of Machpelah' (25.9a). Forced to choose between them in his life, does Abraham register, in his death, one final protest against Yahweh's plans with the two united with their father?[1]

As we look back on chs. 12–25 as a whole, we see that the posterity promise provides much of its connective tissue. The ebb and flow of tension and resolution is almost constantly centred on this one issue. A promise which for Abraham seemed so clear cut at the outset became increasingly complex and confusing, and ultimately resulted in the reversal of his initial expectations. In the beginning Lot (and later Ishmael) was crucial; Sarah was expendable. Eventually he learned that Lot (and all others except Isaac) was expendable; Sarah it was, who was crucial. It began with a promise contingent simply on obeying the command to 'go', but developed into an arrangement dependent on Abraham's blameless behaviour. These shifts are to be explained, perhaps, not so much in seeing Yahweh changing the script as in presenting Abraham with successive drafts—until Isaac arrived. By the conclusion of this story the fulfilment of the promise has on the one hand advanced, and on the other stood still. In the end Abraham does have a son (acceptable to Yahweh), through whom his numerous descendants will come. However, is this any real progress? In the beginning Abraham trusted in one individual (Lot), as his descendant: by the end he has only one descendant who counts (Isaac). All that has progressed is that Abraham

---

[1] Cf. Gordon, 'Hagar', pp. 273-74.

and Yahweh now agree on who the crucial descendant is.

The Promise of Land

We now return to the land promise which runs throughout chs. 12–25. I noted earlier that 12.1 does not contain the promise of land possession[1] but indicates that the issue of land will be of some importance in the plot.[2] The exact role it will play is not yet clear.

Yahweh's promise to show Abraham a certain land and his subsequent trek toward Canaan recalls the previous travels of his father Terah, who similarly set out for Canaan (11.31):

Terah (11.31)				*Abraham (12.5ff.)*		
Terah took:	Abraham	⎫		Abraham took:	Sarah	⎫
	Lot	⎬ A			Lot	⎬ A
	Sarah	⎭			All his possessions	
					Other persons	⎭
Terah went from:	Ur	B		Abraham went from:	Haran	B
to:	Canaan	C		to:	Canaan	C
But:	Settled in Haran	D		But:	Moved on to Egypt	D

The similarities are quite clear, and raise a number of questions, e.g. why did Terah set out for Canaan? There is no evidence that Terah set out in response to a divine call, as Abraham did. Yet Abraham's journey seems to be more of a

---

[1] This remains true despite the observations on the meaning of *gôy* (12.2) by Alexander, *Literary Analysis of Abraham Narrative*, p. 306 n. 14. He believes that the concept of nationhood necessarily carries with it the idea of land in which the nation exists. In support he cites Clements, '״ג *gôy*', p. 427: 'the three aspects of race, government, and territory are all important... Normally all three aspects were combined in the formation of a *goy*...' I can accept this as true without having to affirm, as Alexander does, that there is an explicit promise of land in 12.1-2.

[2] However, I would reject as over-zealous the claim of Jeyeraj, *Land Ownership in the Pentateuch*, p. 27, 'that the theme of the whole story of Abraham is "promise and possession of the land"'. Cf. Clines, *Theme of the Pentateuch*, p. 46. The assessment of von Rad, 'Promised Land', pp. 84-85, is more likely: 'It must be stressed that it is the linking together of the promise of the land and its ultimate fulfilment, with all the tensions this involves, which gives to *the Hexateuch as a whole* its distinctive theological character' (emphasis mine).

resumption of his father's endeavour than a completely new enterprise. They both set out *Canaan-wards*: *wayyēṣᵉû*... *lāleket 'arṣâ kᵉna'an* (11.31; 12.5)—suggesting that they did not know their final *destination*, but had a clear idea of the correct *direction*. But while Abraham sets out in response to a divine imperative, Terah's motivations for such an initiative remain puzzling.[1]

Whatever the answer to these questions is, Yahweh's promise to Abraham in 12.7 is an important development in the role of land in the story and obviously calls out for some comparison with the original enigmatic reference in 12.1e. This is especially true when one considers that 12.1-9 is probably to be taken as a self-contained unit.[2] The usual assumption, on learning of Abraham's arrival in Canaan and hearing Yahweh's promise, 'to your descendants I will give this land' (12.7), is to think that Abraham has now arrived in the land referred to in 12.1e.[3] However, as I have already noted, 12.1e does not actually promise Abraham the *possession* of any land, merely that Yahweh will cause him to see a certain land. In addition, 12.7 promises possession of Canaan not to Abraham himself but to Abraham's *descendants*—a matter distinct from that raised in 12.1. Therefore the relationship between the two verses is certainly not that of promise and fulfilment.[4] Abraham's subsequent behaviour confirms this conclusion. On reaching Canaan, and receiving the promise, *he continues his*

---

[1] Cf. Sarna, *Understanding Genesis*, p. 97, and Dequeker, 'La vocation d'Abraham', p. 3, who conclude that Terah's journey was a purely human initiative.

[2] Kikawada, 'Unity of Genesis 12.1-9', pp. 229-35, believes the verses exhibit rhetorical devices and balances which demonstrate that the whole unit must be read as one if the full impact of the parts is to be appreciated. Cf. Westermann, *Genesis 12–36*, pp. 152-53, who argues similarly, though dismissing vv. 4-5 as secondary.

[3] E.g. Skinner, *Genesis*, p. 245; Gunkel, *Genesis*, p. 163; Alexander, *Literary Analysis of Abraham Narrative*, p. 35.

[4] As argued by e.g. Ruprecht, 'Vorgegebene Tradition', p. 179, although he sees the fulfilment as provisional (*vorläufig*). He also sees 12.5c as carrying the same weight (p. 176). Koch, *Growth of Biblical Tradition*, p. 116, commenting on 12.9-10, sees Abraham as leaving the land which 'has just been given to him'. But cf. Clines, 'What Happens in Genesis', pp. 55-56.

journey southwards—hardly the action of one who believes he
has reached the goal of his travels. He is still 'in search of the
unknown land'[1] mentioned in 12.1. This suggestion is more
satisfying than that which sees Abraham's passing through
the land as a symbolic gesture that he is now in charge, or that
it 'represents the ideal transfer of the country to his possession
for the purpose of the Lord's service'.[2] If this were so one
would not expect the announcement of 13.17 in which the gift
of the land—admittedly an enlarged land, but including the
tract in 12.7ff.—is still seen as future. I conclude therefore,
that 12.7 introduces for the first time a promise of land
possession, but a promise for Abraham's descendants, not for
him personally.

This makes Abraham's journey down to Egypt (12.10)
completely understandable. While it is of interest to Abraham
to learn that his descendants will inherit the land, there is no
indication that this is the land to which he was commissioned
to go, and the famine which hits Canaan (12.10), if not con-
firming this fact, at least confirms Abraham in his desire to
move on. Those who judge Abraham to have been unfaithful
to the land promise in quitting Canaan and going to Egypt do
so unjustly,[3] primarily because the land he quits had not yet
been promised to him. The fact that Abraham did not consult
Yahweh before leaving can hardly be brought forward as evidence.[4] As Miscall points out, nowhere does Abraham talk to

[1] Jeyeraj, *Land Ownership in the Pentateuch*, p. 30. Cf. Miscall,
Workings of Old Testament Narrative, p. 25.
[2] Cassuto, *Genesis*, 2.301. Cassuto's argument rests in part upon
arguing that the altars constructed by Abraham were not cultic altars
(as no sacrifice is mentioned) but are tokens of the sanctification of the
land to Yahweh and of the 'symbolic conquest of the country' (p. 329).
However, I am not convinced that the absence of references to sacrifices renders the altars symbolic. In 12.8, we are told that Abraham
'pitched his tent', but makes no mention of him living in it. Was this
only a symbolic tent? Secondly, even if one grants the symbolic nature
of the altars, why should this signify the conquest of the country?
[3] E.g. Kidner, *Genesis*, p. 116; Klein, 'Yahwist Looks at Abraham',
pp. 44-45.
[4] Cf. Berg, 'Ein Sündenfall Abrahams', pp. 9-10, who argues that this
lack of divine consultation reveals a human act which endangers the
land promise. Cf. Kidner, *Genesis*, p. 116.

God without having first been spoken to: 'If this is to be an indictment of Abraham in 12.10-20, then it is an indictment that applies to Abraham throughout his life'.[1]

I have already had occasion to look briefly at the land promise in ch. 13 when dealing with elements of the posterity promise. I noted then that, up to this point, Abraham knows that the land of Canaan will be given to his descendants (12.7). His offer of part of Canaan to Lot (whom he believes to be his 'descendant'), must be seen therefore as an act of faith in that promise. We now need to look in more detail at the separation of Abraham and Lot.

Helyer looks at the important issue of what exactly Abraham offered Lot in 13.9, 'If you take the left hand, then I will go to the right; or if you take the right hand, then I will go to the left'. He points out that the Hebrews, when talking of directions, faced east.[2] Thus, when looking at 'the whole land', he was offering Lot the north ('left') or south ('right') of the land *of Canaan*. Lot chose neither but journeyed *east* (13.11)—i.e. straight ahead—and removed himself from Canaan, as can be seen clearly by the distinction made in 13.12. Initially the situation seems to be as Helyer contends— that Lot's separation from (rejection of) the land of Canaan separates him from the land of promise and thus eliminates him as a potential heir of Abraham. This must have been Abraham's perspective, for up to this point he has been told that his descendants will receive the land of *Canaan* (12.7). Abraham's feeling of deprivation could not have lasted for too long, however, for no sooner has Lot set off for the Jordan valley, than Yahweh explains to Abraham that the dimensions of the promised land, while including Canaan, extend much further and include the cities of the plain (13.4f.). Thus while Lot is out of Canaan he is still within the promised land.

However, in addition to these observations touched on before, the repetition of the land promise (13.14-17) needs to be scrutinized. Abraham already knows that his descendants will be given the land of Canaan (at least), but he still does not know which is the land the Lord will 'show' him (12.1e). This

---

[1] Miscall, *Workings of Old Testament Narrative*, p. 25.
[2] Helyer, 'Separation', p. 79.

gap in his knowledge is filled in 13.14-17, where the land is formally shown to him for the first time (note *ûrᵉ'ēh*, v. 14; cf. *'ar'ekā*, 12.1e), and promised to *him* (cf. 12.1e)—as well as to his descendants.[1] Thus the initial land promise—severely limited in scope—has been fulfilled and also expanded to reveal that the purpose in 'showing' him the land was to reveal what would one day be given to him and his descendants. So much is clear, in my opinion; however, Yahweh's invitation to Abraham to 'walk through the length and breadth of the land' (13.17) is the subject of some discussion. A common suggestion is that Abraham's perambulation reflects an ancient custom of land acquisition and was the means whereby the promise of the gift of land comes to its fruition.[2] However, as Jeyeraj points out, these arguments are based on Roman practices whose connection with the world of Genesis 13 has not been demonstrated.[3] I am more inclined to follow Calvin who observes that this travelling throughout the land reinforces the impression that he was a nomadic stranger and not its possessor.[4] This in itself would confirm that the land promise, as it is now understood, still looks to the future for its fulfilment.

Thus it is that ch. 15 engages the reader's interest. This chapter is very important generally in the unfolding of the ancestral promise theme, with vv. 1-6, concerned with descendants, flowing into vv. 7ff. in which the land promise is central. The strong connection between these two elements[5] is demonstrated by their amalgamation in vv. 13-16. If proof be needed that the promise of land—or land possession as it has now become—still awaits fulfilment, one need go no further than Yahweh's declaration that he has brought him thus far in his journeys, 'to give you this land to possess' (15.7)—to

---

[1] Jeyeraj, *Land Ownership in the Pentateuch*, p. 34.
[2] E.g. Sarna, *Understanding Genesis*, p. 104; Brueggemann, *Genesis*, p. 130 (citing David Daube, *Studies in Biblical Law*, pp. 28-36); Westermann, *Genesis 12–36*, p. 180 (citing Daube, p. 37). Cf. Victor, *Theme of Promise*, pp. 115, 118.
[3] Jeyeraj, *Land Ownership in the Pentateuch*, p. 34.
[4] Calvin, *Genesis*, 1.376.
[5] Snijders, 'Genesis XV', p. 265; Rendtorff, 'Genesis 15', p. 76; Anbar, 'Genesis 15', p. 40.

which Abraham responds, 'O Lord God, how am I to know that I shall possess it?' (15.8). Whether we interpret this question as expressing doubt, or merely a request for information,[1] it is clear that for Abraham the fulfilment still lies in the future.

Yahweh's response to this question, part of which takes the form of killing and dismembering an assortment of animals, raises a number of questions for the reader. Foremost among these is—what is the meaning of all this carnage? Hasel has conveniently summarized several suggestions, and also looked at ancient Near Eastern parallels.[2] While some of the examples cited by Hasel are not as cogent as he claims,[3] his conclusions seem to be generally sound. The most important of these for my present purpose is that an animal rite such as outlined in ch. 15 amounts to an act of treaty/covenant ratification:

> The animal rite in Gen 15 may... be considered as a covenant ratification rite in which Yahweh binds himself in a promise to the Patriarch. In this sense it may not be off the mark to call the *berît* of Yahweh with Abraham in Gen 15 a promissory covenant.[4]

This interpretation of vv. 9-11 is really confirmed by Yahweh's words in vv. 13-16, 18. Here, Yahweh gives a solemn promise that Abraham's descendants, though sojourners in a foreign land for a long period, will eventually return and they will then be given the land. In other words the promise of land possession remains a promise.[5] The relationship of Yahweh's speech to Abraham's question demonstrates this. Abraham had asked, 'how am *I* to know that *I* shall possess it?' (15.8). Yahweh's answer is, 'to *your descendants* I give this land'

---

[1] Victor, *Theme of Promise*, p. 135; Westermann, *Genesis 12–36*, p. 224.
[2] Hasel, 'Animal Rite', pp. 61ff.
[3] E.g. pp. 64-65, where examples from the Mari letters and the Abba-AN treaty text are adduced as parallels. However, in neither of these is there a division of animals nor does either party pass through the middle, as is the case in Gen. 15.
[4] Hasel, 'Animal Rite', p. 69.
[5] Cf. Brueggemann, *Genesis*, p. 150; Wenham, 'Animal Rite', p. 134 (possibly); Gibson, *Genesis*, 2.55; Westermann, *Genesis 12–36*, pp. 215, 229.

(15.18). This shows quite clearly that it is not Abraham himself who will possess the land but only his posterity (and even they only after a considerable delay).[1] Victor is of the opinion that 'the possession of the land by Abraham's descendants is equivalent to the possession of the land by Abraham himself'.[2] This conclusion is based on a theory of Israelite corporate personality that may be arguable from some passages, but is not present here.[3] The pericope makes a clear distinction between the two parties, rather than collapsing them into the same category: 'Know of a surety that *your descendants* will... *they* will be oppressed... *they* shall come out... As for yourself (*wᵉ'attâ*)...' (15.13-15). Similarly, notice the contrast in 17.7-9. Here, what is said of one party is carefully distinguished from the other, and it is only Abraham's descendants who are specifically promised the gift of the land. Any possibility of the promise of land possession being fulfilled in Abraham's lifetime is killed off by Yahweh's announcement; even Abraham's descendants will not possess it for at least four hundred years (15.13; cf. *wᵉdôr rᵉbî'î*, v. 16); additionally, a precondition for the return of Abraham's seed to the land is the full maturation of Amorite iniquity, and this will not be achieved for some time. The only problem for Abraham to solve is to ensure that he has descendants around when the time comes, and his course of action in that area we have already covered. As ch. 15 concludes, the promise of land possession is clarified further. The land to be possessed is now shown to be even larger than previously stated and will stretch from the river of Egypt to the Euphrates.[4]

---

[1] As seen correctly by Habel, 'Gospel Promise to Abraham', p. 351.

[2] Victor, *Theme of Promise*, p. 138.

[3] Such a theory has come under searching criticism from, e.g., Porter, 'Legal Aspects of "Corporate Personality"' (who limits himself to legal texts); Rogerson, 'Corporate Personality'; *idem*, *Anthropology*, pp. 55-59. Porter questions the cogency of key texts used by Wheeler Robinson in his classic formulation of the theory, while Rogerson considers its anthropological basis to be insecure.

[4] The recipients of the promise had previously been 'you and your descendants' (13.15; cf. v. 17); the recipients of the land outlined in 15.18-21 are simply 'your descendants' (v. 18). The difference between these two designations is probably no more significant than the fact that the focus of the verses leading up to this latter declaration by

The land promise is mentioned explicitly once more in 17.8, which is one of several points of contact between chs. 15 and 17.[1] As with the posterity promise, the new element of conditionality is applied to the land promise. It is not to be given *gratis* (the impression one has received so far), but in response to Abraham's 'blameless' behaviour (17.1; cf. 18.19). The dimensions of the promised land are here confirmed to be 'all the land of Canaan', probably to be taken in the general sense of 'Greater Canaan' as outlined in 15.18-21. However, a problem arises concerning the recipients of the promise. No sooner have we been informed that the land is to be given to Abraham's descendants, with no immediate reward for the patriarch himself (ch. 15), than he is told, 'I will give to *you*, and to your descendants after you... all the land of Canaan' (17.8). Does this indicate that Abraham himself will be given the land? We should note, however, that it is immediately added, 'And I shall be *their* God' (*wᵉhāyîtî lāhem lē'lōhîm*); so even with Abraham in the picture, the emphasis is still on his descendants rather than himself. Perhaps 17.8 should be read as containing waw explicativum, 'And I will give to you, *that is* to your descendants after you, the land of your sojournings...'

As the Abraham story moves toward its conclusion a number of incidental details reinforce the fact that Abraham does not have possession of the land. The magnanimity of Abimelech's offer, 'my land is before you; dwell where it pleases you' (20.15), cannot hide the truth that Abraham is living as a sojourner in another's land outside the borders of what was promised him (Philistia [cf. 26.1] presumably being outside Canaan [17.8] even in the more detailed description of 15.18-21; and if it is in fact within the land, the text still demonstrates that the land does not belong to Abraham.) By the time of his

Yahweh has been on the descendants of Abraham who will enter the land after Abraham's death (cf. vv. 13-16).
[1] Noted e.g. by Skinner, *Genesis*, p. 290:

(a) Self-introduction of deity	17.1 // 15.7
(b) Covenant	17.1ff. // 15.9ff.
(c) Promise of numerous seed	17.4ff. // 15.5
(d) Promise of land	17.8 // 15.18
(e) Promise of son	17.19, 21 // 15.4
(f) Abraham's incredulity	17.17 // 15.3, 8

death, Abraham's total real estate property in Canaan amounts to two holes in the ground: a well at Beersheba (21.25f.) and a grave at Machpelah (23.1ff.).[1] The non-fulfilment of the land promise in Abraham's lifetime is underlined by the negotiations he has with Ephron the Hittite for the cave of Machpelah. Ephron counters Abraham's initial offer to buy (23.9) by offering the property as a gift: 'I *give* (*nātattî*) you the field, and I *give* you (*neˁtattîhā*) the cave… I *give* it (*neˁtattîhā*) to you' (23.11). However, Abraham insists on *buying* it: 'I will give (*nātattî*) the price of the field' (23.13).[2] He then agrees to pay the exorbitant sum of four hundred silver shekels, which even allowing for the trauma of bereavement suggests he has more money than sense. The purchase of the property means that he now has the deeds to a small portion of the promised land, but it hardly fulfils the spirit of the promise. Yahweh had promised to *give* the land; Abraham turns down the offer of a gift in order to buy the cave. If *buying* property could be construed as fulfilling the promise, one wonders why Abraham—laden down with this world's goods—had not made similar offers for desirable properties before. He had used his own initiative in trying to push the posterity promise along, but even Abraham realizes that land bought—at any price—is not a *gift* from Yahweh. It would appear that by now he realizes that those who will receive the land as *gift* are his descendants. (Hence the reason why Isaac must stay in the land at all costs—24.6-7.) Until then, Abraham must bear the cost. His purchase of this small plot simply emphasizes the non-fulfilment of the promise.[3]

---

[1] Contra Alexander, *Literary Analysis of Abraham Narrative*, p. 60, who believes that by ch. 21, 'God has substantially fulfilled all his promises to Abraham'. Abraham's puny possessions show that the land promise awaits its fulfilment.

[2] Some have suggested that Ephron's offer is not to be taken too literally, but is a typical part of oriental bartering. E.g. Sarna, *Understanding Genesis*, p. 169; von Rad, *Genesis*, p. 247; Brueggemann, *Genesis*, p. 195. Even if this is granted—and the evidence adduced is far from compelling—the irony of the situation is clear to the reader. However, Goldingay, 'Patriarchs', p. 6, has seen correctly the distinction between gift and purchase. I would disagree, however, with his judgment that this was a 'sinful act' of Abraham.

[3] I see no reason for supposing with Brueggemann, *Genesis*, p. 196,

In reviewing the land promise, we can see that while it is important, it does not have the dominating role of the posterity promise. It shares some common features with it, however. Just as Abraham was kept guessing about the identity of Yahweh's choice for true descendant, so here he has to puzzle out a number of features, e.g. the exact dimensions of the land; is the land to be given to him, or to his descendants only, or to both? On the other hand it differs from the posterity promise. At least the goal of the nation/posterity promise was clear from the start, but the same cannot be said for the land promise. Finally, like the posterity promise, it has not progressed very far by the end of the story. By then he owns a tomb and a well, which is no more progress toward possessing the land than the birth of Isaac is toward becoming a great nation.

Blessing

The elements of the divine Announcement concerned with 'blessing' contain some problems of translation with which I dealt in the Introduction to this chapter. Before I proceed with my analysis of this section let me summarize my previous conclusions. Contrary to common suggestions I maintain the form and force of the imperative *wehyēh bᵉrākâ*—'be a blessing!' (12.2), and see the following clauses as consequential ('so that...'). I will assume a broad definition for the term 'blessing': the receipt of 'happiness, success, and increase of earthly possessions'.[1] The problem of whether to translate

that getting a legal right to the grave was 'a symbolic but concrete guarantee of possession of the whole land'. The assertion by Klein, 'Yahwist Looks at Abraham', p. 49, that 'at death the patriarchs were no longer mere aliens, but they got possession of the land... Their burial was a down payment on the promise of an everlasting possession of the land' similarly lacks any support. Cf. Kidner, *Genesis*, p. 145. (Von Rad, *Genesis*, p. 250, has seen the weakness of this argument.) I also disagree with Coats, *Genesis*, p. 164, and Westermann, *Genesis 12–36*, p. 376, who argue for no connection whatsoever with the land promise. There is a very close connection—but not that of promise/fulfilment.

[1] Scharbert, '*brk; bᵉrākhāh*', p. 293. Terrien, *Elusive Presence*, p. 74, suggests that *bᵉrākâ* 'designates far more than the pseudo-magical

nibr^eḳû (12.3) passively or reflexively is not so crucial for my
present aim; either possibility demands that the nations will
have a positive assessment of Abraham—in having been
either directly blessed by Abraham or in invoking his name
when uttering blessings. The context provided by the Abraham story as a whole may help deciding between options.

On his journey to the land which Yahweh would show him,
the first foreigners mentioned are the Canaanites who 'were
in the land' at that time (12.6). Yahweh immediately promises
their land to Abraham's descendants (12.7), which although a
blessing for Abraham's descendants would probably not strike
the Canaanites in the same way. On the other hand we do not
yet know how those descendants will conduct themselves and
so it is *possible* that the Canaanites will welcome such a
takeover. However, this is set for the future and remains
beyond the ken of the first-time reader.

At this stage Abraham has the land promise primarily in
mind and he 'journeys on', disregarding the opportunity of
being a blessing to the Canaanites. The famine which hits the
land forces him down to Egypt, and it is here that the first real
opportunity for altruism raises its head. However, it is clear
that Abraham feels no burden to be a blessing to anyone
(except himself). That he is not a blessing to his wife goes without saying. This is equally the case with regard to Pharaoh.
Abraham's sole motivation is 'that my life will be spared'
(12.13); any moral considerations are also spared. As a result,
'the Lord afflicted Pharaoh and his house with great plagues'
(12.17). So much for the blessing. The reversal of roles in the
promise of blessing should also be noted. It is Pharaoh (a
representative of the nations if ever there was one) who
blesses Abraham—at least in terms of material wealth: 'for
her sake he dealt well with Abram; and he had sheep, oxen,
he-asses, menservants, maidservants, she-asses, and camels
[but no longer any wife!]' (12.16). In this light it is hard to
sustain the view that the punishment on Pharaoh was done to

virtue of material wealth, physiological fertility, and immediate success. It evokes well-being in a corporate sense, and it implies social
responsibility.'

protect Abraham from the might of the nations.[1] It was Pharaoh who needed protecting.

One of the most interesting facets of this pericope is the characterization of Pharaoh. He realizes that Sarah is the cause of his problems, but we are never told how Pharaoh discovered that Sarah was Abraham's wife; simply that he correctly interpreted events.[2] He certainly stands out as Abraham's moral superior, seeing quite clearly the wrong that has been done, while Abraham expresses no regret for placing Pharaoh in such a situation. The foreigner is the wronged party—as is highlighted by his words of accusation, 'What is this you have done to me?' Abraham's silence condemns him more eloquently than any words.[3] Quite obviously Pharaoh does not consider himself to have been blessed by Abraham, and is not likely to invoke Abraham's name in any future blessing he himself might utter. The story ends with words which ironically echo the opening events in this chapter. Previously Yahweh said, 'Go!' (*lek*)... 'so Abram went' (12.1a, 4a); now Pharaoh says, 'Go!' (*lek*)... 'so Abram went' (12.19; 13.1).[4] This parallel serves to highlight that an endeavour begun with such high hopes has temporarily, at least, foundered. Rather than being a blessing, Abraham is unceremoniously deported by the first foreigner who has the pleasure of making his acquaintance.

Having been bundled out of Egypt, the party returns to Canaan, which, as I noted previously, is probably still in the grip of the famine. This cannot have been unmitigated good news for the Canaanites who must have suffered some economic disruption when Abraham brought in tow 'all that he had' (13.1), including Lot, and we are not surprised to learn that 'the land could not support both of them dwelling together' (13.6). With no mention of Canaanite opposition, we might wonder if they would have been so tolerant if they had

[1] Cf. Westermann, *Genesis 12–36*, p. 165.
[2] Skinner, *Genesis*, p. 250; Koch, *Growth of Biblical Tradition*, p. 123; Petersen, 'Thrice-Told Tale', p. 37; McEvenue, 'Narrative Styles in Hagar Stories', p. 71.
[3] Petersen, 'Thrice-Told Tale', p. 38; Westermann, *Genesis 12–36*, pp. 166-67.
[4] Cf. Berg, 'Ein Sündenfall Abrahams', p. 14.

been privy to the promise of 12.7.

Lot's choice of the Jordan valley brings Abraham increased opportunities to mingle with the nations of the earth. In bringing back his descendant from exile he manages to 'rout' (14.15, RSV) Lot's captors who represent the nations. The verb *nkh* (hiphil) has a semantic range from 'hit' to 'destroy',[1] but no matter at which end of the spectrum we place it here, the recipients of Abraham's action would hardly feel themselves blessed. Here of course it must be allowed that Abraham has been provoked, and the nations are not innocent parties as Pharaoh was, but the reader can observe clearly that either as a coward (12.10-20), or as a hero (ch. 14), Abraham brings no blessing to these nations. (Any blessing the Sodomites might experience is purely coincidental.) However, the curious episode with Melchizedek, with which the chapter closes, may temper our judgment slightly. The king of Salem pronounces a blessing over Yahweh and Abraham (14.19-20). According to 12.3a this should result in blessings coming to Melchizedek, but the story breaks off without giving any sequel. However, Abraham effects no blessing at all in this passage, by word or deed. We cannot even be certain from the MT who pays tithe to whom (14.20c). The king of Salem's relationship to Abraham cannot be discerned from this enigmatic piece. Abraham has already taken advantage of one foreigner (12.16); it is certainly possible for him to do so again. One is left with the curious impression that so far in this story Abraham is doing his best to be a blessing to no one but himself[2]—even the rescue of Lot in this chapter was prompted by his desire to keep alive his promise of descendants.

Abraham's stance toward the nations seems to be inherited by his descendants, if Yahweh's predictions in 15.13ff. are to be believed. Again, like Lot, they will be sorely pressed in enslaved exile (15.13). While the cynic may feel that this enslavement could be a blessing for their Egyptian masters, and will last for a considerable time, they will be emancipated and leave with

---

[1] Koehler and Baumgartner, *Lexicon*, pp. 615-16.
[2] I cannot agree with Gibson, *Genesis*, 2.45, who suggests that Abraham's defeat of the kings demonstrates that the blessing (of 12.1-3) was working. Abraham has been commissioned with the blessing of the nations, not their destruction.

great possessions—in a similar fashion to Abraham's recent expulsion from Egypt. Even granting that Abraham's descendants will be innocent victims of Egyptian thuggery, this scenario of their masters' dispossession does not bode well for Israel being a blessing to this particular nation. If this were not enough, once out of Egypt they will receive the territory of the Kenites *et al*. This may be a blessing for Israel, but hardly for those who lose their ancestral real estate. That this dispossession, like that of the Egyptians, will be a judgment from Yahweh showing that their iniquity is complete (cf. 15.14, 16) merely emphasizes that whatever else Abraham's descendants do, they will not be blessing these nations.

Chapter 15 reflects the promise on the grand scale; ch. 16 reduces it to personal relationships. In a neat reversal of roles from 15.13, Abraham and Sarah have a female slave who just happens to be an Egyptian. While initially she may seem to be a blessing to Sarah and Abraham in being used as a surrogate mother for Sarah's missing child, the aged couple are certainly no blessing to Hagar. She looks with contempt (*qll* [cf. 12.3]) on Sarah (16.4, 5), who responds by treating Hagar harshly (16.6), when given a free rein by Abraham—who could not have doubted the outcome. We hardly see the reciprocal milk of human kindness in these sharp exchanges. Even the angel's words offer no improvement in the situation: 'Return to your mistress and submit to her' (16.9b). What was writ large in the earlier predictions concerning Egyptians and Kenites is here worked out in individual eyeball to eyeball confrontations. There is not a blessing to be found anywhere; the 'blessing' of 16.12 is hardly the kind that any normal mortal would lust after.[1]

We now reach a lull in the narrative as far as developments in this promise are concerned. We catch a fresh scent as the judgment on Sodom is being organized, with Yahweh's statement in 18.18 that 'all the nations of the earth shall bless themselves by him'. This declaration is illuminated if it is read

---

[1] The contention of Gibson, *Genesis*, 2.63-64, that this story shows the unfolding of the blessing to the nations, is, on my interpretation, unsupportable. Klein, 'Yahwist Looks at Abraham', p. 46, observes correctly that Hagar 'is a representative of "all the families of the earth", from whom Abraham and Sarah withheld blessing'.

in the light of the unfolding posterity promise. Wolff points out that Abraham's intercession (18.23ff.), if successful, would result in the nations being blessed (Sodom, for him, representing all the nations of the earth).[1] However, there are two important considerations to bear in mind. First, we have already seen that Abraham's major concern is the rescue of Lot; the salvation of Sodom is really a means to this end. Secondly, Sodom is destroyed but Lot is rescued. Even if we concede that Abraham intended to save Sodom in order to bless the nations, he does not succeed. However, Yahweh's disregard of the conditions agreed to in the bartering of 18.23ff. suggests that he read between the lines of Abraham's pious posturing and gave him what he was really after— Lot—with Sodom being expendable; 'when God destroyed the cities of the valley, God remembered Abraham, and sent Lot out of the midst of the overthrow' (19.29).

The nations have been spared a visit from Abraham for some time, until he turns up unexpectedly in Gerar (20.1). True to form he acts as though he had never heard the imperative to be a blessing. Once again Abraham is guilty of deceit, which this time endangers the life of Abimelech king of Gerar (20.3). The king's innocence and moral integrity contrast with Abraham's guilt and expediency. (The plague sent on Abimelech's house is to be seen more as a heavy-handed attempt by Yahweh to prevent the sin of adultery than as a punishment.)[2] The contrast is compounded by Abraham's crass admission that his deception had been done because he thought 'there is no fear of God at all in this place' (20.11). Abimelech's conduct shows how wrong Abraham had been. He conducts himself in an admirable way: 'In the integrity of my heart and the innocence of my hands I have done this' (20.5).[3] In this light it is nothing short of amazing that

---

[1] Wolff, 'Kerygma of the Yahwist', p. 148. Also, Habel, 'Gospel Promise to Abraham', p. 349; Klein, 'Que se passe-t-il en Genèse 18?', pp. 84-85. Klein, 'Yahwist Looks at Abraham', p. 46, is too sympathetic toward Abraham when he suggests that as Ammon and Moab emerge from Sodom, Abraham is also praying for the likes of these. This is to impute knowledge to Abraham that has not yet been divulged.

[2] Westermann, *Genesis 12–36*, p. 323.

[3] Cf. von Rad, *Genesis*, p. 229; Coats, *Genesis*, p. 150; Brueggemann,

Yahweh should tell Abimelech that Abraham 'is a prophet, and he will pray for you' (20.7). Equally amazing is the fact that Abraham does just that (20.17), with the result that Abimelech's household is healed. This is a significant development in that it is the first time Abraham does something positive for one of the nations—but even here this assessment must be tempered by the knowledge that the 'blessing' which ensues is merely the lifting of the plague induced by Abraham's own behaviour. In any case, this prayer in itself is not sufficient to allay Abimelech's fears, for just a little while later we have him forming a covenant so that 'you [Abraham] will not deal falsely with me or with my offspring or with my posterity...' (21.23). The man obviously still has his suspicions. The covenant, designed merely to prevent Abraham from acting in unprincipled ways, brings no other obvious blessing to Abimelech.

From this point onward the narrative gives but fleeting references to the blessing theme. After the Mount Moriah episode Abraham is told: 'by *your descendants* shall all the nations of the earth bless themselves' (22.18). Previously such blessing has been predicted of Abraham alone. Does this change signify that Yahweh has given up on Abraham ever fulfilling the role himself? One is tempted to think that Yahweh would have been justified in doing so.[1] Upon Sarah's death, Abraham is shown with foreigners, but this is nothing more than a financial transaction (ch. 23). Abraham may have paid over the odds for the tomb, but this cannot be construed as any conscious blessing on the nations. In fact, Abraham's attitude toward the nations—at least the Canaanites—is clearly antagonistic, as one can see by his instructions to his servant concerning Isaac's wife (24.3). This is Abraham's last

Genesis, p. 178; Westermann, *Genesis 12–36*, p. 325; McEvenue, 'Elohist at Work', p. 321.

[1] Cf. Chew, *'Blessing for the Nations'*, p. 63:

> It therefore appears that this particular universal destiny and responsibility... is not to be transmitted to Abraham's seed, until the patriarch proved himself to be a suitable agent, as a 'fearer of God' (22.12) would be, to bring about blessing for others.

However, even though Abraham may now have proved himself, *his* attitude toward the nations does not change in any way.

significant act, and a telling testimony to the fact that he lived
his life as though he had never heard Yahweh say, 'Be a
blessing!'

As one reviews chs. 12–25 looking at Abraham's relations
with the nations, one is hard pressed to find any example
where Abraham does anything positive for anyone which was
not motivated by self-interest. (The only possible exception is
his prayer in 20.17—but even here he merely reverses the
havoc his actions have wrought.) Paradoxically, I might note
that Abraham finds himself blessed on a number of occasions
at the expense of foreigners (e.g. 12.16)—surely the reverse of
Yahweh's intention in 12.3b. Defining the exact connotation of
nibr^e*kû* in 12.3, a seemingly important task at the time, has
turned out to be a purely academic pursuit. The unfolding of
the plot in general, and of Abraham's actions in particular,
give no help whatsoever in deciding between the passive and
reflexive possibilities. Abraham does little to bless the nations,
and Abraham's treatment of them makes his absence from
the blessing formulas of foreign dignitaries no surprise at all.

Conclusion

We are now in a position to draw some general conclusions. As
we look back on the Abraham story we can now see that the
initial promises given to him by Yahweh were imprecise. In
this way the story of Abraham differs, as we shall see, from
that of Jacob or Jacob's family in which the divine will is set
out fairly clearly at the outset (though there are still some
surprises in store for the participants). However, in 12.1-3
only certain elements of the promise are present, and even
these are vague. For example, land is mentioned, but it is not
made clear that the land to be shown to Abraham will become
the possession of his descendants; this is clarified only later.
Also, he is told that he will become a great nation, but it is
certainly not clear that this nation will result from the biological son of himself and Sarah. Abraham and the reader are fed
just one piece of information at a time as the plot unfolds.[1] This

---

[1] I am therefore only in partial agreement with Mitchell, 'Abram's
Understanding', p. 38, who states that 'God never made any material

complicates the task of answering the question, Is God's promise being fulfilled or hindered? When we talk of *the* promise, do we mean, the promise so far revealed?, or the promise as we understand it once having read the whole story? As White says,

> The promise is a word which has been explicitly separated from its referent. The promisor offers a word *in place of* a thing which will be supplied at a future time. This separation of the word from its referent injects an element of uncertainty into the relation of the signifier to the signified. When a man promises to bring me apples, I know what *I* think apples are (i.e. the signified of the signifier, apples), but I will not know what *he* thinks they are until he produces them.[1]

When we break down the issue into these elements, Abraham elicits a certain amount of sympathy. We see him taking some initiatives to fulfil God's promise. For example, in the posterity promise, he works with Lot; risks his life for him; is clever enough to think of the ruse of Sarah as his sister, etc. These are understandable actions (though not all are beyond moral reproach). Given Abraham's knowledge of the promise at the time he takes these initiatives, his actions not only make sense, but may also be seen as faithful responses to God's promises. However, from *hindsight*, we see that most of his best efforts served only to complicate their fulfilment. From hindsight, all that would have been necessary was for Abraham to have patiently 'waited for the Lord'. If he and Sarah had simply continued in their usual marital relationship, Isaac would have been born—eventually. All of his activity outside of this ambit merely complicated matters. As Magonet says,

> Oft kehrt die Frage in den Erzählungen der Genesis wieder: Warten sie auf Gott, daß er sein Wort einlöse, oder unternehmen sie ihre eigenen menschlichen Schritte, um die Dinge zu beschleunigen, selbst wenn sich am Ende heraus-

additions to the provisions set forth at the first. God did give further explanations, spelling out details of the promises and obligations. But nothing of substance was added.' I would argue that developments of substance do occur.

[1] White, 'Word Reception', p. 77.

stellen sollte, daß es gegen Gottes Willen war?[1]

We see, therefore, that even faithful initiatives can work havoc with the promise. Apparently Yahweh was looking for Abraham to give complete passive acceptance to the promise, trusting in Yahweh to bring about the result. This he eventually gets in ch. 22. In succeeding chapters I will suggest a similar theme working in the stories of Jacob and Jacob's family, in the relationship between the fulfilment of Yahweh's promises on the one hand and human activity and/or passivity on the other.

In the light of what I have said above, Yahweh's behaviour must be questioned. Has he been fair to Abraham? If from the beginning Yahweh knows, for example, that the nation would come from Abraham's biological son—and presumably he does know—then why does he not say so? By keeping Abraham guessing, is he not risking the fulfilment of his own promises? Or was the whole enterprise an elaborate process of character development for Abraham, who finally comes to realize that he must obey Yahweh with no ifs, buts, or ideas of his own (ch. 22)? But if it is, why does Yahweh want this kind of divine-human relationship? Ultimately, these are questions raised by the narrative, but not answered by it.

If we return to the simple issue with which this chapter started—the fate of the imperatives and promises in 12.1-3—we have a rather depressing picture. Of the two imperatives, one is partially obeyed, and the other hardly at all. Yahweh had said, 'Go!', and Abraham went, but not exactly as the Lord had told him. Yahweh had said, 'leave your kindred'; for the best of reasons, Abraham took Lot. It might be Yahweh's fault for not explaining clearly enough—but nevertheless, and especially from hindsight, less than complete obedience. More blame attaches to Abraham with the second imperative, 'Be a blessing!' He lived his life as if unaware of its existence. His one prayer in 20.17 hardly absolves him from this accusation. When we come to the major promises, we fare little better. Yahweh had promised, 'I will make of you a great nation'. By the end of the story Abraham has one legitimate son. This is

[1] Magonet, 'Die Söhne Abrahams', p. 206.

some progress, but hardly an outstanding success. The precise form of the land promise in 12.1e has been fulfilled—Abraham was *shown* the land—but the purpose for thus showing him, i.e. *possession*, is almost as far away as ever at the end of the story; a well and a grave hardly constitute all the land from the river of Egypt to the Euphrates (15.18). I would suggest a causal relationship between Abraham's less than full obedience of the imperatives and the stumbling progress of the promises. I noted at the beginning of this chapter that 12.1-3 taken as a whole strongly implied that the fulfilment of the promises was contingent upon obedience to the imperatives. Having surveyed the narrative, the correlation between these two aspects should come as no surprise. (It is only toward the end of the story, in ch. 22, that the reader sees the kind of obedience expected from the beginning.)

In closing I must comment on 24.1, 'Now Abraham was old, well advanced in years; and the Lord had blessed Abraham in all things'. As a statement of general material prosperity this is obviously true. However, it cannot be taken to mean that the promises of 12.1-3 have been fulfilled.[1] In 24.35f. Abraham's servant spells out exactly *in what sense* Abraham has been blessed—material prosperity and a son in his old age. This obviously falls far short of a complete fulfilment of 12.1-3 as it has now been defined. As yet, there is no great nation nor any real possession of the land. While it shows that Yahweh can bless to some degree a less than blameless (*tāmîm*) man, it is also eloquent testimony to the failure of the divine promises of 12.1-3 to materialize in any real way during Abraham's lifetime.

---

[1] As argued by Golka, 'Die theologischen Erzählungen im Abraham-Kreis', p. 190; Goldingay, 'Patriarchs', p. 6.

Chapter 3

THE JACOB STORY

Introduction

In the previous chapter I looked at the ways in which the plot
of the Abraham story related to the initial Announcement
delivered in 12.1-3. In this chapter I will investigate how the
Announcement of plot contained in the divine oracle to
Rebekah (Gen. 25.23), and Isaac's blessings on Jacob (27.27-
29) and Esau (27.39-40), carries hints and promises of how
the Jacob story is going to develop, and whether in fact such
aspirations are converted into reality.

Gen. 25.23 fits the pattern of crucial statements setting out
God's purpose which introduce the individual narrative cycles
in the ancestral history. It also assumes prominence not only
for its content but also for its rarity in containing the words of
Yahweh; in the Jacob narrative, unlike the primaeval history
and the Abraham cycle, divine speeches occur only occasionally and at crucial moments. This importance of 25.23 is generally recognized. For von Rad, 25.21-28, of which v. 23 is the
kernel, forms 'an expository preface to the whole [Jacob story]'
which 'acquaints the reader with those facts which are
important for understanding the following stories'.[1]

The importance of 27.27-29, 39-40 also is self-evident. These
words by Isaac introduce the crucial theme of blessing. The

---

[1] Von Rad, *Genesis*, p. 265. See also Fishbane, 'Composition and
Structure', p. 33; Fokkelman, *Narrative Art in Genesis*, p. 94, 'By its
centre of power scene 1 [Gen. 25.19-26]... obliges the reader to read all
of the events of Jacob's life in the light of the oracle...'; Brueggemann,
Genesis, p. 208, 'Clearly the oracle of designation (25.23) governs the
narrative'; p. 215, 'The oracle of 25.23 casts its power over the entire
Jacob narrative'; Coats, *Genesis*, p. 185, 'It sets the tone for the entire
scope of the Jacob story...'

amount of space devoted by the narrative to the intrigue and risks involved in the acquisition of the blessing highlights its significance, as does the burning ambition of Rebekah and willing cooperation of Jacob.[1] The fact that Isaac pronounces the words 'before Yahweh' (*lipnê yhwh* [27.7]) reveals their solemnity and suggests the hope that Yahweh will honour what he says.[2] In addition, there are many specific connections between these blessings and the subsequent fate of the brothers. The importance of these texts is acknowledged by several scholars,[3] with some seeing part of their importance as providing a commentary on the oracle of 25.23.[4]

Unlike many scholars who have written on the Jacob story I shall argue that these key passages are not to be read *exclusively* as relating to the political relationship between Israel and Edom, as though they had no reference to the fortunes of the main protagonists in the plot of the Jacob story. It is not to be denied that relations between the two nations are envisaged, particularly in 25.23, but Driver overstates his case when he says, 'the future which the verse [25.23] holds out in prospect is the future not of Jacob and Esau, but of *Israel* and *Edom*'.[5] While 25.23 is concerned with nations (*gōyîm*) and

---

[1] Jacob's objection in 25.12 does not concern the proposed deception but only the risk of being caught.

[2] Cf. Scharbert, *'brk; bᵉrākhāh'*, p. 289, who states that the term means that Isaac is uttering God's will. However, it is better to see it as expressing Isaac's seriousness, rather than proof of Yahweh's agreement (cf. pp. 298, 303). This term is not found in Isaac's speech to Esau (27.4), but in Rebekah's report of it. However, it is unlikely to be her invention, given Isaac's invocation of God in 27.28 ('May God give to you...' [*wᵉyitten-lᵉkâ hāᵉlōhîm*]).

[3] E.g. Westermann, *Genesis 12–36*, p. 434, cf. p. 409; *idem, Promises to the Fathers*, p. 89, 'Theologically, the whole narrative cycle of Jacob and Esau is determined by the concept of blessing'; Brueggemann, *Genesis*, p. 207, sees 'blessing' as the dominating influence in the Jacob cycle. However, the sharp distinction he makes between 'religious' *promises* and 'earthly' *blessings* is hardly tenable. God delivers both promises and blessings, making it difficult to designate one category more 'religious' than the other. Also, e.g. 28.13 contains the 'promise' of land, which could hardly be more 'earthly'. The sharp divide between 'religious' and 'earthly' is not inherent to the text itself.

[4] E.g. Kuntzmann, 'Le symbole des jumeaux', p. 36. See also Coats, *Genesis*, p. 203; Brueggemann, *Genesis*, p. 217.

[5] Driver, *Genesis*, p. 247; cf. Skinner, *Genesis*, p. 356; Maag, 'Jakob—

peoples (*le'ummîm*), the context provided by vv. 24ff. picks up elements of the oracle and relates them to Jacob and Esau as individuals: i.e. there are to be two nations (the twins); one is to be stronger (Esau's hairiness); division is to occur between the two of them (Jacob holding Esau's heel suggesting rivalry; Esau is a hunter, Jacob is a domestic individual; the presence of parental favouritism); the reversal of the expected relationship between the 'greater' and the 'lesser' (the haggling over the birthright—an important issue in determining seniority between the twins). Gen. 27.27-29, 39-40 also is assessed by many to have relevance solely for providing insight into the relationship between Israel and Edom. Skinner's view is typical: 'the blessing... deals, of course, not with the personal history of Jacob, but with the future greatness of Israel'.[1] This assessment, which denies any relationship between these blessings and the plot of the Jacob narrative, is not justified either by the content of the passages, the context provided by ch. 27 as a whole, or by the role they play in chs. 25–36 in which elements of the blessings are repeatedly related to the two brothers.

Looking at the final form of the text, the reader may reasonably assume that Yahweh's oracle and Isaac's blessings were intended to exert their influence from the time they were uttered, with reference to Jacob and Esau as individuals, and to extend into the future to cover their descendants in their national, political spheres.[2] Thus, they include the future

---

Esau—Edom', p. 419; Schiltknecht, 'Konflikt und Versöhnung', esp. pp. 522-25; Scharbert, '*brk; berākhāh*', p. 303; Westermann, *Promises to the Fathers*, pp. 80-81; Bartlett, 'Brotherhood of Edom', p. 19; Westermann, *Genesis 12–36*, p. 412.
[1] Skinner, *Genesis*, p. 371. See also Driver, *Genesis*, p. 261; von Rad, *Genesis*, p. 278; de Pury, *Promesse divine et légende cultuelle*, 1.103 n. 32; Speiser, *Genesis*, pp. 210, 212; Westermann, *Genesis 12–36*, pp. 436, 441. See Thompson, 'Conflict Themes', pp. 5-9, for a discussion of recent scholarly approaches which treat the Jacob story (or at least the conflict themes within it) as expressing real historical relationships between Israel and its neighbours.
[2] Cf. Westermann, *Genesis 12–36*, p. 443, '[27.40b] foretells Esau's way of life and that of his descendants...' Cf. Luke, 'Isaac's Blessing', p. 37, 'the historical conflicts between the two peoples had already commenced when their ancestors were in their mother's womb';

of Israel and Edom but do not exclude Jacob and Esau. From
the perspective of the narrative itself, the national histories of
Israel and Edom commence with the life of each nation's
respective patriarch (cf. 25.30; 36.1, 8, 19, 43). As Ahroni says,
'the drama seems to unfold a divine master plan in which the
fate of *individuals* and *nations* is preordained'[1] (emphasis
mine). In addition, Isaac's review of the blessing deceitfully
received by Jacob reminds the reader that the blessing is to
exert its power in the lives of the two brothers: 'Behold, I have
made him your lord, and all of his brothers I have given to him
for servants, and with grain and wine I have sustained him.
What then can I do for you, my son?' (27.37).[2] The use of the
plural 'brothers' here and of 'your brothers and your mother's
sons' in 27.29 cannot be put forward as an objection that 'the
immediate situation is forgotten'.[3] Apart from the fact that if
the plural were taken literally it would not fit the historical
situation of Israel and Edom either, 'brothers and mother's
sons' was a fixed stereotyped pair, which should not be read

Sarna, *Understanding Genesis*, p. 183; Kuntzmann, 'Le symbole des
jumeaux', p. 33, sees 25.23 operating at three levels: (a) personally
between Jacob and Esau; (b) nationally between Israel and its neighbours; (c) psychologically between Jacob himself and his descendants.
[1] Ahroni, 'Why did Esau Spurn the Birthright?', p. 326. Cf. Thompson, *Origin Tradition*, p. 161, 'The episode [25.22f.] makes a prediction
of conflict between *Jacob* and *Esau* and gives the interpretation that
both children will be ancestors of the nations *Edom* and *Israel*'
(emphasis mine).
[2] The difficulty of limiting matters to Israel and Edom can be seen in
the scholarly literature. For example, Westermann, *Genesis 12–36*,
p. 443, believes that Isaac's blessing on Esau in 27.39-40 shows that
'Esau is to have a hard life, but he is to live', yet he also asserts that
'the oracles refer not to the two men, but to the later tribes and
peoples'. The latter statement contradicts the former. If the blessing
refers only to national matters then it can say nothing about Esau. If it
does say something about Esau, as Westermann correctly affirms in
his former statement, then we may legitimately ask concerning the
degree of coherence between the blessing and the subsequent plot of the
Jacob–Esau story. Westermann adds to his uncertainty with the
statement cited above, which I believe is, in fact, the best way of
viewing the blessings.
[3] Bartlett, 'Brotherhood of Edom', p. 19.

woodenly (cf. Judg. 8.19).[1]

I would suggest that if one of the main questions in chs. 12–25 is how and when the initial promises of land and descendants will be fulfilled, and in chs. 37–50 how and when the dreams of Joseph's lordship will become reality, then an important question in chs. 25–36 is 'how and when will the promises and aspirations contained in the oracle (25.23) and blessings (27.27-29, 39-40) come to fruition?' In fact, de Pury is of the opinion that the fulfilment of the blessing is the dominating theme throughout the Yahwistic Jacob story.[2]

This chapter questions most of the approaches which have previously been made concerning the relationship of these passages to chs. 25–36 as a whole. Scholars have in the main taken one of two stances: first, that these verses are indeed fulfilled in the Jacob story; second, that they are not fulfilled within chs. 25–36 either because they are secondary additions unrelated to the plot of the story or because they refer exclusively to Israel and Edom. None of these approaches has, to my knowledge, undertaken to study in any *detail* the relationship between these pericopes and the narrative cycle as a whole. I will attempt to do so, and will argue that the predictions and hopes within these pericopes remain unfulfilled in various degrees and that this lack of coherence is an integral part of the plot of the Jacob cycle.

The Announcements

Our study of the passages in question will be helped by noting their major motifs.

Yahweh's Oracle to Rebekah

25.23	Two nations are in your womb,	(a) Two peoples
	and two peoples, from your body, shall be divided;	*divided*
	and [one] people shall be stronger than [the other] people.	(b) One *stronger*
	The greater shall serve the lesser.	(c) *Servitude* of greater

---

[1] Luke, 'Isaac's Blessing', p. 40.
[2] De Pury, *Promesse divine et légende cultuelle*, 1.103. I would argue that it is in fact the *non-fulfilment* of the oracle and blessings which dominates chs. 25–36 (see below).

Isaac's Blessing on Jacob

27.27b-29 See, the smell of my son [is] as the smell of a field which Yahweh has blessed!	
May God give to you of the dew of the heavens and of the fatness of the earth, and much grain and wine.	(d) *Fertility* and *prosperity*
Let peoples serve you, and nations bow down to you. Be lord over your brothers, and may your mother's sons bow down to you	(e) *Lordship* over others in general and brothers in particular
Cursed be everyone who curses you and blessed be everyone who blesses you!	(f) *Curses* and *blessings*

Isaac's 'Blessing' on Esau

27.39b-40 Lo, away from the fatness of the earth your dwelling shall be, And away from the dew of the heavens on high.	(g) *Lack* of fertility and prosperity
And by your sword you shall live,	(h) Live by *sword*
and you shall serve your brother;	(i) *Servitude*
but when you break loose you shall break his yoke from your neck.	(j) *Breaking* of servitude

It will be noticed that there is a considerable degree of over-lap in content, with Isaac's blessings, in effect, expanding some important points of the divine oracle. To facilitate our discussion I group together similar motifs found in more than one pericope and deal with these as a whole. Points of detail peculiar to individual passages will nevertheless be looked at so that important nuances will not be lost. The primary motifs are:

 (i)   Service (points c, e, i, j)
 (ii) Fertility/prosperity (points d, g)
 (iii) Division (points a, b)
 (iv) Living by the sword (point h).

1. *Service*
The verb *'ābad* occurs in all three passages under considera-tion, reinforcing the concept that in the Announcement peri-copes Esau is intended to serve Jacob (25.23d; 27.29a, 40b). The

same root occurs many times in the Jacob cycle and it is instructive to see how the narrative uses the motif. *'ābad* describes Jacob serving Laban (29.15, 18, 20, 25, 27, 30; 30.26, 29; 31.6, 41). *'ebed* is used of Jacob as servant of God (32.1) and of Esau (32.17, 19; 33.14), while *ᵃbōdâ* again describes Jacob's service of Laban (29.27).[1] Thus apart from passages which *promise* or *desire* that Esau will serve Jacob, every use of the root *'bd* in the Jacob cycle depicts *Jacob* as serving or assuming the posture of servant. On this point the divine oracle and Isaac's blessings do not come to fruition anywhere in chs. 25–36, and significantly the scenario they depict is inverted by the story as a whole. Let us now see in more detail how this is achieved.

(It should be noted that the specific terms 'elder'/'younger' are not used in 25.23, rather the more general 'greater' (*rab*) and 'lesser' (*ṣā'îr*). Speiser claims that the word pair has an exact parallel in Akkadian family law where it designates elder and younger son.[2] However, we cannot be certain that terms based on common Semitic roots necessarily carry identical connotations in different cultures. On the other hand the immediate context of the oracle prompts the reader to make the connection between greater/lesser and elder/younger.)

There is a degree of irony in the relationship which Jacob strikes up with his uncle Laban. Jacob, the lord-designate, flees from the one appointed to be his servant, only to become a servant himself. His relationship with his uncle is characterized by service and wages (29.15); he even serves for his two wives (29.18, 20, 25, 30).[3] The relationship between Jacob

---

[1] *'ebed* is used in the divine speech to Isaac in 26.24 to describe Abraham as Yahweh's servant. In Gen. 27.37 Isaac uses the same term in explaining to Esau the blessing he has just given to Jacob.

[2] Speiser, *Genesis*, p. 95.

[3] The introduction of Leah and Rachel obviously echoes the elder/younger motif first encountered with Esau and Jacob, and seen most obviously in Laban's statement, 'It is not so done in our country, to give the younger before the first-born' (29.26). The divine oracle had stated that 'the greater (elder) shall serve the lesser (younger)' (25.23); with Laban's trickery it happens, in a different sense, that the younger (Jacob) serves (for) the elder (Leah). Also, it is just possible that Laban's foisting Leah onto an unsuspecting Jacob could be an echo of Jacob's previous deception of his father. There, Jacob deceived Isaac

122   *Announcements of Plot in Genesis*

and Leah is given an ironic twist, when having been duped
into working seven years for the woman he did not love, Jacob
finds himself to be the servant of this same unloved wife when
she hires him from Rachel: 'When Jacob came from the field
in the evening, Leah went out to meet him, and said, "You
must come in to me; for I have hired you with my son's
mandrakes". So he lay with her that night' (30.16). This, as
clearly as anything in the story, reveals his role as a servant—
one who serves his uncle for his wives and who is *hired* out in
order to make his wife a mother. The one designated 'lord' in
his father's blessing (27.29) becomes subservient not only to
Laban, but also to Laban's daughter, with the fruit of that
night's hire, Issachar, perpetuating in his name the nature of
his conception with a play on *śākar*, 'hire'.[1] This life of servitude is clearly recognized (and resented?) by Jacob who, on his
first attempt to leave for home, sums up his relationship to his
uncle and wives with a three-fold repetition of *'bd*: 'Give [me]
my wives and my children for whom I have served (*'ābadtî*)
you, and let me go, for you know the service (*'bōdātî*) [with]
which I have served you (*'badtîkā*)' (30.26).

The narrative uses Jacob's eventual escape from Laban and
return home as an opportunity to develop the 'service' theme
further. Laban may be behind him, but Esau is before him,
and it is this encounter which calls to mind Isaac's desire,
'may your mother's sons bow down to you' (27.29c), and 'you
[Esau] shall serve your brother' (27.40b). The scene is set for
the fulfilment of this part of the blessing; instead we get the
opposite. Jacob's prayer which he offers as he anticipates
meeting Esau, 'Deliver me, I pray thee, from the hand of my
brother' (32.12), and his subsequent ploy of sending ahead a
present for Esau (32.14), highlight the fact that up to this point
the lord-servant relationship envisaged by the earlier oracle
and blessings has not yet come to fruition, and if anything, is in

whose eyes were weak (*wattikhênā 'ênāyw*, 27.1); here, Leah whose
eyes are weak (*rakkôt*, 29.17) is party to deceiving Jacob—a neat reversal (Zucker, 'Jacob in Darkness', p. 407; cf. Matthews and Mims,
'Jacob the Trickster', p. 188).
[1] See Fokkelman, *Narrative Art in Genesis*, p. 138, '[Issachar] is by
far the most important name in the whole Story of Jacob after that of
Jacob himself'.

danger of being reversed. In fact Jacob does present that very
reversal when he instructs his servants with the words,
'When Esau *my brother* meets you... you shall say, "They
belong to *your servant* Jacob"' (32.17-18). Whether or not this
is merely an insincere act of self-deprecation to save his own
skin, Jacob's words amount to an inversion of the blessing he
had earlier risked so much to gain. This unexpected development is taken one step further in ch. 33. Gen. 27.29 had
expressed the desire that his mother's sons would 'bow down'
(*wᵉyištaḥᵃwu*) to Jacob. Apart from this reference, the only
occurrences of *ḥwh* in the Jacob cycle are in ch. 33 and they
depict *Jacob and his family bowing down to Esau*: e.g. 'He
[Jacob]... went... bowing himself (*wayyištaḥû*) to the ground
seven times, until he came near to his brother' (33.3; see also
33.6, 7[2×], 9). This is the action of a vassal before his suzerain.[1]
   On this scene generally, Gibson observes:

> This was not the elder serving the younger of Rebekah's
> private oracle (25.23), nor was it his mother's sons bowing
> down to Jacob as forecast in the blessing he had stolen
> (27.29). Rather, it was as if Rebekah had been hopelessly
> deluded and as if Isaac had pronounced the blessing on
> Esau as he had meant to.[2]

Gibson is correct in seeing the lack of coherence between
oracle/blessing and subsequent plot; whether it represents
delusion for Rebekah and success for Isaac I will discuss in the
conclusion.
   It should be noted that the failed fulfilment has been largely
guaranteed by the 'separation' motif which runs throughout
the cycle. The separation of the two brothers while Jacob is in
Paddan-aram makes it physically impossible for Esau to serve
Jacob, the impossibility being continued by the later (token?)
subservience of Jacob to Esau, combined with their reconciliation (ch. 33) and eventual separation yet again (33.12-17; 36.6-

[1] Westermann, *Promises to the Fathers*, p. 82.
[2] Gibson, *Genesis*, 2.209; cf. Fokkelman, *Narrative Art in Genesis*,
p. 200; Brueggemann, *Genesis*, p. 232. Bar-Efrat, 'Analysis of Structure', p. 166, sees chs. 32–33 as an example of 'plot reversal' but curi-
ously does not make any connection with the divine oracle or Isaac's
blessings.

8). We may conclude that at no point in the Jacob cycle does Esau serve Jacob; if anything the 'service' motif is used to show Jacob's subservience to Laban, Leah and *Esau*. On this point the divine oracle and Isaac's blessing founder.

(As my interest is with the plot of the Jacob story I will not enter here into a detailed analysis of the way in which the oracle/blessings relate to the national histories of Israel and Edom. It should be noted, however, that the usual assumption that the words of Yahweh and Isaac in these passages are *vaticinia ex eventu* and thus accurate indicators of Israelite/ Edomite relationships does not lack problems. Over the centuries one was stronger than the other and the elder *did* serve the younger *sometimes*, but if the evidence from the OT historical books is accurate, Edom spent as much time as an independent nation as it did under Israelite control. There is also evidence that Edom joined Babylon in the destruction of Jerusalem [cf. Ps. 137.7; Lam. 4.21-22; Obad. 10-16]. This act was a decisive annulment of any superiority Edom's neighbour may have had over it and would be an accurate 'fulfilment' of 27.40b: 'but when you break loose you shall break his yoke from your neck'. However, for a number of reasons arising from traditional Pentateuchal source-criticism, the throwing off of Israelite dominion is usually taken to be the loss of control experienced during Solomonic times (1 Kgs 11.11ff.)[1] or the revolt during the reign of Joram (2 Kgs 8.20ff.)[2]

Some scholars have noted the difficulty of the standard view. For example, Keukens cites Blank who believes the blessings are

> pious wishes, which, however, subsequent history did not fulfil. The accepted interpretation makes of them vaticinia ex eventu; we however, would regard them as unrealized hopes.[3]

[1] E.g. von Rad, *Genesis*, p. 279.
[2] E.g. Westermann, *Genesis 12–36*, p. 443.
[3] S.H. Blank, 'Studies in Post-Exilic Universalism', *HUCA* 11 (1936), p. 176, cited in Keukens, 'Der irreguläre Sterbesegen Isaaks', p. 54. (However, Keukens' view that the lack of fulfilment of Isaac's blessings is due to Isaac not following the correct protocol in their delivery is less than convincing.)

3. *The Jacob Story* 125

2. *Fertility and Prosperity*
While blessings take many forms in Genesis, the major
recurring elements concern fertility and prosperity which are
found in both of Isaac's blessings (27.28, 39).[1] Most commentators take *min*, which occurs in both pericopes, in two different senses:[2] partitively in 27.28—*w*ᵉyitten-lᵉkâ hā*ᵊlōhîm
miṭṭal haššāmayim* ('May God give to you *of* the dew of the
heavens...'); privatively in 27.39—*hinnēh mišmannê
hā'āreṣ* ('Lo, *away from* the fatness of the earth'). A few
believe it should be translated partitively in both cases.[3] This
latter approach sees the contrast between the two blessings not
in Jacob's prosperity and Esau's deprivation, but solely in
Jacob's lordship (27.29) and Esau's servitude (27.40).
However, the context in which Isaac pronounces these words
argues strongly for seeing a contrast between vv. 28 and 39.
Isaac tells Esau quite plainly, '... with grain and wine I have
sustained him [Jacob]. What then can I do for you, my son?'
Skinner is correct therefore in concluding that 27.39, though
expressed in a very similar way to 27.28, is 'virtually a curse'.[4]
It may well be that the inversion of the usual heaven–earth
sequence in Isaac's words to Esau is used to underline this
distinction:

This point has been treated more recently by Thompson, 'Conflict
Themes', esp. pp. 15-16:

It is very difficult to understand this narrative [25.19-34] as an
historiographical reference to a past or contemporary hegemony
of Israel over Edom... the past 'ancestral event' is not oriented
by the narrator to either his contemporary world or to the world
of the historical past of Israel and Edom.

[1] Pedersen, *Israel*, 1.204-205, enumerates four major elements which
include: (a) The power to multiply—ch. 9; 12.2; 13.16; 26.24; 28.14; cf.
v. 3; 35.11; 48.4. (b) Numerous progeny—'to be blessed and to have a
large progeny amounts to the same thing' (p. 205). (c) Wealth and prosperity—24.35; 26.12-14; 27.27-28. (The fourth element is power over
enemies.) Cf. von Rad, *Genesis*, p. 278, who sees a contrast between
Isaac's blessings and the usual ancestral promises.
[2] E.g. Skinner, *Genesis*, p. 373; von Rad, *Genesis*, p. 279; Kidner,
Genesis, p. 157; Speiser, *Genesis*, pp. 207, 210.
[3] E.g. Calvin, *Genesis*, 2.98; Driver, *Genesis*, p. 260.
[4] Skinner, *Genesis*, p. 373. Cf. the *double entendre* in 40.13, 19, noted
in Kidner, *Genesis*, p. 157.

27.28a	... of the dew of the *heavens*	A	Jacob
	and of the fatness of the *earth*	B	
27.39b	... the fatness of the *earth* ...	B	Esau
	... the dew of the *heavens*	A	

'The sense of Isaac's words is clear enough: all fertility has been granted to Jacob and so Esau cannot expect anything in that sphere.'[1] Thus, Jacob's blessing is prosperity and lordship; Esau's 'blessing' is deprivation and servitude.

In some ways, it is true, Jacob does see the fulfilment of this part of the blessing. Yahweh blesses him in his work as herdsman, and despite Laban's dirty tricks, Jacob 'grew exceedingly rich, and had large flocks, maidservants and menservants, and camels and asses' (30.43). If his uncle's words are to be taken at face value, he too is materially blessed by Yahweh because of Jacob (30.27). Yet, this is only part of the picture. Jacob's flocks may be fertile, but only after his favourite wife has suffered infertility for a long period, causing conflict in the family. Rachel 'said to Jacob, "Give me children, or I shall die!" Jacob's anger was kindled against Rachel, and he said, "Am I in the place of God, who has withheld from you the fruit of the womb?"' (30.1b-2). In contrast, the hated (elder!) wife is fruitful (29.31ff.). The fulfilment of this aspect of the blessing is complicated. Jacob receives the blessing of fertility and prosperity with his flocks but only after the 'wrong' wife has conceived and fertility has been withheld from the 'loved' wife until eventually 'God remembered Rachel' (30.22a). Only after a considerable wait is 27.28 fulfilled at the two levels of Jacob's flocks and his wives.

Isaac's blessings on his two sons had predicted fertility for Jacob but material deprivation for Esau. With Jacob exiled in Paddan-aram, the reader must wait until ch. 32 to discover whether the elder brother's 'blessing' has become reality. Jacob returns home with living proof of the efficacy of his blessing, sending a present to Esau which includes 'two hundred she-goats and twenty he-goats, two hundred ewes

---

[1] Luke, 'Isaac's Blessing', pp. 38-39. Luke attempts to argue for the reversal of word order in the remainder of the verses, but his argument is less than convincing, presumably requiring reading *ḥwh* for *ḥyh*.

and twenty rams...' (32.14-15), and accompanied by 'his two wives, his two maids, and his eleven children' (32.22). If Esau's 'blessing' has been equally efficacious, Jacob should encounter an impoverished individual. However, Esau has prospered, despite the 'blessing', as can be seen in his leadership of four hundred men (32.6; 33.1). Perhaps the most telling detail of all is in Jacob's urging of Esau: 'Accept, I pray you, my gift [*'et-birkātî*]...' (33.11 RSV). Jacob urges Esau to take his *b*e*rākâ*, the same term used for the *blessing* he had previously deceitfully wrested from Esau's grasp (27.41). The fact that Esau can initially refuse this, 'I have enough (*rab*), my brother, keep what you have for yourself' (33.9), underlines the fact that though he may not have received the blessing, he has nevertheless been blessed. Esau's prosperity comes to light again in ch. 36 when the brothers decide once again to live separate lives because the possessions of *both* of them make it impossible to live together in Canaan. Thus 'Esau took his wives, his sons, his daughters, and all the members of his household, his cattle, all his beasts, and all his property which he had acquired in the land of Canaan' (36.6). For Esau the 'virtual curse' of 27.39 has been converted into an actual blessing (almost as if the narrative is playing on the two possibilities of *min* noted above).

Within the Jacob cycle therefore, the blessing of fertility and wealth comes to fruition in Jacob's life, but Isaac's intended aim of giving Esau a blessing of material deprivation founders. Both brothers are equally blessed.[1] This equality neutralizes the distinction between the two which was Isaac's intention when the blessings were delivered.

---

[1] Westermann, *Genesis 12–36*, p. 526, observes on 33.9:

> Esau has obviously suffered no disadvantage through the loss of his prerogative as firstborn. He has even prospered and become powerful without it, and to such an extent that he can do without the substantial gift representing considerable wealth.

However, Westermann does not relate this observation to Isaac's blessings (which for him represent a different source—see p. 436, and cf. p. 524), and the observation remains for him a mere curiosity.

3. *Division*

> Two nations are in your womb,
> and two peoples, from your body, shall be divided [*yippārēdû*]
> (25.23a).

An initial question to be asked before investigating this part of the divine oracle concerns the force of 'divided'. Does it connote merely physical *separation* or an *enmity* between the two parties? *Prd* is used seven times elsewhere in Genesis, where it connotes (in Niphal) the separating of rivers (2.10), nations (10.5, 32), and (in Hiphil) lambs from the flock (30.40). These examples do not carry any sense of enmity or strife. However, it is also used (in Niphal) to describe the separation of Lot from Abraham (13.9, 11, 14). Here, while the word itself does not connote strife, the separation of Abraham and Lot is a consequence of the strife between their herdsmen (see 13.7-8). The background provided by 25.22-34 places *yippārēdû* in 25.23a in a similar context. The 'struggle' in the womb (25.22) portends strife in the lives of the yet unborn sons, while one being stronger than the other suggests a contest of strength (25.23c), as does Jacob's taking hold of Esau's heel at birth (25.26).[1] The distinction made between the two in 25.27-28 anticipates strife in the family, with Esau the hunter being favoured by the father, and Jacob the domestic individual being favoured by the mother; this suspicion is confirmed by the haggling over the birthright in 25.29-34. The flight-return structure of 27.46–33.20 shows clearly the correlation between 'strife' and 'separation'. Strife with Esau causes Jacob's flight into exile and strife with Laban is the cause of his return. Read within this context therefore, *prd* suggests more than merely separation, but includes *antagonism*.[2]

[1] Westermann, *Promises to the Fathers*, p. 80, sees rivalry 'hinted at obliquely' in this detail.
[2] For a similar position, see Cohen, 'Two that are One', p. 335, who sees the sibling rivalries (Jacob/Esau; Rachel/Leah) as sustaining the narrative. However, his development of the theme is not exegetical but follows a midrashic model. The following are examples of those who see 'conflict between brothers' as the main theme of chs. 25–36: Hauge, 'Struggles of the Blessed I', p. 11 n. 32; Westermann, *Promises*, p. 79; Gammie, 'Theological Interpretation', pp. 118-19; Thompson, *Origin Tradition*, pp. 104ff.; Brueggemann, *Genesis*, p. 205, sees

Strife characterizes the relationship between most of the individuals in the story: between Isaac and Rebekah in their favouritism of different children; Jacob and Esau over the blessing; Jacob and Laban over wives and possessions; Rachel and Leah over Jacob and children. (Even ch. 26 which according to most commentators disrupts the flow of the Jacob story with a chronologically displaced narrative concerning Isaac fits in perfectly with this major motif. Chapter 26 presents another story centring on conflict. While it may disrupt plot development, it fits its context thematically.)[1] In this respect the Jacob cycle picks up and expands a motif from the Abraham cycle (the strife that affects the relationship between the servants of Abraham and Lot, and that between Isaac and Ishmael), a theme continued in the story of Jacob's family with Joseph and his brothers. While the object of strife differs in all of these examples, the theme of contention itself is sustained throughout the ancestral history.[2]

Does the plot of the Jacob cycle develop the 'division' motif in a manner compatible with the words of the divine oracle: 'Two nations are in your womb, and two peoples, from your body, shall be divided' (25.23a)? A reaction to two recent, important studies by Coats,[3] who investigates the related themes of strife and reconciliation, will help to answer this question.

Coats observes that several studies of the ancestral narratives have concluded that the 'promise' theme is a secondary addition. Accepting these conclusions, Coats aims to discover what was originally the primary theme and concludes that it was 'strife within the family' or more specifically 'strife without reconciliation'.[4] Taking the Jacob-Laban story (chs. 29–31) first, he observes the strife between Rachel and Leah (29.15-30) and Laban's deceit which causes strife with Jacob (30.25-43). Chapter 31 brings some resolution of the tension, but, importantly for Coats, no reconciliation. The covenant

'the juxtaposition of *special designation* and a *life of conflict* [as] the mainspring of the narrative'.
[1] Thompson, *Origin Tradition*, p. 103.
[2] Hauge, 'Struggles of the Blessed I', pp. 15-16.
[3] Coats, 'Strife and Reconciliation', pp. 15-37; *idem*, 'Strife without Reconciliation', pp. 82-106.
[4] Coats, 'Strife without Reconciliation', p. 83.

between Laban and Jacob does nothing to alleviate the strife, but merely puts the strife on a formal level, as is witnessed by Laban's farewell to his daughters and grandchildren and his shunning of Jacob. 'The story ends without reconciliation for the striving parties. It confirms that the subject of the story is... strife without reconciliation.'[1] This theme is revealed once again in the Jacob-Esau story within which the Jacob-Laban story has been inserted. Jacob flees from Esau and when the two meet again (ch. 33), the strife continues with the two continuing to live separate lives (33.15-17). Coats concludes, 'the framework story itself develops entirely on the theme, strife without reconciliation'.[2]

Coats' conclusion depends to a large degree upon his interpretation of the two incidents in which Jacob once again meets his adversaries Laban (ch. 31) and Esau (ch. 33). However, far from the covenant between Jacob and Laban 'institutionalizing' strife, as Coats argues, the oath taken indicates a formal acceptance that reconciliation has been achieved and must be solemnly upheld: 'This heap is a witness, and the pillar is a witness, that I will not pass over this heap to you, and you will not pass over this heap and this pillar to me, for harm' (31.52). Having been reconciled to Jacob, Laban takes his leave by kissing and blessing his daughters and grand-children, not because he wishes to *exclude* Jacob, as Coats argues, but to *include* these members into the new reconciled relationship.

Coats' conclusion that the strife between Jacob and Esau continues in ch. 33 rests upon his contention that 'reconciliation cannot occur if the reconciled parties continue to live apart'.[3] This would be true if the reason for their continued separation is strife, but the narrative seems to counter this explicitly. First, ch. 33 simply does not read like an exercise in managing strife but as a reconciliation. Esau is genuinely pleased to see Jacob (33.4) and whether Jacob's *subservience* is genuine or not, he shows no signs of wishing the *strife* to continue. It is true that the brothers are again separated by the

---

[1] Coats, 'Strife without Reconciliation', p. 90; cf. Fokkelman, *Narrative Art in Genesis*, p. 192.
[2] 'Strife without Reconciliation', p. 102; cf. 'Strife and Reconciliation', p. 26.
[3] 'Strife and Reconciliation', p. 26.

time we reach the end of the chapter, but separation may be caused by many factors, not only strife. I would agree with Westermann's assessment:

> The narrator wants to say that a reconciliation between brothers need not require that they live side by side; it can also achieve its effect when they separate and each lives his own life in his own way... Jacob and Esau remain brothers, though each in his separate living space.[1]

This conclusion is supported by two further pieces of information regarding the brothers' relationship. Jacob and Esau are together at the burial of their father (35.29), while 36.6-8 gives a specific reason for their separation—prosperity:[2] '[Esau] went into a land away from his brother Jacob. For their possessions were too great for them to dwell together.' This final statement shows that the reason for separation, far from being the inexorable outworking of the divine will in 25.23a, is in fact the non-fulfilment of Esau's 'blessing' in 27.39.

I conclude that the strife which is the cause of the initial separation is overturned by the reconciliation of ch. 33. However, the physical separation is maintained after this except for the brief encounter in 35.29. By the end of the story *prd* still accurately defines the relationship between the two, but in a different sense from that suggested by its context in 25.22-34. Separation caused by strife has become separation within reconciliation.

4. *Living by the Sword*

> By your sword you shall live (27.40a).

This is an element in Esau's blessing which conceptually is closely connected to the strife/separation motif, but which is not really developed in the story. Nevertheless it may not be without significance that in the rest of the narrative it is *Jacob*

---

[1] Westermann, *Genesis 12–36*, p. 527. On ch. 33 as reconciliation see also Vischer, 'La réconciliation', p. 50; Hauge, 'Struggles of the Blessed II', p. 120; Fokkelman, *Narrative Art in Genesis*, p. 88; Miscall, 'Jacob and Joseph Stories', p. 36; Westermann, *Promises to the Fathers*, p. 89; Gibson, *Genesis*, 2.208; Cohen, 'Two that are One', p. 338; Thompson, *Origin Tradition*, pp. 110-11.
[2] As seen correctly by Thompson, *Origin Tradition*, p. 114.

rather than Esau who is explicitly connected with the sword (*hereb*). Laban complains that Jacob carried away his daughters 'like captives of the sword' (31.26), while Jacob's sons 'slew Hamor and his son Shechem with the sword' (34.26).[1] This association is reiterated in the story of Jacob's family where Jacob gives to Joseph the mountain slope which he 'took from the hand of the Amorites with my sword and with my bow' (48.22). Gen. 49.5 reminds us of the violence Jacob's sons Simeon and Levi wielded with their swords. In contrast, at a time when we (and Jacob) expect Esau to use his sword, marching with four hundred (armed?) men, he appears as a pacifist: 'Esau ran to meet him and embraced him...' (33.4). To be sure, this theme is not developed in any systematic way, yet within the story there is no evidence to show that Esau did 'live by the sword', rather the reverse,[2] while the only persons mentioned as using swords are Jacob and his family. This evidence *may* suggest that Esau's 'blessing' fails in this detail also.

Conclusion

Reviewing the fate of the hopes and predictions in the three passages we have investigated, it is clear that either they do not come to fruition at all or they do so in ways not originally envisaged. Jacob's lordship is never seen. He serves Laban and Leah, and most importantly assumes a posture of subservience before Esau, until once again the two separate and neither can serve the other. Esau never serves Jacob and thereby the hope that Esau would break Jacob's yoke from his neck (27.40c) is rendered redundant. The blessing of fertility and prosperity is fulfilled for Jacob but not without tension and a considerable delay. Esau's 'blessing' of lack of fertility and prosperity is overturned; he prospers in a similar manner to Jacob. This equality effectively reverses the intention of the

---

[1] The irony of 34.26 is noted by Gammie, 'Theological Interpretation', p. 124.
[2] It is true that Esau plans to kill Jacob (27.42), but he has been sorely aggrieved and Rebekah realizes that this is simply an impetuous reaction which will disappear after 'a while' (27.44). Chapter 33 proves her to be correct.

blessings, which was to distinguish between the brothers. The prediction that the two would be divided is indeed fulfilled, but in an unexpected manner. While separation caused by strife (the reader's expectation) occurs initially, by the end of the story we have separation within reconciliation. Finally, if references to 'sword' are relevant, far from living by the sword, Esau is a pacifist; only Jacob and his sons are mentioned as taking it up.

The conclusions I have drawn counter the way in which the Jacob cycle is usually viewed. For example, Miscall believes that when looking at biblical narrative one must distinguish between divine and human words in the following way: with divine words (e.g. prophecy, oracle), 'It is a question not of whether it *will* be fulfilled but of *how* it will be fulfilled', whereas with human words (e.g. blessing, prediction), 'it is a question of whether it will be fulfilled, and not just of how'.[1] With Isaac's blessing reiterating, as it does, the divine oracle to Rebekah, 'any question of the fulfillment of this human word is answered; only the issue of how remains, and the rest of the Jacob story details the process'.[2] Miscall receives

> the impression that everything is carefully orchestrated by Yahweh: all works out in the end and the parts fit the whole. The neat accord between the divine will and human activity appears to be the effect of God's initiative and direction.[3]

In this way, Miscall sees the Jacob and Joseph stories as analogies, in which, despite differences, 'the endings are in accord with the divine plan and promises'.[4] On the contrary, I would argue that the similarities between the two stories lie rather in the lack of accord with the initial promises. (See Chapter 4 for a discussion of Joseph.) Miscall believes that the Jacob story as a whole fulfils the oracle/blessings, but he does not provide any detailed analysis of the passages concerned.

---

[1] Miscall, 'Jacob and Joseph Stories', p. 32.
[2] Miscall, 'Jacob and Joseph Stories', p. 33.
[3] Miscall, 'Jacob and Joseph Stories', p. 33. Miscall concedes that the text does not explicitly make this point, because God is only involved in the human story at certain points, and is not to be seen as a divine puppeteer. Cf. p. 39.
[4] Miscall, 'Jacob and Joseph Stories', p. 34.

He merely assumes that because seemingly authoritative statements are made at the outset 'the general outcome of the story is clear from the start',[1] and then reads the rest of the narrative in this blinkered fashion apparently unaware of any problems the story itself presents for such a position.

The following representative statements illustrate that Miscall is not alone in his basic assertion. According to Fokkelman, Jacob and Esau's

> whole lives are going to pass under a very special sign, whose destiny and mutual relationship were decisively determined and predicted by Providence before their birth.[2]

Brueggemann believes that

> without a very explicit statement, the narrative [33.1-17] affirms that the initial oracle of 25.23 has come to fruition.[3]

According to Goldingay the reader is intended

> to read the story in the context of 25.23 and to marvel at how Yahweh's word is fulfilled in extraordinary ways.[4]

Similarly, Blenkinsopp states:

> Even before birth there occurs the oracular prediction of the ascendancy of the younger brother (25.23). Having listened to many such stories since childhood we know that this will indeed happen, but... it will take a great deal of pain and absence before it happens in the way it was meant to happen, after strife and reconciliation.[5]

I can only reply to such assertions by stating that the narrative does not develop the motifs found in the oracle and blessings in such a way. Rather than showing their inexorable, or perhaps simply inevitable, fulfilment, the reader may

[1] Miscall, 'Jacob and Joseph Stories', p. 33.
[2] Fokkelman, *Narrative Art in Genesis*, p. 94.
[3] Brueggemann, *Genesis*, p. 208. Turner, 'Rebekah', p. 46, sees 25.23 fulfilled as early as Isaac's blessings in ch. 27, 'the tension surrounding the oracle given to Rebekah before the twins were born was finally resolved. What Yahweh had ordained—the younger son to dominate the older—had come to pass.' It is obvious of course that this is a misinterpretation of the narrative.
[4] Goldingay, 'Patriarchs', p. 8.
[5] Blenkinsopp, 'Biographical Patterns', pp. 39-40.

perceive a well-documented succession of incidents which guarantee their non-fulfilment.

The Abrahamic Announcement in the Jacob Story

With the fortune of Yahweh's oracle and Isaac's blessings providing the main interest in the Jacob story, the unfinished agenda begun by the divine Announcement of 12.1-3 does not command as much attention. Yet the Jacob story gives periodic reminders that it has not abandoned this previous focus of interest and that in a number of ways the oracle blessings serve as reinforcers of the Abrahamic Announcement. All three elements of the Abrahamic Announcement are repeated in 26.3-4 and 28.13-15, and two elements—those of numerous descendants and land—in 28.3-4 and 35.11-12 also, with Abraham's name being mentioned in all four passages lest the reader fail to make the connection.

1. *Nationhood*

When one learns at the outset that 'Isaac prayed to Yahweh for his wife, because she was barren' (25.21a), one experiences feelings of *déjà vu*, wondering whether *this* story will take us down a tortuous path similar to that found in the Abraham story, before the promise of nationhood can be seen to be on course again. On this occasion, however, the obstacle is overcome in the same breath with the news that 'Yahweh granted his prayer and Rebekah his wife conceived' (25.21b). Only with the narrative of the birth do we learn that Rebekah has suffered twenty years of barrenness (25.20; cf. 25.26).

Rebekah's enquiry regarding the meaning of her difficult pregnancy elicits Yahweh's response that 'two nations' are in her womb, echoing the previous divine promise to Abraham that 'I will make nations of you' (17.6). The trend started with the two genealogical lines of Isaac and Ishmael gains momentum here with Jacob and Esau. The narrative drops reminders to the reader, via divine statements, that Yahweh will multiply Isaac's descendants (26.4, 24), with a progress report on how the future nation is developing: 'And Abimelech said to Isaac, "Go away from us; for you are much mightier than we"' (26.16).

Although he has wrested the birthright and blessing from Esau, Jacob still has an important obstacle to overcome, identical to that of Isaac in ch. 24. Nationhood can come to Jacob only if he gets an acceptable wife and has children.[1] Thus, he is sent off to Paddan-aram with Isaac's words in his ears, 'God Almighty bless you and make you fruitful and multiply you, that you may become a company of peoples' (27.3), the importance of which is reiterated by Yahweh's words to him on his first night on the run, 'your descendants shall be like the dust of the earth...' (28.14a).

The power of these two blessings seems to be at work when the first woman Jacob meets in the land of the east is not only beautiful and a kinswoman, but also allows him to kiss her before he has introduced himself (29.11-12).[2] Even Laban's deception with Leah could be seen as furthering the nationhood promise, for with two wives the potential number of children is that much greater. However, the recurring barrenness theme intrudes once more ('When Yahweh saw that Leah was hated, he opened her womb; but Rachel was barren', 29.31), and as Jacob underlines, barren because God wants it that way (30.2b). Not for the first time in the ancestral narrative, Yahweh appears to be making matters deliberately difficult. However, as with Rebekah's infertility this problem is overcome quickly, with Leah, Bilhah and Zilpah producing sons in quick succession and finally Rachel herself conceiving Joseph (30.22-24). Perhaps not much more success in this area can be expected than for Jacob to father a family of twelve sons and one daughter, and regular hints are inserted into the narrative that remind us of how well this aspect of the Abrahamic promise is progressing (cf. 32.10, 12; 35.11). It should be noted, however, that a golden opportunity to increase the size of the ancestral family is by-passed in ch. 34. There, an opportunity is given for Jacob's family to become

---

[1] Coats, *Genesis*, p. 200.

[2] With the exception of the harlot's embrace (Prov. 7.13), Gen. 29.11 contains the only example in the OT of kissing between two individuals who are not formally known to each other. The OT evidence does not support the idea that strangers would normally greet one another with a kiss.

'one people' with the people of the land (34.16, 22). Unfortunately, two of Jacob's sons, driven by moral considerations, exterminate these potential family members. We are not surprised to hear Jacob (never one to dwell too long on ethical issues) complaining to his sons that their action has had severe personal consequences for him. His sons are more concerned about their sister's honour (34.31). Nevertheless, the reader can see clearly that the nationhood promise has gained impetus in the Jacob story. By the close of the Abraham story there was only one descendant who counted. But in 35.22ff. the full extent of multiplication is tabulated, and it makes impressive reading, especially when read together with 36.1ff. in which Esau's descendants are listed. There is some room for confidence that not only is *the* nation beginning to form, but that Abraham is gradually becoming the father of 'nations' and 'kings' (17.6).

2. *Land*
The land promise, like that of nationhood, gets off to a shaky start with the news that a famine in Canaan forces Isaac to migrate to Philistia. While 15.18-19 had promised a huge tract of land to Abraham's descendants the land of the Philistines had not been included explicitly and the reader assumes that the action will now take place outside of the land of promise. However, once Isaac becomes a sojourner there, Philistia too is promised to Isaac and his descendants (26.3). However, Yahweh's command to *sojourn* (*gûr*) in Philistia clearly shows that possession is still future, and no amount of digging and re-digging of wells can be seen as bringing it any closer.

Isaac eventually returns to Canaan (26.31) and in his senility is duped by Rebekah and Jacob. Esau's anger means, however, that no sooner has Jacob received Isaac's blessing than he is exiled from the land of promise. The irony of this is compounded by Isaac's blessing in 28.4 as Jacob is making his exit from Canaan, 'may you take possession of the land of your sojournings which God gave to Abraham', presumably referring to Canaan, since Jacob's Mesopotamian destination was not promised to Abraham. This is confirmed by Yahweh's promise to him that night, 'the land on which you lie I will give to you and to your descendants' (28.13b), which necessitates the subsidiary promise, 'I will bring you back to this land' (28.15a). Jacob's first attempt to return home (30.25ff.) does not succeed, but Yahweh's direct command to him to do so (31.3) is more successful, supplemented as it is with reminders of the promises given at Bethel (31.13, 17). The high hopes with which Jacob set off for home must have been somewhat muted when he enters the land limping after his nocturnal wrestling match at the Jabbok.

Once back in Canaan he buys a piece of land and erects an altar (33.19-20), but, as I noted concerning Abraham's purchase of Machpelah, buying property falls far short of receiving the *gift* of land. Shechem's rape of Dinah opens the possibility of some significant progress for the land promise with Hamor's offer, 'You shall dwell with us; and the land shall be open to you; dwell and trade in it and be settled in it (*wᵉhēʼāḥᵃzû bāh* [RSV 'and get property in it'], 34.10). The moral sensibilities of Simeon and Levi soon scotch this possibility, however, ethnic and economic cooperation being demolished by their slaughter of the Shechemites (cf. 34.30). The repeated land promise in 35.12 is a reminder of the unfulfilled agenda: 'The land which I gave to Abraham and Isaac I *will give* to you, and I *will give* the land to your descendants after you'. Yahweh's promise, containing a three-fold repetition of *nātan*, places the gift of the land to Jacob and his descendants in the future, which necessitates a qualified interpretation of the qal perfect used of Abraham and Isaac. (In addition, we have already observed the minimal amount of real estate Abraham and Isaac actually possessed.) The true status of the land promise is revealed in the epilogue of ch. 36, in which both Jacob and Esau cannot dwell together in 'the land of their *sojournings* (*ʼereṣ mᵉgûrêhem*)' (36.7b; cf. 17.8). Neither Jacob nor Esau possesses any land yet. However, the transition from the story of Jacob to that of Joseph contains a significant contrast. While Esau's genealogy projects the action to a time beyond that recounted by the main plot, it concludes with the words, '... according to their dwelling places in the land of *their possession* (*ᵃḥuzzātām*)' (36.43). Thus we learn that the Edomites have taken possession of their land. The next verse, however, informs us that 'Jacob dwelt *in the land of his*

father's sojournings (bᵉʾereṣ mᵉgûrê ʾābîw)ʾ (37.1). Jacob has
taken possession of no more of the promised land than he
could buy for 'one hundred pieces of money' (33.19). He lives
in the land, but as a sojourner in the midst of people whose
land remains theirs.[1]

3. Blessing

When we turn to the third element of the Abrahamic
Announcement—blessing to the nations—the Jacob story
provides a catalogue of unmitigated disaster. The divine oracle
of 25.23 predicts division and servitude as the relationship
between the two nations in Rebekah's womb, which to the
first-time reader makes it seem unlikely that the inferior will
feel blessed by the superior. In the parenthetical ch. 26
Yahweh repeats that 'by your descendants all the nations of
the earth shall bless themselves' in the same breath as ceding
their land to Isaac (v. 4; cf. v. 3), and his relationship with the
Philistines in this chapter undermines international har-
mony. Abimelech justifiably complains that Isaac could 'have
brought guilt upon us' (v. 10); Isaac's possessions become a
source of envy rather than blessing (vv. 13-14); Abimelech
feels threatened by Isaac (v. 16) and the dispute continues,
culminating in Isaac's candid acknowledgment of Abimelech's hatred (v. 27) and a covenant necessitated by Abimelech's view of Isaac as a threat (v. 29a). No sooner has this
dispute been settled than we are told that Esau had a rather
more generous attitude to foreigners than the rest of his
family, taking two Hittite women as wives. We are saddened
to learn that 'they made life bitter for Isaac and Rebekah'
(26.35). As the story progresses we are given more reminders
of the less than amicable relationship between the chosen
people and the nations, in Isaac's blessings (27.29, 40),
Rebekah's complaints about Esau's wives (27.46) and Isaac's
charge to Jacob not to marry a Canaanite (28.1). Again, Esau
exhibits a much more ecumenical spirit (28.6-9). All of this
makes Yahweh's statement at Bethel, 'by you and your

---

[1] I can see no reason for supposing with Cassuto, *Genesis*, 2.304, that
the erection of an altar here and in 35.7 shows Jacob conquering the
land 'ideally in the name of the Lord'.

descendants shall all the families of the earth be blessed/bless themselves' (28.14b), seem impossibly optimistic. While it is true that Laban seems to reap some benefits from his association with Jacob (30.27), a point not overlooked by his nephew (30.28ff.), the reader is also aware that Laban is Jacob's kith and kin—not a representative of the nations.[1]

It is only when he is back in the land that Jacob has the opportunity to improve international relations. But as with the other aspects of the Abrahamic blessing, this opportunity is squandered with the Shechemite massacre in ch. 34. True, Hamor's son has committed a grave sin, and the Shechemite's motives for a closer relationship are less than altruistic (34.23a), but Jacob's complaint against his sons is eloquent testimony to the scuttling of this element of the Abrahamic Announcement: 'You have brought trouble on me by making me odious to the inhabitants of the land...' (34.30).

Thus the Jacob story shows progress in only one of the three key areas, that of the nationhood promise. This represents a marked improvement over Abraham's efforts in this matter. Unfortunately, the land promise advances not one step, while Jacob, like Abraham and Isaac before him is of no tangible benefit whatsoever to the nations.

It is obvious, of course, that the narrative does not develop the elements of the Abrahamic Announcement in a systematic way. While the major themes are mentioned, and some development can be seen, the fortune of these particular points does not hold the reader's attention in the same way it did in the Abraham story. That is to say, they no longer provide the main impetus of the plot, but the reader is notified nevertheless that they maintain *some* importance. Now, it is Yahweh's oracle and Isaac's blessings that dominate both the plot and the motivation of the characters. A good illustration of this is the Bethel incident (28.10-22). Gen. 28.13-15 repeats the Abrahamic promises which had already been given by Isaac to Jacob as he set off on his journey (28.1-4). Jacob's response to Yahweh's speech reveals that he does not have much interest in the promise given there. His vow (vv. 20-22) is inappropriate as a response to Yahweh's promises in vv. 13-

---

[1] Contra Wolff, 'Kerygma of the Yahwist', p. 150.

15, but is more appropriate to the content of his father's blessing (27.27-29).[1] He asks for material sustenance ('bread to eat and clothing to wear', together with a promise to tithe 'all that you give me', v. 22), echoing Isaac's promise of prosperity, and returning home in peace (*bᵉšālôm*, v. 21), presumably necessitating Esau's acceptance of the reversal of brotherly roles outlined in 27.29, 40. The tone of his vow also reveals that the Bethel incident has not changed Jacob in any way: 'If God will be with me... *then* Yahweh shall be my God' (vv. 20-21).[2] The veneer of piety cannot disguise the same self-interest as was displayed in the selling of stew to his brother and the presentation of kid dressed up as venison to his father. That is to say, Yahweh will be his God if he is true to his initial oracle to Rebekah and to Isaac's blessing uttered before him. The fact that Yahweh is not true to these, *as Jacob understands them*, raises the question of whether Yahweh will continue to be his God.

---

[1] Gen. 27.27-29 and 28.13-15 have clearly distinct concerns. The only point of contact between them is that of fertility/prosperity (27.28) and numerous descendants (28.14)—and even here the correspondence is not exact. It is simply not true to say, as does Aalders, *Genesis*, 2.105, that

> what had been promised to Jacob even before his birth (25.23) and had been confirmed to him in the blessing pronounced by his father (27.27-29; 28.3-4) now was promised to him by God Himself [in 28.13-15].

Gen. 28.13-15 repeats only 28.3-4.

[2] Kodell, 'Jacob Wrestles with Esau', p. 66; Gibson, *Genesis*, 2.164; Matthews and Mims, 'Jacob the Trickster', p. 188; Zucker, 'Jacob in Darkness', p. 406, 'The statements of Jacob seem patently clear. He will continue to serve the God of his fathers only *on the condition* that he continue to receive protection during his protected journey.' Others, however, take Jacob's words as expressing the spirituality of a true vow, e.g. Driver, *Genesis*, p. 266; Skinner, *Genesis*, pp. 378-79; Kidner, *Genesis*, p. 158; Richter, 'Das Gelübde', pp. 42ff.; von Rad, *Genesis*, p. 286. While it is true that *some* OT vows have conditional 'if' clauses, not all do, and the reader who has seen the characterization of Jacob unfold so far is entitled to be cynical of his motives here. Cf. Davies, 'Vows', pp. 792-93.

Chapter 4

THE STORY OF JACOB'S FAMILY

The Story of Jacob's Family

This chapter will investigate the way in which Joseph's dreams (Gen. 37.5-11) function as an Announcement of plot for the story of Jacob's family (chs. 37–50). The dreams received and interpreted in 37.5-11 purport to determine future relationships between Joseph and the other members of Jacob's family, and I wish to ascertain whether subsequent events prove them true. (As Joseph is the focus of interest for much of the story I will refer to the narrative, where appropriate, as 'the Joseph story', but this should not be taken to show my acceptance of the critical assumptions which usually underlie this designation.)[1]

The importance of 37.5-11 for the plot of the story is generally recognized.[2] For example, Brueggemann comments,

---

[1] The introduction to chs. 37-50 informs us that it is in fact 'the history of the family (*tōlⁿdôt*) of Jacob' (37.2). Westermann, *Genesis 37–50*, p. 27, reminds us that all the characters in chs. 37-45 (which for him forms the true 'Joseph story'), except the Egyptians mentioned in chs. 39–41, occur in previous ancestral stories. Therefore, the 'Joseph story' does not mark a completely new beginning. Cf. Coats, 'Redactional Unity', p. 15: '[chs. 37–50] constitute a collection of traditions unified around "Jacob and his sons", itself a theme in a larger narration of traditions about Jacob stretching from Gen 25.19 to Gen 50.14 (15–26)'. However, he sees the collection in chs. 37–50 as being more unified than the 'loosely organized' chs. 25–36 (p. 21). Cf. *idem*, *Genesis*, pp. 259-60; Gibson, *Genesis*, 2.225.

[2] E.g. von Rad, *Genesis*, p. 352; Redford, *Story of Joseph*, p. 69, 'Remove the dreams from chapter 37, and the Joseph Story as a coherent whole is reduced to nothing'; Seybold, 'Paradox and Symmetry', p. 60; Coats, *From Canaan to Egypt*, p. 12; Goldingay, 'Patriarchs', p. 11. Humphreys, *Joseph and his Family*, p. 32, sees 37.1-4 as the

The power and validity of the dream in 37.5-9 emerge as a
main issue. The dream functions in the Joseph narrative as
the oracle does for the Jacob materials... the dream of chapter 37 governs all that follows.[1]

An important matter for assessing the importance of the
dreams is their source. Are they merely a reflection of Joseph's
own psychology, or are they divine revelation? While it is
commonly assumed that the dreams do derive from God,[2] not
all agree.[3] If one reads this pericope in isolation, there is little
evidence to support a divine source for the dreams. Joseph
does not present the dreams as divine when divulging them to

exposition and 37.5-36 as the complication. I prefer to see 37.1-4 as a
general introduction; 37.5-11 as the exposition; 37.12ff. as the
complication.
[1] Brueggemann, *Genesis*, pp. 290, 296.
[2] E.g. Driver, *Genesis*, p. 322, '[the dreams] are divinely-sent presen-
timents of his future greatness'. However, rather confusingly Driver
has earlier stated: 'Joseph is the recipient of no supernatural warn-
ings or promises, directing his steps' (p. 320); Rowley, *The Faith of
Israel*, p. 31; Kidner, *Genesis*, p. 180; Zeitlin, 'Dreams and their Interpretation', p. 1: 'There can be no question that during the Biblical
Period prior to the Restoration dreams were regarded as acts of divina-
tion possessing the power of efficacy'; Stek, 'Dream', p. 992; Gnuse,
'Dreams and their Theological Significance', pp. 167, 171; Brueggemann, *Genesis*, p. 301; Goldingay, 'Patriarchs', p. 11; Greenstein, 'An
Equivocal Reading', p. 123; White, 'The Joseph Story', p. 60; Thompson, *Origin Tradition*, p. 118; Humphreys, *Joseph and his Family*,
p. 35. According to Ottosson and Botterweck, in Mesopotamia and
Mari and among the Hittites, most dreams were thought to be of divine
origin, and a frequent means of revelation to officials in the cult and
also to lay people; see Bergman, Ottosson and Botterweck, '*chalam;
ch*^{a}*lôm*', pp. 424-25. Mendelsohn, 'Dream; Dreamer', p. 868, gives a
similar assessment of the ANE material, and concludes that 'The OT
recognizes one source of dreams; all night visions proceed from God,
and his assistance is sought in interpreting them'. However, he does
concede that some 'night visions' (which for him are equivalent to
dreams), are of no consequence (e.g. Job 20.8; Ps. 73.20; Eccl. 5.7).
[3] E.g. Westermann, *Genesis 37–50*, p. 39. Some note the difficulty of
deciding on a human or divine source. Von Rad, *Genesis*, p. 351,
accepts that they could be viewed as either (a) 'real prophecies', or (b)
'notions of a vainglorious heart' (while admitting that 'the narrator
undoubtedly thinks of them as real prophecies given by God'). Sarna,
Understanding Genesis, pp. 212-13, looks at both sides of the issue, but
does not come to any firm conclusion. Cf. Miscall, 'Jacob and Joseph
Stories', pp. 33-34.

his brothers and father, nor do the dreams themselves make any mention of God.[1] However, when 37.5-11 is read within a larger context, the possibility is raised that the dreams come from God. Dreams have occurred on four previous occasions in the ancestral narratives. To Abimelech, 'God came to Abimelech in a dream by night...' (20.3); twice to Jacob, 'And he dreamed... and behold, the angels of God were ascending and descending on it! And behold, the Lord stood above it and said...' (28.12-13); 'Then the angel of God said to me in the dream...' (31.11); to Laban, 'But God came to Laban the Aramean in a dream by night...' (31.24). All of these dreams have two features worthy of note. First, they are non-symbolic;[2] they simply recount in sober form the words issued by God or the angel of the Lord, and in the cases of Abimelech and Jacob (31.11) the humans reply. Second, they all unambiguously see God as their source.

When we compare this evidence with that of chs. 37–50 we discover that in this latter narrative four individuals receive dreams, all of which differ from those found in chs. 12–36 in the following way. First, they are all symbolic: Joseph sees sheaves bowing down to his sheaf (37.7) and the sun, moon and eleven stars bowing down to him (37.9). The butler dreams of a vine, bunches of grapes and cups of wine (41.9-11). The baker sees cake baskets and birds eating their contents (41.16-17). Finally, Pharaoh is intrigued by the imagery of seven fat cows and seven thin cows coming out of the Nile, followed by seven plump and seven thin ears of grain (42.1-7). Second, *none* of the dreams features God at all, either as an actor or as being acknowledged as the source of the dream by the dreamer. An additional element which distinguishes these dreams from those recounted earlier is that, because they are symbolic, they all require interpretation: Joseph's dreams by his brothers and father, and the Egyptians' by Joseph. (The formal interpretations underline their symbolic nature even though most of the dreams are fairly transparent in mean-

---

[1] This latter point is decisive for Westermann, *Genesis 37–50*, p. 39.
[2] The visual element in 28.12 is not symbolism which requires an interpretation; rather it is a setting for God's unambiguous speech in vv. 13-15. Similarly, the goats of 31.10 do not require an interpretation in order for the dream to be understood; God's word explains all.

ing.) Quite clearly, therefore, the dreams in the Joseph story are of a different type. However, Joseph's interpretation of the Egyptians' dreams reveals that they too come from God. (Or at least, Joseph *believes* them to be divine.) Joseph offers his services as an interpreter to his fellow prisoners with the words, 'Do not interpretations belong to God?' (40.8). It is hardly likely that the dreams could be purely human if their meaning can be derived from God alone. Joseph's rhetorical question suggests quite strongly, therefore, that the dreams are divine revelation. With Joseph's interpretation of Pharaoh's dreams we see this point made unequivocally. Joseph honours God not only as the interpreter of the dream ('God will give Pharaoh a favourable answer' [41.16]), but also as its source, 'God has revealed to Pharaoh what he is about to do' (41.25; cf. v. 28). Joseph's successful interpretation of the dreams lends credence to his judgment regarding their source. We see, therefore, that none of the Egyptian dreamers mentions the divine in his dream report, yet the dream, according to Joseph, derives thence. With this in mind, the lack of reference to the divine in 37.5-11 cannot be offered as conclusive proof for denying the divine nature of Joseph's dreams. To argue this would make Joseph's dreams uniquely 'human', amidst all of the other 'divine' dreams in Genesis. It is surely unlikely that the dreams of one who interprets God's dreams elsewhere with divine aid should himself have dreams which merely reflect his own vaunting ambition. Also, the crucial importance of 37.5-11 for understanding the Joseph story as a whole strongly suggests God as the author of the dreams (as we shall see below). Joseph's report in 37.5-11 may in fact be seen as an example of the 'subdued theology' of chs. 37–50: God works throughout, but is explicitly mentioned only occasionally.

Joseph's dreams continue the spirit of the previous Announcements of plot which introduce the ancestral cycles. All of these were concerned with inverting normal expectations. Thus 12.1-3 promises, among other things, many descendants to a childless man and 25.23 announces that the elder son will serve the younger. In a similar manner, 37.5-11 asserts that the eleventh of twelve sons will assume sovereignty.[1] While both dreams are symbolic and are 'interpreted' by the brothers and Jacob, their meaning is immediately clear to all concerned.[2] The overriding theme in the dreams is that of 'bowing down' (*ḥwh*). The sheaves 'bow down' (v. 7); the sun, moon and stars 'bow down' (v. 9); Jacob wonders if he will 'bow down' (v. 10).[3] In addition, we should note that all of the dreams in chs. 37–50 come in pairs. When Joseph interprets the duplication of Pharaoh's dreams as an indication that their fulfilment is fixed, the reader very naturally draws the connection with Joseph's dreams and wonders whether their doubling has the same significance.[4] Thus, it is not only the clarity but also the duplication of the message that Joseph will be acknowledged as lord by his family, that causes strife with his elder brothers and initial ridicule and modified scepticism from Jacob (vv. 10-11).

Our discussion of Joseph's dreams will be facilitated if we investigate each dream individually, because an awareness of the differences between them is crucial for a correct understanding of their role in the story.[5] The general intention of the first dream (37.7) is obvious, and the reader hardly needs the brothers' interpretation (v. 8). At this stage it is not clear why the brothers should be symbolized by 'sheaves' of grain, for the imagery will only be elucidated as the dream moves toward its eventual fulfilment. By that time we shall realize the peculiar

---

[1] However, given the description of Jacob's favouritism toward Joseph (37.3-4), the reader may wonder to what degree these dreams *predict* such a state of affairs, and how far they *describe* present realities. Cf. Seybold, 'Paradox', p. 60.
[2] Cf. Fritsch, '"God was with him"', pp. 21-34; Redford, *Story of Joseph*, pp. 70-71; Gibson, *Genesis*, 2.229; Westermann, *Genesis 37–50*, p. 38. While it is generally true that the imagery of the dreams is transparent, and the general intention unambiguous, we shall see below that the second dream contains one element of uncertainty.
[3] Brueggemann, *Genesis*, p. 302.
[4] Driver, *Genesis*, p. 322; Stek, 'Dream', p. 992. Westermann, *Genesis 37–50*, pp. 37-38, sees their duplication as merely underlining the importance they have for the narrator in determining and holding together the whole narrative.
[5] The following are examples of those who tend to treat the dreams as though they are identical: Driver, *Genesis*, p. 356; Kidner, *Genesis*, p. 204; Seybold, 'Paradox', p. 66.

significance of the symbolic details.[1] Initially however, any such fulfilment is placed in jeopardy by the brothers' hastily devised plot as they see Joseph arriving on his errand from Jacob: 'Come now, let us kill him and throw him into one of the pits; and we shall say that a wild beast has devoured him, and we shall see what will become of his dreams' (37.20). Joseph's imprisonment down in the pit stands in ironic juxtaposition with the image of elevation contained in the dreams.[2] Upon his arrival in Egypt it is true that Joseph attains a position of authority in Potiphar's household (39.2-4), but this must not be allowed to detract from the fact that Potiphar is his lord who has *bought* him from the Midianites/ Ishmaelites (37.36; 39.1), and his future is determined by his refusal to obey a command from his mistress. Similarly, the keeper of the prison may have placed Joseph in charge of the other inmates (39.22), yet Joseph himself is also a prisoner, and his position merely makes him the first among equals. Thus, the way in which the narrative juxtaposes Joseph's elevation and humiliation may serve to remind the reader that he has been destined for great things (as witnessed by his initial dreams), but that this has been frustrated by his physical separation from those who should serve him and by his descent from the status of favourite son to that of slave, and finally, imprisoned slave. Those who have been opposing the dream either consciously (the brothers) or unwittingly (Potiphar's wife) appear to have succeeded.[3] Joseph's imprisonment in Egypt is almost as effective in frustrating the fulfilment of the first dream as if he had been devoured by a wild beast as Jacob surmised (37.33).

There is a degree of overlap between Joseph's two dreams, with the second (37.9) supplementing the first. Joseph's dream of the sheaves which bowed down to him obviously refers to

[1] Cf. Redford, *Story of Joseph*, p. 70; Alter, *Biblical Narrative*, p. 163. Surprisingly, von Rad, *Genesis*, p. 352, believes it would be incorrect to see any connection between the imagery of sheaves and Joseph's later policy of grain storage, but he gives no reason why this should be so.
[2] For a diagrammatic representation of the whole Joseph story, showing the relationship between descent and elevation in the plot, see McGuire, 'The Joseph Story', p. 24.
[3] Cf. Brueggemann, *Genesis*, p. 301.

his brothers' subservience, and this imagery of prostration is reiterated in the second dream where the 'eleven stars' do the same. However, the second dream includes, in addition to his brothers, his father and mother (37.10). Thus the first dream would be fulfilled by his brothers bowing down to him. (It is likely that the first dream has only his ten older brothers in mind, i.e. those who are his seniors and with whom he has already been in dispute, those likely to be binding sheaves with him in the field and who will later sell him to the traders.[1] Benjamin, as Joseph's junior would probably be too young to be drawn into this family dispute, and would probably accept Joseph's seniority in any case. My interpretation in the rest of this chapter is not materially altered even if the first dream is taken to include Benjamin.) However, the second dream demands that both parents and all eleven brothers do the same. This raises a very serious problem: Joseph's mother, Rachel, is dead. Her death and burial have already been recorded in a preceding narrative (35.19). And chs. 37–50 as a whole seem to assume the fact of her death. For example, 37.11 records the reaction of Jacob and his sons to Joseph's second dream, but makes no mention of Rachel, about whom the second dream is also concerned. Later, having been duped by his sons, Jacob mourns for Joseph and is comforted (insincerely) by those same sons and also by his daughters, but Rachel is conspicuous by her absence from this scene of family tragedy. When Joseph meets his brothers in Egypt, he enquires concerning the welfare of Jacob, but makes no mention of his mother (43.27), suggesting that Joseph knew of her death *before* he went to Egypt.[2] In 48.7 Jacob states quite

---

[1] I am in agreement here with Lowenthal, *Joseph Narrative*, pp. 60, 180 n. 5.

[2] It could be argued that he gained this fact from the brothers' summary of their family situation in which Rachel is omitted (42.13): 'We, your servants, are twelve brothers, the sons of one man in the land of Canaan; and behold, the youngest is this day with our father, and one is no more'. However, if this were the first intimation Joseph had had of his mother's death we would expect some reaction, when just the sight of Benjamin is sufficient to induce a fit of weeping (43.30). On Joseph's omitting any reference to his mother in 43.27-29, Humphreys, *Joseph and his Family*, p. 195, suggests:

clearly that Rachel died on their journey from Mesopotamia to Canaan—many years before Joseph had his dreams. Thus, the case for arguing that Rachel was already dead at the time Joseph had his dreams is compelling.

If it is argued that Rachel was still alive, a different problem is created. Rachel died giving birth to Benjamin (35.16-19). Therefore, if she was still alive when Joseph dreamed, Joseph had only ten brothers, and not the *eleven* stipulated by the dream; if Joseph at that time had eleven brothers, then his mother must have been dead.[1] It is clear therefore, that there is something inherently impossible about the dream.[2] In fact Rachel's previous demise may explain Jacob's response to his son's dream report, which could be paraphrased as, 'how is it *possible* that I and your mother [who is already dead!] and

> this is the story of men, of the complex relationships of a father and his sons... It appears that the complexity that the presence of Joseph's mother would have brought to this matrix is avoided.

However, the final form of the text shows quite clearly that she was dead before Joseph was taken to Egypt.

[1] Older scholars tend to make light of the problem. For example, Driver, *Genesis*, p. 322, suggests the possibility that Rachel's earlier death notice was the work of J, while E authored Joseph's dreams. Skinner, *Genesis*, p. 440, believes that the 'extreme youth' of Benjamin in the later stages of the story suggests that he had not yet been born when Joseph left home. If Rachel is mentioned as though she were alive, then she must be alive. However, this ignores the problem of having eleven brothers and a live Rachel. Also, it may be contested that the story portrays Benjamin as being in his 'extreme youth'. He is described as being the son of Jacob's 'old age' rather than being in his 'extreme youth'. Judah uses the term *na'ar* to describe him (44.30, 31), but this does not demand 'extreme youth'. According to 46.21 Benjamin is the father of ten children at the time he goes down to Egypt. Cf. Koehler and Baumgartner, *Lexicon*, p. 623.

[2] The impossibility may have a bearing on the source of the dreams. Rachel's bowing down is ridiculous regardless of whether it represents Joseph's human ambition or divine revelation. But by now the reader of Genesis has learned not to be surprised by Yahweh predicting the unusual and the bizarre. From a literary point of view the second dream is hardly something a human being would 'dream up' of his or her own accord. Therefore, the seeming impossibility of the dream renders it more likely to be divine revelation than human ambition.

your brothers will bow down to you?"[1]

Aalders, it is true, makes a detailed attempt to overcome the problem by suggesting that much of ch. 37 precedes the action of ch. 35. He suggests two possibilities: either Rachel died between Joseph's two dreams, or after the two dreams and before Joseph's visit to his brothers at Dothan.[2] It can be seen quite clearly that Aalders' suggestions merely confirm the problem. If Rachel died before the second dream, she should not be included in it; if she did not die until after it, the reference to 'eleven stars' would not be possible. Yet even Aalders effectively concedes defeat when he states,

> As far as the fulfillment of this dream is concerned we would do well not to dwell on the details with too much emphasis. To do so could lead to serious difficulties.[3]

Aalders concludes that the general intention of the dream is to place Joseph in a position of power and authority within the

---

[1] This possibility was already accepted in rabbinic literature. (Cf. Ginzberg, *The Legends of the Jews*, 2.8.) Rashi understood Jacob's speech to mean, 'I cannot come with thy mother, *since she is dead*, so the whole dream is an impossibility' (Lowe, *'Rashi' on the Pentateuch*, p. 396; cf. Rosenbaum and Silbermann, *Pentateuch*, p. 181). Similarly, Hershon, *Rabbinical Commentary*, p. 220: 'Thy mother is already dead and therefore thy dream is a lie'. Cf. Hertz, *Pentateuch and Haftorahs*, p. 311. *Genesis Rabbah* 34.11 notes two interpretations in light of Rachel already being dead: (i) 'Jacob thought that resurrection [of Rachel] would take place in his days'; (ii) that 'mother' here should be taken to refer to Bilhah.

[2] Aalders, *Genesis*, 2.179. A similar point is made by Humphreys, *Joseph and his Family*, p. 24, who suggests that Benjamin must have been born during the time Joseph was away in Egypt. However, later (p. 195), Humphreys solves the problem by arguing that the Jacob and Joseph stories have different chronologies.

[3] Aalders, *Genesis*, 2.183. In a similar way, Coats, *Canaan to Egypt*, p. 14, recognizes the problem of the moon imagery, but suggests that

> it simply facilitates the sun-moon motif at the center of the dream as a symbol of the family. The reference to the mother, in that case, would appear only because of the astral imagery of the dream.

But this 'solution' begs the question as to why the astral imagery was used when it does not cohere well with the realities it intends to portray; such a correlation is important in all the other dreams in chs. 37–50 (see below).

family.[1] However, this generalized interpretation does not accord with Jacob's understanding in which each element of the imagery has significance. In addition, all of the other dreams in the Joseph story show a very close and detailed relationship between imagery and reality. The butler and baker see *three* bunches of grapes and cake baskets respectively because their fate will be decided in *three* days; in addition the imagery is peculiarly appropriate to their respective vocations. Pharaoh sees *seven* fat and thin cows emerging from the Nile followed by *seven* plump and thin ears of grain, because the agricultural prosperity of the country will go through two contrasting *seven* year cycles. As we shall see below, the imagery of Joseph's first dream has a similar significance. Thus the dreams of the Joseph story as a whole do not allow us to treat the details of Joseph's second dream in a cavalier manner, as if they were of no importance. They must be treated seriously and the problems which arise from doing so frankly acknowledged.[2]

In summary, Joseph's dreams present the reader with related but not identical pictures. The first dream predicts the subservience of the (ten) brothers; the second dream, the subservience of father, mother and eleven brothers. We have already seen how the first dream has seemingly been frustrated by Joseph's descent into Egypt; this situation obviously threatens the second dream, yet it also carries within itself the seeds of its own non-fulfilment; only two of its three elements (subservience of father and brothers) can possibly be ful-

---

[1] Aalders, *Genesis*, 2.183; cf. Calvin, *Genesis*, 2.262.
[2] Thompson, *Origin Tradition*, pp. 118-19, notes the incongruities of the second dream but suggests that

> the minor narrative discord that this dream brings with it pales in contrast to the striking imagery of the sun and the moon and all the stars bowing down before Joseph. Could any storyteller resist such magic for the sake of consistency?

However, the story of Jacob's family reveals that its narrator had an eye for detail, and such an important incongruity in the introductory programmatic pericope would have constituted far more than a 'minor narrative discord'. It is difficult to see such a narrator including traditional material regardless of whether it 'fitted' his narrative or not.

filled—taken as a whole, it is an *impossible* dream.[1]
As long as Joseph remains enslaved and imprisoned in
Egypt, it is impossible for his dreams to be fulfilled. However,
his successful interpretation of the dreams of the butler and
baker raises the possibility that his own dreams too may
become reality. Although the butler forgets Joseph for two
years, the failure of the court officials to give an interpretation
for Pharaoh's dreams provides Joseph with the opportunity to
interpret them and to receive the royal accolade. With
Joseph's promotion to second position in the empire, the
groundwork has been laid for the possible consummation of
his boyhood dreams. The reader does not have to wait long.
The famine pictured in Pharaoh's dreams hits Canaan and
Jacob despatches ten of his sons to Egypt to buy grain (42.1-5):
'And Joseph's brothers came, and bowed themselves
(*wayyištaḥ⁰wû*) before him with their faces to the ground'
(42.6). The connection with Joseph's original dreams is abun-
dantly clear and the explicit reminder, 'Joseph remembered
the dreams which he had dreamed of them' (42.9), is hardly
necessary. The reader can now see the significance of the
imagery of sheaves bowing down (37.7): the dream is fulfilled
when Joseph's brothers prostrate themselves before him on
the floor of a granary. The fulfilment of the first dream is not
confined to 42.6 but is repeated in 43.26, 'they... bowed down
(*wayyištaḥ⁰wû*) to him to the ground'; 44.14, 'his brothers
came... and they fell (*wayyippᵉlû*) before him to the ground';
50.18, 'His brothers also came and fell down (*wayyippᵉlû*)
before him'.[2] However, I must emphasize an important point.

---

[1] An ancient proposal is that 'mother' of 37.10 refers not to Joseph's
biological mother but to Bilhah. See Hershon, *Rabbinical Commentary*, p.220; Lowe, *'Rashi' on the Pentateuch*, p.396; *Genesis Rabbah*
34.11. Gibson, *Genesis*, 2.230, pursues a similar line of argument,
suggesting Leah was intended. However, Aalders, *Genesis*, 2.179,
plausibly suggests that in polygamous marriages each wife was
'mother' of only her own children.
[2] This is commonly observed by commentators, e.g. Driver, *Genesis*,
p.356; Kidner, *Genesis*, p.204; Speiser, *Genesis*, p.378. Westermann,
Genesis 37–50, p.133, sees the use of *nāpal* rather than *ḥāwâ* in 44.14
(and 50.18) as expressing the stronger concept of 'complete submis-
sion'. He takes this to show that 'as the dreams are fulfilled, the act of
bowing is varied; it has a different nuance on each occasion'. If this is

The obeisance of the brothers in 42.6 fulfils at most only the first dream. (If one feels the first dream refers to all eleven brothers, then it is not completely fulfilled until 43.26.) At this point the second dream remains unfulfilled. Only ten brothers have come down to Egypt; the second dream requires *all* family members.[1]

The fate of this second dream now needs to be investigated. This task will be facilitated if we look also at another problem—that of Joseph's harsh treatment of his brothers. We will find that these two seemingly unconnected issues help to shed light on each other.

The major problems in understanding Joseph's bizarre behaviour toward his brothers are that it is given no explicit explanation in the narrative, and also, that it does not fit easily

---

so, then the repetition of the brothers' obeisance serves not only to reinforce but also to intensify the first dream's fulfilment.

[1] This point is overlooked by most commentators. Cf. von Rad, *Genesis*, pp. 352, 383; Alter, 'Joseph and His Brothers', p. 62 [= *Biblical Narrative*, p. 163], states, 'Joseph's two dreams are here literally fulfilled'. Yet, to reach this conclusion he must see the imagery of the sun, moon and stars as foreshadowing Joseph's role as Egyptian vizier—which is unconnected with Jacob's interpretation of the imagery in ch. 37 (cf. *Biblical Narrative*, p. 169). Lowenthal, Letter, p. 18, rightly takes Alter to task by pointing out that the dream spoke of *eleven* stars, but only *ten* brothers bow down in 42.6. Unfortunately, he does not develop this insight. Gibson, *Genesis*, 2.273, writes: 'We are left in no doubt that this was a fulfilment, partial maybe but real, of the dreams in chapter 37'. (Similarly, Kidner, *Genesis*, p. 199.) It would be closer to the truth to say that the first dream has been fulfilled, but that none of the three elements of the second dream (obeisance of father, mother, and eleven brothers) has been fulfilled. Seybold, 'Paradox', p. 69, points out that in 42.6 'the second dream remains unfulfilled', but he is very vague on its actual fulfilment (cf. p. 72). Richter, 'Traum und Traumdeutung im AT', p. 208, believes that the fulfilment of the first dream (42.6ff.) prepares the way for the fulfilment of the second, which is achieved, though not literally (*wörtlich*), in ch. 47. He too remains vague on how the second dream works out. I would ask, if it is not fulfilled literally, how can it be said to have been fulfilled, when all other dreams in the story are fulfilled literally? Recently, King, 'The Joseph Story', p. 593, has stated, 'At this point in the story Joseph's adolescent dreams come true... he does rule over the whole family as his adolescent dreams had foretold'. This view, of course, does not give enough detailed attention to what the dreams actually predicted.

with the belief that Joseph is being presented as an ideal
administrator and the archetypal Wise man.[1] He repeatedly
torments his brothers by accusing them of crimes of which he
knows them to be innocent, e.g. 'You are spies, you have come
to see the weakness of the land' (42.9). In addition, by imprisoning Simeon and demanding Benjamin's presence in Egypt,
he puts his frail father through torture, as can be seen in
Jacob's words to his sons: 'You have bereaved me of my children: Joseph is no more, and Simeon is no more, and now you
would take Benjamin; all this has come upon me' (42.36).

What motivates Joseph's behaviour? A possibility which
immediately suggests itself is that Joseph is out for revenge
against the brothers who had wronged him when he was a

[1] Von Rad, 'The Joseph Narrative and Ancient Wisdom', pp. 292-300;
idem, Genesis, pp. 435-39. Von Rad has been followed, with varying
degrees of agreement, by several scholars: e.g. Meinhold, 'Die
Gattung der Josephsgeschichte', pp. 321-24. Coats, 'The Joseph Story
and Ancient Wisdom', p. 296, sees Wisdom as one of many influences
on the Joseph story:

> the Joseph story lives in an atmosphere larger than wisdom
> tradition, larger than a total devotion to stereotyped theological
> formulation. It draws on both, and even more. It is the atmo-
> sphere of an artist with wide-ranging experience.

However cf. *idem, Canaan to Egypt*, p. 90, where Coats confirms that
Wisdom provides the best context for understanding parts of the
Joseph story, e.g. 40.8; 41.16, 25. Cf. also *idem*, 'The Joseph Story and
Ancient Wisdom', pp. 289ff.; *idem, Genesis*, p. 266. For a presentation
of Joseph as an ideal administrator and ideal human being, see
Dahlberg, 'Unity of Genesis', pp. 364-65. Apparently Dahlberg does not
see Joseph's behaviour as a problem for this view, as he makes no
mention of it.
Nevertheless, significant protests have been raised against the view
that the narrative should be categorized as Wisdom. E.g. Crenshaw,
'Determining Wisdom Influence', esp. pp. 135-37; Redford, *Story of
Joseph*, p. 103, points out that Joseph's behaviour in chs. 37 and 42-44
does not accord with the Wisdom ideal, and concludes, 'there is no
reason to believe that the story *per se* originated in, or belongs to, the
sphere of Wisdom Literature' (p. 105); Westermann, *Genesis 37-50*,
p. 247, sees only chs. 39-41 as having any connection with Wisdom, but
the Joseph story as a whole 'is neither a didactic narrative nor a
wisdom narrative'. More recently Humphreys, *Joseph and his
Family*, pp. 139-51, has argued that Wisdom is a helpful model for
understanding some aspects of the Joseph material.

youth, and it is true that there seem to be a number of 'tit-for-tat' measures in which the brothers relive Joseph's experiences, e.g. their three-day imprisonment (42.17) parallels their earlier 'incarceration' of Joseph in the pit (37.23ff.).[1] However, a major objection to this possibility is the fact that on several occasions Joseph's emotions get the better of him (42.24; 43.30), and at times he treats them in a kindly manner (e.g. 42.25-27). These actions are hard to reconcile with someone who is motivated *solely* by vindictiveness. It is not necessary to deny that revenge may have been part of the picture, but his apparently contradictory actions—both harsh treatment and tender emotions—show that this single motive does not explain everything.[2]

By far the commonest suggestion for explaining Joseph's actions is some variation of the following. Joseph's intention is to test his brothers to see whether they have reformed, repented and shown loyalty to Benjamin and Jacob, as preconditions for his forgiveness and his reconciliation with them.[3] Since the text is not explicit on the matter any investigation of Joseph's motives involves reading between the lines, but we may well wonder what evidence there is to support this almost universal suggestion. It is *possible* that Joseph's replacement of the money bags in the sacks is a test of their honesty (42.25)—but the narrative nowhere confirms this suspicion. Joseph's enquiry about Jacob's welfare (43.27) *could* be a test question concerning his brothers' treatment of the old man, but as Jacob is in Canaan at the time, Joseph has no way of knowing whether their reply, 'Your servant our father is well, he is still alive' (43.28), is the truth or a bare-faced lie. In addition, it could be argued that since Judah's speech in 44.18-

---

[1] Sternberg, *Poetics of Biblical Narrative*, p. 228. Cf. Ackerman, 'Joseph, Judah, and Jacob', pp. 89ff.

[2] Interestingly, while many commentators discuss this possibility, most of those I have encountered dismiss it. Cf. Driver, *Genesis*, p. 320; Kidner, *Genesis*, p. 199; Alter, *Biblical Narrative*, p. 163; Gibson, *Genesis*, 2.274.

[3] See Greenstein, 'Reading Strategies', pp. 7ff., for a helpful summary of approaches to this issue. Cf. Driver, *Genesis*, pp. 320, 349; Fritsch, '"God was with him"', p. 28; Kidner, *Genesis*, p. 199; Seybold, 'Paradox', p. 70; Westermann, *Genesis 37–50*, p. 106; Ackerman, 'Joseph, Judah, and Jacob', p. 94.

34 shows the brothers in a generous light, with Judah as
spokesman for the group, expressing genuine love for Jacob
and Benjamin, once Joseph is reassured on this issue, he
reveals his true identity (45.3) and the family reconciliation is
accomplished. However, was it Joseph's aim to elicit such a
speech from Judah? It may be the *result* of Joseph's ploy, but
was it the *aim*? As we shall see, the Joseph story as a whole
would seem to counter such a suggestion.

If we look in more detail at the conventional explanation of
Joseph's behaviour, we may ask why Joseph should ever think
that the brothers would treat Benjamin badly. The story states
clearly the understandable reasons for their previous hatred
of Joseph: Jacob's excessive love for him (37.4) and his tale-
bearing and dream reports (37.2, 8, 11, 19-20).[1] The reasons
for the brother's hatred were based on the unique relationship
between Jacob and Joseph, and Joseph's behaviour as a
braggart. There is nothing to suggest that either of these
factors would be repeated in Benjamin's case.[2] (It is true that
Jacob treats Benjamin preferentially [43.28], but this piece of
information is for the reader's consumption only; it is not
divulged to Joseph.) In the same manner we may ask why
Joseph should think that the brothers would treat Jacob in a
disrespectful or harmful way. Although the reader knows
how the brothers deceived Jacob with the cloak dipped in
goat's blood, Joseph does not.[3] That is to say, the view that

[1] Some see the presentation of these points as being the main function
of the introduction to the story (37.1-35), e.g. Meinhold, 'Die Gattung
der Josephsgeschichte', p. 311. Westermann, *Genesis 37–50*, p. 37,
attempts to defend Jacob by suggesting that as Joseph was born during
Jacob's old age it was only natural for him to treat him in a special
way and therefore the reader should not pass any moral judgments.
That Jacob may have had a special regard for Joseph is understandable; that he should so flagrantly display his favouritism is not.
[2] Sternberg, *Poetics of Biblical Narrative*, p. 289, is an example of those
who make this unwarranted assumption. He says:

> What fate (Joseph asks himself) has this gang of fratricides
> devised for Benjamin, his full brother and the next object of
> jealousy, allegedly at home now but quite possibly likewise put
> out of the way?

[3] Cf. Hyman, 'Questions in the Joseph Story', pp. 437-55; Miscall,
'Jacob and Joseph Stories', p. 31, reminds us that we must maintain a

Joseph's harsh treatment is designed to discover whether his brothers have repented and are now acting properly toward Jacob is a question which seems reasonable to the *reader*, who knows how they deceived Jacob, but is not so reasonable to ascribe to *Joseph*, who knows nothing of the deception of his father.

In addition, 42.21-22 amounts to a confession by the brothers that they were wrong to have treated Joseph as they did in ch. 37. If Joseph is looking for a 'confession' or 'reformation' before he reveals himself, then here he has it. Yet instead of being overjoyed at this revelation, which would allow him to drop the masquerade and be reconciled to his brothers (which is surely what one would expect if the conventional explanation of the 'test' is correct), Joseph's only response is to weep (42.24).

It is maintained by some that Joseph has to put his brothers through such agonies if true reconciliation is to be achieved. Westermann believes that

> the narrator wants to say that at the very moment that he saw his brothers before him, Joseph had decided to heal the breach... The structure as a whole allows this conclusion. It is to this purpose that Joseph allows his brothers to undergo the severe trial of being at the disposition of the potentate. A quick pardon at this moment could not have led to a real solution, as the continuation shows.[1]

It is difficult to see why a 'quick pardon' could not have produced a reconciliation. In fact Joseph subjects his family to such severe treatment that any reconciliation is threatened. It is instructive to observe that when Joseph meets his brothers he is in an análogous situation to that of Esau in ch. 33.[2] Both he and Esau meet the agents of their previous injustices after an absence of twenty years, and are both in a position of power—Joseph as Grand Vizier, Esau with four hundred men. Yet Esau acts in a completely different manner. He does not concoct an elaborate series of self-concealments and

---

distinction between the narrator's, reader's and characters' knowledge of a story.
[1] Westermann, *Genesis 37–50*, p. 107.
[2] Cf. Miscall, 'Jacob and Joseph Stories', p. 32.

deceptions, nor does he demand any repentance or bottle up
his emotions for use at a more propitious time, but immediately 'ran to meet [Jacob], and embraced him, and fell on his
neck and kissed him, and they wept' (33.4). An immediate
(unspoken) pardon was Esau's response to a brother who had
cheated him, and this resulted in a true reconciliation. It
would be unfair to demand that Joseph act in exactly the same
manner as Esau, but ch. 33 shows that testing, trial and confession are not a *necessary* route to reconciliation. Esau has
shown a better way.

I conclude therefore, that the narrative provides no support
for the view that Joseph treated his brothers harshly in order
to ascertain or provoke their repentance.

Does the narrative give *any* clues about Joseph's motives? I
noted above that the brothers' prostration in 42.6 fulfilled only
the first dream (37.7); the second dream (37.9) remains
unfulfilled. The narrator rarely divulges the inner thoughts of
his characters, but this occasion is an exception. On seeing his
brothers with their faces to the earth, 'Joseph remembered the
dreams which he had dreamed of them; and he said to them,
"You are spies, you have come to see the weakness of the
land"' (42.9). As Ackerman observes, 'Like the reader, Joseph
remembers not the betrayal or suffering wrought by his
brothers, but his dreams'.[1] This rare insight into Joseph's
mind must be significant.[2] The verse seems to link Joseph's
decision to treat his brothers harshly with his remembrance of
his dreams.[3] At first there seems to be no logical connection,
especially if, with the majority of scholars, one assumes that
both dreams have already been fulfilled. But if it is recognized,
as it surely must be, that only the *first* dream has been fulfilled,
then a possibility suggests itself. Joseph's accusation of his

[1] Ackerman, 'Joseph, Judah, and Jacob', p. 87.
[2] Westermann, *Genesis 37–50*, p. 107.
[3] As observed correctly by Ackerman, 'Joseph, Judah, and Jacob',
p. 87:

> In the unusual description of Joseph's thoughts in 42.9, the
> syntax connects his remembering the dreams with his accusing
> his brothers, launching a new series of events. That syntactical
> connection suggests that everything that follows is related to his
> dreams.

brothers is the beginning of an attempt *to fulfil the second dream.*[1] This suggestion is given credence when after the initial thrust of claim and counter claim between the two parties, Joseph utters his ultimatum, 'By this you shall be tested: by the life of Pharaoh, you shall not go from this place unless your youngest brother comes here' (42.15). In terms of the dispute between them, this 'test' would hardly prove anything. The group may well be brothers, and have a younger sibling in Canaan, but they could still be spies. Later, when the nine brothers return with Benjamin, Joseph would have no way of knowing whether he were their brother or an imposter used to buttress their deception. That is to say, there is no logical connection between the accusation and the test.[2] However, Joseph's test does have a logical connection with the second dream: Benjamin must come down to Egypt if the *'eleven* stars' (37.9) are to bow down before him. In fact, once the party return from Canaan with Benjamin, and present themselves before Joseph, this is exactly what happens: 'When Joseph came home, they [all eleven brothers]... bowed down (*wayyištaḥᵃwû*) to him to the ground' (43.26); 'And they bowed their heads and made obeisance (*wayyištaḥᵃwu*)" (43.28). This act of social etiquette fulfils the letter of the dream imagery, but despite this, Joseph continues his deception by planting evidence on Benjamin (44.1ff.), which elicits the following confession from Judah, 'Behold, we are my lord's slaves, both we and he also in whose hand the cup has been found' (44.16). Joseph's deception has resulted not only in all his brothers bending the knee, but also in their *confessing* their subservience. Thus Joseph has succeeded in bringing about the fulfilment of one element of the dream: the 'eleven stars' have bowed down. This situation has been brought about solely as a result of Joseph's strange actions.

(Sternberg sees the possibility that an explanation for

[1] Ackerman, 'Joseph, Judah, and Jacob', p. 91, commenting on Joseph's three-day imprisonment of his brothers, states, 'He had wanted his brothers to relive in part the hardships that he had experienced. But his major purpose is to bring his dreams to fulfillment, and this necessitates a change in strategy.' It is a pity that Ackerman does not properly develop this most important observation.
[2] As noted by Humphreys, *Joseph and his Family*, p. 44.

Joseph's request to see Benjamin is his desire to fulfil the dreams. However, Sternberg dismisses the notion immediately because he believes that 'the dreams make no sense to Joseph, either singly or paired', and because of this assumption wonders how 'anyone [can] hypothesize a wish to fulfil the dreams and causally relate it to the insistence on Benjamin's showing himself'.[1] I hope that my argument above has demonstrated how this is not only possible but even essential. I can find no substantiation in the text itself for Sternberg's position that Joseph did not understand the dreams. That Joseph did understand them is clearly shown by his remembrance of them at the same instant that his brothers bowed down before him. Yet Sternberg effectively concedes the weakness of his argument by suggesting that Joseph may have acted in the way he did toward his brothers not in order to fulfil the dreams but 'to test and elucidate [the dreams]'. But since the only way Joseph has of elucidating the dreams is to try to fulfil them, Sternberg really confirms the position he seeks to discredit.)

It might be objected to the foregoing account of Joseph's behaviour toward his brothers that if Joseph wished to fulfil the second dream and have all his family do obeisance to him, why did he require the presence of only Benjamin in Egypt? Why did he not request Jacob as well? For a while this remains a puzzle for the reader. However, a perfectly plausible reason is provided a little later in the story. Judah's plea to Joseph (44.18-34) recounts the previous discussion between Joseph and his brothers (42.7ff.). In his speech, however, Judah reminds Joseph of a detail not divulged to the reader on that previous occasion: 'We said to my lord, "The lad cannot leave his father, for if he should leave his father, his father would die"' (44.22; cf. 42.13). Despite being told this, Joseph had persisted in demanding Benjamin. Why? I suggest that in requesting Benjamin Joseph thought he would get Jacob automatically, if, as Judah stated, the two were inseparable.

---

[1] Sternberg, *Poetics of Biblical Narrative*, p. 292. A few scholars allude briefly to the possibility that a desire to fulfil the dreams explains Joseph's behaviour, but to my knowledge none argues that this is in fact the case. Cf. Ackerman, p. 160 n. 1; Miscall, 'Jacob and Joseph Stories', pp. 34, 37; Greenstein, 'Reading Strategies', p. 8.

This suggestion is supported by Joseph's words to his brothers when they return to Egypt with Benjamin. His *first* recorded words to them are, 'Is your father well, the old man of whom you spoke? Is he still alive?' (43.27). Joseph had expected to see Jacob. When he sees that he is absent, it occurs to Joseph that his ploy may have backfired and, as Judah had said, the separation had killed Jacob. When he is reassured that Jacob is still alive (43.28), Joseph realizes that he must try another ploy to get Jacob—and this he does by threatening to imprison Benjamin over the silver cup incident. To let the other brothers return to Canaan while Benjamin remains in Egypt serves no useful purpose unless Joseph still has his mind on the unfulfilled dream. Benjamin's imprisonment is necessary for the next element of the dream to be fulfilled, with Jacob pleading for clemency for Benjamin, and, presumably, prostrate before Joseph. However, at this point, the unexpected happens, with Judah's impassioned plea (44.18-34). Joseph's subterfuge was based on the assumption that the old man could not be separated for long from his youngest son. Judah's speech shows that Joseph has miscalculated.[1] Imprisoning Benjamin, rather than bringing Jacob to Egypt, would actually kill Jacob: 'When he sees that the lad is not with us, he will die' (44.31). In response to this unwelcome reminder, the love Joseph has for his father and family overcomes his hubris, he breaks down, and reveals his true identity (45.1-3). He had not reacted this way on the first occasion Judah had told him of the effect separation from Benjamin would have on Jacob. But now, Judah offers himself as prisoner in an attempt to prevent Joseph's plan. This brings home to Joseph the terrible seriousness of what he has been doing—playing with death. Thus Joseph's plan is never put into action. Even though Jacob does come to Egypt he comes as Joseph's *father* (e.g. 46.29; 47.1), with all his rights and privileges within the family. Significantly, not only is the first element of the second dream never fulfilled,[2] but it is actually reversed when Joseph brings his

---

[1] I see this as the main issue in the speech, rather than demonstrating that 'the bothers have passed the great test which Joseph set them' (von Rad, *Genesis*, p. 395). Cf. Hyman, 'Questions in the Joseph Story', p. 447.

[2] Zeitlin, 'Dreams', p. 2, states, 'According to the Bible, Joseph

sons to Jacob for blessing: 'Then Joseph removed them from
his knees, and he bowed himself (*wayyištaḥû*) with his face to
the earth' (48.12).[1] Joseph, despite his elaborate plans and
callous calculations, receives his come-uppance, to the delight
of the reader. (The fact that Rachel is dead and cannot bow
down to Joseph means that this element of the second dream
was always doomed to fail. The reader, however, is left to
ponder whether *Joseph* considered this to be impossible. Does
he attempt to fulfil only those parts of the dream which can be
fulfilled, or has he become so intoxicated with power that he
believes he is capable of anything, and if his plans to get Jacob
had not been thwarted, would have plotted even the fulfilment
of the element concerning his mother?)

In contrast to this reading, Ackerman's attempt to see the
fulfilment of the second dream in the incident in which Jacob
slumps exhausted on the head of his bed is hardly convincing.[2]
I would agree with Gibson who comments,

> It is not so commonly pointed out, however, that the second
> dream is *not* fulfilled in the epic... Joseph's dream of the
> sun and moon and stars must have been a false one, sug-
> gested by his own arrogance and ambition, and not at all by
> God's prompting.[3]

I agree with Gibson's comments on the non-fulfilment of the
second dream, but I suggest a different reason (see below).

The above interpretation still needs to take account of the
occasions when Joseph's emotions get the better of him. Can
these be accommodated to the picture I have presented so far
of Joseph as a calculating and scheming individual? I would
suggest that the characterization of Joseph is a subtle one. He
is presented neither as complete villain nor complete saint, but
like most humans has elements of each. It would seem that

became ruler of Egypt, and when his father and brothers came to
Egypt, they bowed down before him'. However, there is no evidence
whatsoever that Jacob bowed down to Joseph.
[1] It is possible that 46.29 also presents a (partial) reversal of the
dream. Joseph 'presents himself' (*wayyērā'*) before Jacob. Depending
upon the weight one places on the verb, this could be seen as the opposite of what the dream envisaged.
[2] Ackerman, 'Joseph, Judah, and Jacob', pp. 108-109.
[3] Gibson, *Genesis*, 2.230-31.

Joseph retains genuine love for his family, yet the old hubris he had before, at home with the family,[1] reasserts itself when he meets his brothers. There is something about his family that brings out the worst in Joseph. He wants to have the best of both worlds: he wants to be reunited with his family but on his own terms, with himself their superior. Rather than accepting the opportunity of reconciliation offered by the initial meeting with the brothers, he desires to enforce the fulfilment of the second dream (or, at least, as much of it as he possibly can). I conclude that the love for his family and his own hubris militate against one another, and produce the emotional fluctuations described in the narrative.[2]

Joseph's dreams dominate the narrative so much that a survey of the attitudes to the dreams on the part of the characters in the narrative and the effect of such attitudes on their fulfilment is a necessary task. The characters relate to the dreams in a number of ways. First, Joseph's brothers explicitly attempt to frustrate them (37.18ff.). Yet, para-doxically, this actually creates the circumstances in which the first dream can be fulfilled (42.6).[3] Second, Joseph's personal relationship to the dreams is quite complex and has at least three aspects. For much of his sojourn in Egypt Joseph is *unable* to do anything about the dreams. In his position as a slave and then a prisoner he does not have enough control over his personal circumstances to make the dreams work; yet events actually move inexorably toward the fulfilment of the first dream (42.6). Not only is he unable to effect the fulfilment of the dreams, he also exhibits an *apathy* toward

---

[1] Peck, 'Genesis 37.2', pp. 342-43, attempts to give a positive assess-ment of Joseph's behaviour in ch. 37. However, he seems to work from the assumption that Joseph must behave consistently throughout the story; I believe that Joseph is a much more complex character than this. In addition, Peck assumes that Joseph's behaviour toward his brothers in chs. 42–44 (in keeping with the rest of the narrative), reveals 'his nobility and innocence'. I find this simply hard to believe.
[2] I disagree therefore, with Skinner, *Genesis*, p. 475, who sees Joseph as being utterly inscrutable, his motives defying analysis. Calvin, *Genesis*, 2.341, states, 'nothing is more common than for great and unexpected felicity to intoxicate its possessors', and that Joseph resisted this temptation. I believe he succumbed.
[3] White, 'The Joseph Story', p. 61.

them. In the naming of his firstborn, Manasseh, Joseph
explains the child's name with the curious statement, 'For...
God has made me forget all my hardship and *all my father's
house*' (41.51). (This is reinforced by the fact that despite being
in such a position of authority for more than seven years,
Joseph makes no attempt to contact his family in Canaan.) If
he has 'forgotten' his 'father's house' (*bêt 'ābî*) then he must
also have 'forgotten' the dreams, because they relate to family
relationships. (This is underlined by the contrast between
41.51 'God has made me *forget* [*naššanî*]... all my father's
house', and 42.9, 'And Joseph *remembered* [*wayyizkōr*] the
dreams'.) Therefore, it is in the state of not caring about the
fulfilment of the dreams that the first dream actually comes to
fruition. Finally, having seen the first dream fulfilled with no
effort on his part, he attempts to fulfil the second dream
through his series of elaborate ruses designed to get Benjamin
and Jacob down to Egypt to acknowledge his sovereignty.
Paradoxically this actually *frustrates* its fulfilment. Joseph
succeeds in seeing his eleven brothers accepting his majesty,
but Jacob never does accept it; that element is reversed by
Joseph's prostration before his father. And of course his
mother cannot, for she is dead.

Conclusion

As we have seen, the first dream is fulfilled in 42.6 (and also in
43.26; 44.14 and 50.18). Joseph's elder brothers bow down to
him without his having done anything actively to bring it
about. The second dream is not fulfilled. While one element,
the obeisance of his mother, *cannot* occur, that of his father's
obeisance *could*, but does not occur; only one element, the
prostration of all eleven brothers, is realized. I suggest that the
reason why this dream as a whole fails is that Joseph tried to
make it happen through his playing God with his family
(despite his later protestations, 'Fear not, for am I in the place
of God?' [50.19]). The usual scholarly position on the power of
the dreams is summed up by Brueggemann: 'All sorts of
enemies of the dream try to resist: the brothers, the woman
(chap 39), the famine (chap 41), all resist the dream and fail.

They cannot!'[1] It is true that the active opposition of these foes is overcome; but Joseph's attempted enforcement of the second dream, paradoxically, successfully 'resists' it. I will investigate the relationship between fulfilment and non-fulfilment in the Conclusion when discussing the way in which plot Announcements in general are integrated into their respective narratives.

My conclusions outlined above may be illustrated by ch. 48. In the preamble to his act of blessing, Jacob refers to the death of Rachel (48.7). The precise reason for this reminiscence eludes us.[2] However, Jacob's words, whatever their motivation, reinforce for the readers what they already know. Rachel is dead and cannot bow before Joseph; so this element was always doomed to fail. Another aspect of the dreams comes into focus during the blessing ritual, where Joseph bows before Jacob (48.12). This reverses the first element of the second dream, where father should have bowed to son. In addition, in blessing Joseph first before all the rest of his sons, and giving him preferential treatment ('... I have given to you rather than to your brothers one mountain slope...', 48.22), we see the results of the fulfilment of the first dream, and of the third element of the second: Joseph is superior to his brothers. Thus, this one episode encapsulates the way in which the Announcement of plot has fared: the first dream and third element of the second dream—Joseph's superiority over his brothers—are fulfilled; however, the first two elements of the second dream—obeisance of father and mother—never materialize.

This interpretation of the Joseph story counters the way in which it is usually viewed, as the following representative statements illustrate. Goldingay writes:

> The main theme of the story from Genesis 37–47 is then how Joseph's dream [i.e. both dreams] comes true despite and even through the affliction and humiliation brought about... [by the brothers, Potiphar's wife, etc.].[3]

---

[1] Brueggemann, *Genesis*, p. 301.
[2] For an outline of the various proposals see e.g. Skinner, *Genesis*, pp. 504-505; Westermann, *Genesis 37–50*, p. 186.
[3] Goldingay, 'Patriarchs', p. 11.

Redford asserts that the plot of the story is

> intent... upon showing how despite the inherent improba-
> bility the dreams were literally fulfilled.[1]

Brueggemann believes that Joseph is bound to be
triumphant because not only does he control the food supply
and has knowledge (wisdom), but also,

> He will win because he has had a dream [i.e. both dreams]
> dreamed over him [which results in]... his full triumph
> and his assertion of rule.[2]

The dreams are seen by these writers as having a predestinating power, which I believe is at odds with the way the dreams
are envisaged in the narrative. I believe that these citations
represent a tradition of interpretation which has failed to note
the essential difference between Joseph's two dreams, and
Joseph's relationship to them.[3] Typically, they speak of
Joseph's dream, not his dreams.

Many scholars see divine 'Providence' or 'Sovereignty' as
being a major theological theme of chs. 37–50,[4] and the narrative is usually taken to provide the supreme example in
Genesis of God's will as an irresistible force, as the following
quotations show:

> ... what had been fixed by a celestial decree, was at length,
> in its proper time, carried forward through circuitous
> windings to its completion.[5]

> God's providence and 'hesed'... shape the world of creation
> and his elect people... The entire scheme of history has been
> programmed to serve the high purposes of divinity.[6]

> This divine election is one of the themes of Genesis (cf. Rom
> 9.11ff), and God's design is seen to be no more thwarted by

---

[1] Redford, *Story of Joseph*, p. 69.
[2] Brueggemann, *Genesis*, p. 336.
[3] Cf. Seybold, 'Paradox', p. 59; Miscall, 'Jacob and Joseph Stories',
p. 34.
[4] Cf. Heaton, 'The Joseph Saga', pp. 134-35; von Rad, *Genesis*, p. 439;
Savage, 'Rhetorical Analysis of the Joseph Narrative', pp. 90ff.
[5] Calvin, *Genesis*, 2.260.
[6] McGuire, 'Joseph Story', p. 20. Cf. Baldwin, *Genesis 12–50*, p. 189,
who believes that Joseph's life 'perfectly illustrates the overruling
providence of God'.

the indiscretion of its allies (here Israel and Joseph) than by the malice of its opponents.[1]

If one accepts such a position, then it follows that the narrative of chs. 37–50 presents human activity as being either predestined to conform to God's plans, or as being irrelevant in the light of God's guaranteed success.

This all-sufficiency of divine sovereignty makes human action almost irrelevant (cf. Prov. 21.30).[2]

It [chs. 37–50] urges that in the contingencies of history, the purposes of God are at work in hidden and unnoticed ways. But the ways of God are nonetheless reliable and will come to fruition... the main point is that the ways of God are at work, regardless of human attitudes or actions...
... this story takes a high view of God, so high that human action is declared irrelevant.[3]

Yahweh is wholly free to dispose of the issue as he will. What then remains for man to do?... According to this doctrine, all earthly events are subject to a law which is wholly beyond the grasp of the human mind.[4]

If all this were true, we would be forced to agree with Redford's conclusion that

God had manipulated the principals of the drama like so many marionettes.[5]

However, I do not believe that such conclusions do justice to the entirety of the story of Jacob's family.[6] They ignore

[1] Kidner, *Genesis*, p. 180.
[2] Von Rad, *Genesis*, p. 438. Cf. White, 'The Joseph Story', p. 67: 'The dream system is thus incorporated into a larger deterministic, mystical perspective which virtually negates the meaning of the conscious intentions of the brothers'.
[3] Brueggemann, *Genesis*, p. 289.
[4] Von Rad, 'The Joseph Narrative', p. 298. Cf. White, 'The Joseph Story', p. 60, who suggests that the dreams articulate 'an ideology of fate by suggesting to the characters that their lives are determined in advance by transcendent forces beyond their comprehension'.
[5] Redford, *Story of Joseph*, p. 74. Cf. Humphreys, *Joseph and his Family*, p. 128: 'We do not suddenly discover at the end that we have been an audience in some grand puppet show staged by a divine puppeteer', because the characters have made real choices.
[6] For an interesting discussion of the concept of providence in the OT,

entirely the fact that the second dream, which reveals God's will as much as the first, does not come to fruition. This makes it impossible to talk of its aspirations as being 'fixed by a celestial decree' or of the scheme of history as being 'programmed'. In addition, if it is possible to sustain my suggestion that the reason why such divine plans are thwarted is due at least in part to Joseph's actions, then human activity cannot be dismissed as being 'almost' or actually 'irrelevant'.

The scholarly positions presented above, against which I have been arguing, usually appeal to the 'key texts' 45.5, 'And now do not be distressed, or angry with yourselves, because you sold me here; for God sent me before you to preserve life', and 50.20, 'As for you, you meant evil against me; but God meant it for good...' These sentences are not to be taken, as they are so often, as predestinarian theologoumena; within their context they are addressed to the brothers by Joseph, and simply confirm a point presented in previous ancestral stories, that attempts to thwart God's purpose merely speed its triumph. I do not see 45.5 and 50.20 as stating that God's plans succeed regardless of any human activity. They say nothing of Joseph's attempts to fulfil God's plan in his own way. This shows us that divine providence is essentially 'reciprocal'; that is, the degree of success it enjoys is related to the type of activity humans engage in when responding to its dictates. While it may succeed in reaction to human opposition, or in sympathy with human inability or despite apathy, it cannot be fulfilled if humanity attempts to take matters into its own hands and tries to force the issue. Such human strategies lead to the frustration of providence. If this is indeed the nature of divine providence presented by chs. 37–50, then the 'predestinarian' model usually accepted by interpreters of this narrative needs to be reassessed.

---

which takes Gen. 45.5-8 and 50.20 as its starting point, see Rogerson, 'Doctrine of Providence', pp. 529-43. He concludes that 'the Old Testament writers [did not] believe in history as a process, with a goal towards which God was guiding it' (p. 542).

The Abrahamic Announcement in the Story of Jacob's Family

1. *Nationhood*

With the fate of Joseph's dreams providing the main interest, the development of the nationhood promise is not at the forefront of this story; nevertheless the events presented in chs. 37–50 obviously relate to it in a number of ways. On the broader scale, the famine which hits Canaan threatens the future of the ancestral family, but Joseph's presence in Egypt guarantees its survival (though this outcome is seen only when one comes to the end of the story). At the outset matters do not seem to be so promising, with the conspiracy of the brothers to kill Joseph threatening to reduce Jacob's progeny by one. Joseph's eventual sale into slavery is only one degree better than this.

However, despite this unpromising start, the reader is given a number of glimpses into ways in which the progeny promise survives and grows. The information that Judah marries a Canaanite woman, resulting in offspring (38.2-5), bodes well, but is complicated in ways which require an unusual solution. The sin of Er (whatever it was) results in his premature death before begetting any progeny. Onan's contraceptive practice (38.9) obviously stifles fertility, and his despatch by Yahweh compounds the problem, leaving Judah with only one son. Nevertheless, the increase of this one branch of the ancestral family is continued through a remarkable example of female scheming (38.12ff.).

Joseph marries in exile and has two sons but it is Jacob's journey to Egypt which provides the occasion for the most explicit connections with the progeny promise. First, God appears to him in a night vision, assuring him that 'I will there make of you a great nation' (46.3). No sooner has this assurance been given than a full catalogue of the ancestral family is given (46.8-27), showing exactly how much progress has already been made toward becoming a 'great nation'. Considering the inordinate length of time it took Abraham to produce one son acceptable to Yahweh, this list of seventy souls makes comparatively impressive reading. In addition, once in the land of Goshen the reader is informed that they 'were fruitful and multiplied exceedingly' (47.27). The further reminder of the promise given at Bethel (48.4; cf. 28.14; 35.11), together with Jacob's blessing on Joseph's sons (48.16b, 19) predicting further increase, adds to the impression that while Abraham's progeny have not yet become a 'great nation' in their own right, by the end of Genesis that prospect seems at least a possibility.

2. Land

In contrast, the land promise does not fare so well. At the beginning we receive the reassuring though not spectacular statement that Jacob lived within Canaan (37.1). However, the main thrust of the plot from that point onward is in showing how first Joseph and then all of the family eventually migrate to Egypt. In addition, the famine which comes to Canaan marks it out as an undesirable place in which to live. The family is given a new land by no less a personage than Pharaoh himself (47.6), but this royal generosity does not hide the fact that this is not the land promised by Yahweh. (Ironically, they are *given* a land outside of Canaan, while the only possession they have in Canaan is a burial plot which had to be *bought*.) This explains why Jacob, ever the one to recognize a good bargain, prefers to live in Goshen, but be interred in Canaan. Despite Jacob's choice of burial place, the funeral entourage returns from Canaan and we are told quite baldly that 'Joseph dwelt in Egypt, he and his father's house' (50.22). So with the exception of the deceased Jacob, the entire ancestral family now lives in exile. And at this point the reader is confronted by an intriguing question. Why did the brothers and Joseph remain in Egypt even after the famine had ended? Jacob lived in Egypt for seventeen years before his death (47.29; cf. v. 28); but as we know from Joseph's dreams, the famine lasted for only seven years. Did Jacob remain because Yahweh had promised him that there he would make of him a great nation (46.3)? In order for the nationhood promise to be fulfilled, does the land promise have to be postponed, and if so, for what reason? Such questions are not answered in Genesis, but form part of the unfinished agenda carried over into Exodus and beyond.

3. *Blessing*

The two main characters, Joseph and Jacob, act in ways which see the third element of the Abrahamic Announcement—being a blessing—brought once again to the reader's attention. Apart from the discord he causes at home, Joseph appears to be a blessing to all he meets: to Potiphar's household (39.4ff.); to the keeper of the prison (39.21-23); to Pharaoh (41.46ff.); to the Egyptians (41.56); and eventually to the whole earth (41.57). Having dispensed his blessing to all and sundry in exile it comes as a shock to see him being anything but a blessing when he meets his brothers, by putting them through such a severe trial (42.9ff.), and by subjecting his old father to psychological torture (43.26), although in the end, once Joseph's elaborate plots to secure the fulfilment of the second dream fail, he does dispense material blessing to Jacob and his family (45.10ff.).

Joseph's relationship to the Egyptians is more complex. Through his agricultural policy Joseph does save the lives of the Egyptians, but does so at a price—their enslavement (47.13ff.).

As for Jacob, in his old age he appears to have become more generous with blessings. In being ushered into Pharaoh's presence, Jacob blesses him (47.7). Previously Jacob has either received blessings, or failing that, stolen them. Never before has Jacob *given* a blessing. Yet he still cannot resist the temptation of standing usual expectations in this area on their heads by inverting the expected blessings on Manasseh and Ephraim (48.9ff.). And finally, the 'blessings' (cf. 49.28) he pronounces on his sons (49.1ff.) are a strange mixture of positive (49.8-13, 20-26), negative (49.3-7, 13) and a balance between the two (49.14-15, 19).

By the end of Genesis, therefore, the three main elements of the Abrahamic Announcement have fared differently. The nationhood promise has not been fulfilled, but at least it is on its way to fulfilment with seventy people in Goshen being fruitful and multiplying. The land promise is much more problematical. The entire ancestral family are in exile, while Abraham, Isaac and Jacob lie in their graves in Canaan. They have not given up the vision of the land, however, for Joseph promises his exiled brothers that 'God will visit you, and you shall carry

up my bones from here' (50.25). Nevertheless, one cannot but
contemplate the cyclical route that the land promise has
taken. The ancestral story began with the call of Abraham in
Haran; it concludes with his descendants in a similar
situation, outside of the land of promise.

The issue of being a blessing develops in a complex way.
Joseph is eventually a blessing to his family, but one is left
wondering whether his hand was forced on this issue as he
saw the plans for the enforcement of his dreams disintegrat-
ing before him. To the Egyptians he is a blessing, but only in
the sense that losing one's freedom is preferable to dying of
starvation. And Jacob pronounces blessings, albeit of a highly
unorthodox kind, inverting the rights of primogeniture in the
case of Manasseh and Ephraim, and dispensing to his sons
'blessings' in which the negative outweighs the positive.

CONCLUSION

A summary of the way in which the Announcements of
Genesis govern the plots of their respective narratives shows
that they struggle to translate themselves into reality. In the
primaeval history the command to be fruitful, multiply and fill
the earth makes slow progress, but is at least on the way to
success by the end of this section even though interest has
narrowed down to Terah's three sons and to Abraham in particular—whose wife is barren. This comparative success is
achieved despite opposition from factors such as painful
childbirth and universal death. The two remaining elements
do not fare so well. The command to 'subdue' the earth is
effectively eliminated altogether. Yahweh's curse on the
ground (3.17-19) renders it impossible to fulfil absolutely; the
earth will always successfully resist total human domination.
This is demonstrated in the cosmic upheaval of the Deluge in
which humans succumb to the ferocity of the earth and also in
common death, where humans return to the ground from
which they were made. The absence of this element from the
post-Deluge edict (8.21–9.7) suggests that Yahweh has eliminated it as a requirement. The imperative to have dominion
over the animals has a more complex development. The
limited dominion granted to humans in ch. 1, which denied
them the right to kill animals for food, degenerates into a situation where animals will stand in 'fear and dread' of
humans, and may be consumed for human sustenance (9.3).
Yet the curse of 3.14-15 indicates that humans will not exert
this despotism effortlessly over the entire animal kingdom.

The Abraham story derives much of its interest from the
way in which the progeny/nationhood promise progresses.
This element is itself a continuation of the 'multiplication'
motif of the primaeval history. Despite the problems Abraham
experiences in understanding the exact focus of this promise,

by Abraham's death a son through whom the future great nation will be generated is on the scene, with an acceptable wife—though like her mother-in-law she too is barren (25.21). Therefore, while this element does not see any spectacular success, at least it remains viable. The promise of land possession (as it eventually becomes) similarly remains on the agenda but has hardly moved forward at all—apart from possession of a grave and a well and knowing *which* land will be given *to his descendants*, the land promise remains exactly that—a promise. By contrast, the command to Abraham to 'be a blessing' is an almost unmitigated disaster. Abraham does next to nothing to bless anyone, but prefers to look after his own interests. When the Abrahamic Announcement is traced through to the end of the book, we see the nationhood promise making steady, though not spectacular progress; in Egypt the seventy members of the ancestral family form the nucleus for the future potential nation. Unfortunately, the land, though still promised, has been abandoned by these same people in favour of a higher standard of living in Egypt. Yet Yahweh, who approves of the emigration, and has even engineered it, also promises that one day they will return to possess Canaan. So the land promise remains tied up with their destiny. Yet despite such evidences of Yahweh's involvement with the ancestral family, the patriarchs as a whole remain almost as resistant as Abraham to the command to 'be a blessing'.

The Announcement prefacing the Jacob story is developed in a subtle way. While Jacob's lordship over his brother is simply negated (with Jacob's own words reversing the proposed relationship), the other elements exert their influence on the narrative in a more complex manner. The blessing of fertility and prosperity (the latest modification of the 'multiplication' and 'nationhood' motifs of the previous cycles), comes to Jacob as predicted, yet also to Esau—countering the prediction of distinction between the two. The equality between the two brothers on this point effectively negates the intention of the Announcement. In an even subtler move the prediction of division between the two parties is fulfilled, but in a way not guessed at by the reader. Division caused by strife (our expectation) is converted into separation within reconciliation.

The story of Jacob's family presents a seemingly simple picture of two dreams, of which the first is fulfilled and the second (taken as one unit) is not. However, this narrative probably raises more questions regarding the reasons for the failure of its Announcement as a whole to become reality than any of the others.

It is quite clear from reviewing this evidence that individual elements of the Announcements exert their influence on the plot of Genesis in several different ways. Only one element— Joseph's first dream—seems to be fulfilled to the letter, and is the only element which might legitimately be seen as predestinating subsequent events. Other elements also exert their influence strongly, but in a modified form from that which was announced at the outset. Human dominion over animals, and the separation and fertility/prosperity elements of the Jacob story would be included in this category. Other elements may be seen as enjoying qualified success, inching their way to fulfilment, but certainly not dominating the plot as predeterminators of action; among these would be the Abrahamic land motif. Some evolve during the book: the prime example of this is the 'multiplication' motif of the primaeval history which is modified into the progeny/nationhood promise to Abraham and continued in the prediction of fertility/prosperity to Jacob. Others evolve within individual narrative blocks, for instance the land element in the Abraham story. Perhaps most importantly some elements are negated. Each of the Announcements prefacing the four narrative blocks of Genesis contains one element which simply fails to assert itself. In the primaeval history, it is the command to subdue the earth; in the Abrahamic Announcement, the command to be a blessing; in the Jacob story, it is Esau's subservience to Jacob; and with Joseph, his second dream is never converted into reality. Taken as a whole, therefore, the Genesis Announcements seem to have an unpredictable relationship to the narratives they purport to govern. Can any reason for this be found?

Having come to the end of Genesis, the reader can observe a paradoxical relationship between human activity on the one hand and the fulfilment of individual elements of the Announcements on the other. This is seen most clearly in the ancestral narratives. For example, the Abraham story presents a series of initiatives taken by Abraham of which many, though understandable and 'justifiable' at the time, place obstacles in the way of the Announcement of 12.1-3. These include his taking of Lot despite being told to leave his kindred (12.1, cf. v. 4); his pretence on two occasions that Sarah is his sister (12.10-20; 20.1-17); agreeing to Sarah's scheme which results in the birth of Ishmael, etc. It is not without significance that God's command to Abraham which threatens the life of the son of promise (22.2) meets with Abraham's utter resignation. He travels to the appointed spot, places his son on the altar, but at the last minute God changes his mind, and at the same time announces 'because you have done this... I will indeed bless you, and I will multiply your descendants as the stars of heaven and as the sand which is on the seashore' (22.16, 17). Abraham's initiatives had previously placed the promise under threat; his unquestioning, passive obedience has now confirmed its permanence. The difference between Abraham's two relationships to the Announcement (and its later modifications) is not simply a matter of disobedience versus obedience. It is a matter of inventing schemes to fulfil what God has promised as opposed to resigning himself not only to the promise but also to God's way of achieving it. (Yet it is precisely at this point that the reader feels sympathy for some of the characters. Many of the actions taken by characters which are later revealed to be inappropriate can be explained by Yahweh's habit of not clarifying the exact nature of the Announcement at the outset. For example, the way in which the promise that Abraham will become the father of a great nation will be fulfilled goes through several stages of clarification before Abraham knows exactly what Yahweh has in mind. It is this aspect which complicates the task of knowing whether Announcements are successful or not, i.e. whether an Announcement in its original form or as it is later clarified or modified is exerting its influence.)

The story of Jacob's family repeats these dynamics seen in the Abraham story. Chapters 37–50 fall into two distinct sections when we investigate the relationship between Joseph's active initiatives and apathetic inactivity. At the outset, apart from the opening verses of ch. 37, Joseph is the passive, used individual: i.e. he is 'sent' (37.13); 'stripped' (37.23); 'taken' and 'cast' into the pit (37.24); 'sold' (37.26), etc. The vast majority of verbs in chs. 37–41 which are associated with Joseph have him as their object rather than subject. When he is not passive, his activity does not relate in any self-conscious way to the fulfilment of the dreams. However, from ch. 42 onwards, Joseph takes the initiative: he 'sells' (42.6); 'treats' and 'speaks' roughly to his brothers (42.7ff.); 'puts' his brothers in prison (42.17ff.), etc. I have tried to demonstrate that the first dream is fulfilled during his 'passive' phase and the second frustrated during his 'active' phase. This perspective gives added irony to Joseph's statement to his brothers, 'Fear not, for am I in the place of God?' (50.19). In his attempt to manipulate events so that the divine dream would come to fruition, he had indeed put himself in the place of God. However, he was forcefully reminded of his humanity with the disintegration of his ambition. Also, we must not forget that Joseph's brothers' attempts to counter the Announcement actually facilitate the fulfilment of the first dream.

These dynamics may be expressed by the following formula: human attempts to frustrate the Announcements tend to fulfil them; human attempts to fulfil the Announcements tend to frustrate them. This is clearly presented by some of the material in the Abraham and Joseph narratives but can also be plausibly suggested as a perspective on the Jacob story. Jacob, like his grandfather and son, attempts to *make* the divine oracle happen through deceiving his father over the blessing and taking advantage of his brother over the birthright. Just as Abraham's initiatives (worthy or not) do not facilitate the promise of progeny, and Joseph's elaborate charade is counter-productive in getting the second dream to convert its imagery into reality, so, I would suggest, it is precisely *because* of Jacob's efforts to secure his destiny as lord that he actually becomes the servant. Jacob's own words suggest his recognition that despite being the 'blessed', the blessing received through deceitful human initiative has turned out to be a curse: 'Few and evil have been the days of my life' (47.9). This is the very reverse of the suggestion that 'subsequent

"deceptions" [by the patriarchs] will not negate the promise'.[1]
The implication of all of this is that the Announcements would
have had a better chance of fulfilment if the human characters had done less to attempt to fulfil them and allowed
Yahweh to do more.

The dynamics of paradox, however, do not explain all of the
problems associated with translating the aspirations of the
Announcements into reality. God himself seems to place
impediments in the way of the Announcements being fulfilled.
These impediments fall into two broad categories; those which
exist from the outset, and those introduced at a later stage by
Yahweh. The former raise doubts in the mind of the reader
and challenge the faith of the characters (e.g. the reversal of
primogeniture in the stories of Jacob and Jacob's family). The
latter make the reader question whether Yahweh has
abandoned his original intentions outlined in the Announcement (e.g. the curses of 3.14-19). These latter kinds of impediments enter the narrative largely as responses to human
actions. Some Announcements which seem plausible at the
outset become seemingly less so because of later divine modifications or amplifications (e.g. the promise of a son to Abraham
and Sarah [as it is finally defined] is inherently less likely than
Abraham, through some means, becoming the father of a
great nation).

Actually only three aspects of the Announcements which
present *inherent* difficulties remain unfulfilled. In the Jacob
Announcement it is that Esau should serve Jacob, and in the
Joseph Announcement that first his father, and secondly his
mother should bow down to him. But even here, I have suggested above that the dynamics of paradox may well explain
why the first two of these three aspects do not occur.

However, it is Yahweh's subsequent actions which have a
far greater effect in deciding whether Announcements
succeed or fail. This is seen most clearly in the primaeval history. Yahweh's responses to human disobedience in ch.3 have
far-reaching effects on the Announcement of 1.28. The curse
on the serpent, while not negating human dominion over
animals, gives notice that humans will not wield that domin-

[1] Martens, *Plot and Purpose*, p. 32.

ion effortlessly over all creatures. The curse on the Woman does not negate the command to multiply, but makes it a less attractive proposition to women. But the curse on the earth has far more ramifications. The earth becomes far less tameable and a much less hospitable environment in which the Man may exert his dominion—indeed the earth will successfully resist and receive the Man in death. This last point is confirmed by Yahweh's decision to omit the subjugation of the earth from his post-Deluge edict. He has decided to annul this element.

There is one recurring element which seems to attract Yahweh's solicitous attention more than any of the others. The 'multiplication' motif which appears in various forms—the command 'be fruitful, multiply and fill the earth' (1.28); the progeny/nationhood promise of 12.1-3; the fertility/ prosperity promise of Isaac's blessings. All of these are challenged, but in each case Yahweh acts to facilitate their fulfilment. Admittedly, Yahweh's 'help' in the primaeval history amounts to no more than an amelioration of the curse he himself has placed on the Woman: that is, although she will experience pain in procreating, her 'desire will be for her husband'. Thus, human multiplication will not cease just because it has become less enjoyable. In the ancestral stories the major impediment to reproduction is the barrenness of generations of matriarchs (bearing in mind that Sarah's barrenness is only revealed to be a problem after Yahweh's announcement of the necessity of her maternity in ch. 18). Yahweh systematically, though not immediately, removes these problems by granting conception to Sarah, Rebekah and Rachel. One receives the impression that *this* element *must* succeed. Other aspects can be abandoned or modified but Yahweh must keep faith with this aspect or the Genesis story would end in utter nihilism.

In the final analysis, I must conclude that the Announcements are misleading indicators of how the plot of Genesis will develop. Too many other factors impinge on the narrative for these to be taken as predetermining plot. A great deal depends on how Yahweh relates to the Announcements; whether he is willing to persevere with an individual element (e.g. human multiplication), or is willing to annul it (e.g. human subjugation of the earth or Esau serving Jacob), or modify it (e.g. dominion over animals or the separation of Jacob and Esau). The development of the Announcements in Genesis does not present Yahweh as predetermining from the outset what his creatures will do. Commands may be disobeyed—and often are. In addition, promises may be modified and curses reversed. Announcements may be seen as declarations of Yahweh's initial intention—what Yahweh would *like* to happen—but no more than that. A great irony arises from the recognition of this fact. The Announcements give the impression to the first-time reader that Yahweh will be in total control of the story. But the stories reveal that humans just as often call the tune. In the majority of cases it is their actions which result in Yahweh's modifications and negations. Whether a divine Announcement governs its narrative or not depends to a large extent, not on Yahweh forcing it through, or systematically overcoming all opposition, but on how humans behave.

My conclusions indicate that Genesis is a sophisticated piece of literature. The way the Announcements are integrated into the narrative constitutes a warning to readers not to place faith in seemingly authoritative statements, but to read with caution, carefully and questioningly. The book delights in teasing its readers, forcing us to read the text closely to see what is *actually* happening and not, like many commentators, just taking statements, even divine statements, at face value. (The prediction that Joseph's mother will bow down to him is the prime example of this. Its impossibility makes it the book's ultimate misleading indicator of plot development.) As we have seen, the plot of the Genesis stories is not predetermined by the Announcements, but neither is it completely open-ended. While plots do not simply show an enactment of the agenda presented in the Announcements they do develop in some relationship to them. Sometimes the correlation between the two is that of modification or even negation; rarely is it that of fulfilment.

There is here, therefore, no high view of divine providence. The plot confirms or denies individual elements of the Announcements for a variety of reasons—not always easily discernible. This conclusion counters the way in which most commentators view most of the Announcements. Of course, by no means all scholars see every Announcement as moving smoothly toward its fulfilment. In the Abraham story in particular it is difficult to deny the tension between promise and fulfilment, and such views have been noted in the chapters above. What I hope to have demonstrated in this study is that *none* of the Announcements 'guarantees and effects the hoped-for success',[1] is 'fixed by a celestial decree'[2] or demonstrates that the 'entire scheme of history has been programmed to serve the high purposes of divinity'.[3] Not one demonstrates that 'everything is carefully orchestrated by Yahweh: all works out in the end...'[4] or that Yahweh's 'will cannot be frustrated by any circumstances'.[5] The story of Genesis is certainly not 'the story of the fulfillment of the divine promises of blessing'.[6] These may be the expectations of the first time reader who could be forgiven for assuming that what is *supposed* to happen will actually happen. However, a close reading of Genesis disabuses one of that notion. The power exerted by the Announcements on the plot is far more complex, and far more interesting, than that.

---

[1] Wenham, *Genesis 1–15*, p. 24.

[2] Calvin, *Genesis*, 2.260.

[3] McGuire, 'Joseph Story', p. 20, commenting on the Joseph story.

[4] Miscall, 'Jacob and Joseph Stories', p. 33, commenting on the Jacob and Joseph stories.

[5] Brueggemann, 'Kerygma of Priestly Writers', p. 401. (This comment is limited to the position of 1.28 in the so-called 'P' tradition.) Cf. Sarna, *Understanding Genesis*, p. 104, who makes similar comments regarding the nationhood and land promises of the Abraham cycle. Numerous similar comments could be referred to, some of which have been cited in the main chapters above.

[6] Wenham, *Genesis 1–15*, p. 24.

BIBLIOGRAPHY

Aalders, G. Ch. *Genesis*. 2 vols. Bible Student's Commentary. Trans. W. Heynen, Grand Rapids: Zondervan, 1981.

Aberbach, Moses and Bernard Grossfeld (eds.). *Targum Onkelos to Genesis*. New York: Ktav, 1982.

Ackerman, James S. 'Joseph, Judah, and Jacob', *LIBN* 2: 85-113.

Ahroni, Reuben. 'Why did Esau Spurn the Birthright? A Study in Biblical Interpretation', *Judaism* 29 (1980): 323-31.

Aland, Kurt et al. (eds.). *The Greek New Testament*. 3rd edn. London: United Bible Societies, 1975.

Alexander, T. Desmond. 'Genesis 22 and the Covenant of Circumcision', *JSOT* 25 (1983): 17-22.

—*A Literary Analysis of the Abraham Narrative in Genesis*. Unpublished Ph.D. Thesis, University of Belfast, 1982.

—'Lot's Hospitality: A Clue to His Righteousness', *JBL* 104 (1985): 289-91.

Alter, Robert. *The Art of Biblical Narrative*. London: George Allen and Unwin, 1981.

—'Joseph and His Brothers', *Commentary* (November, 1980): 59-69.

Anbar, Moshe. 'Genesis 15: A Conflation of Two Deuteronomic Narratives', *JBL* 101 (1982): 39-55.

Andersen, Francis I. *The Sentence in Biblical Hebrew*. The Hague/Paris: Mouton, 1974.

Anderson, Bernhard W. 'Creation and Ecology', in B.W. Anderson (ed.), *Creation in the Old Testament*. Philadelphia/London: Fortress/SPCK, 1984, pp. 152-71.

—'From Analysis to Synthesis: The Interpretation of Genesis 1–11', *JBL* 97 (1978): 23-39.

—'Human Dominion over Nature', in M. Ward (ed.), *Biblical Studies in Contemporary Thought*. Somerville, Massachusetts: Greeno, Hadden & Co., 1975, pp. 27-45.

—'Unity and Diversity in God's Creation: A Study of the Babel Story', *CurrThM* 5 (1978): 69-81.

Asselin, David Tobin. 'The Notion of Dominion in Genesis 1–3', *CBQ* 16 (1954): 277-94.

Auffret, Pierre. 'Essai sur la structure littéraire de Gn 12,1-4aα', *BZ* 26 (1982): 243-48.

Baldwin, Joyce G. *The Message of Genesis 12–50: From Abraham to Joseph*. Leicester: Inter-Varsity Press, 1986.

Bar-Efrat, S. 'Some Observations on the Analysis of Structure in Biblical Narrative', *VT* 30 (1980): 154-73.

Bartlett, J.R. 'The Brotherhood of Edom', *JSOT* 4 (1977): 2-27.

Berg, Werner. 'Der Sündenfall Abrahams und Saras nach Gen 16,1-6', *BN* 19 (1982): 7-14.

—'Nochmals: Ein Sündenfall Abrahams—der erste—in Gen 12,10-20', *BN* 21 (1983): 7-15.

Bergman, Jan and Magnus Ottosson. *"erets'*, *TDOT* 1:388-405.

—and G.J. Botterweck. *'Chālam; ch*ͣ*lôm'*, *TDOT* 4:421-32.

Berlin, Adele. *Poetics and Interpretation of Biblical Narrative*. Sheffield: Almond, 1983.

Bledstein, Adrien Janis. 'The Trials of Sarah', *Judaism* 30 (1981): 411-17.

Blenkinsopp, Joseph. 'Abraham and the Righteous of Sodom', *JJS* 33 (1982): 119-32.

—'Biographical Patterns in Biblical Narrative', *JSOT* 20 (1981): 27-46.

Boomershine, Thomas E. 'The Structure of Narrative Rhetoric in Genesis 2–3', *Semeia* 18 (1980): 113-29.

Bright, John. *Covenant and Promise*. London: SCM, 1977.

Brown, Francis, S.R. Driver, and Charles Briggs. *A Hebrew and English Lexicon of the Old Testament*. Oxford: Clarendon, 1959.

Brueggemann, Walter. *Genesis: A Biblical Commentary for Teaching and Preaching*. Atlanta: John Knox, 1982.

—'The Kerygma of the Priestly Writers', *ZAW* 84 (1972): 397-414.

—'Kingship and Chaos: (A Study in Tenth Century Theology)', *CBQ* 33 (1971): 317-32.

—'A Shape for Old Testament Theology, II: Embrace of Pain', *CBQ* 47 (1985): 395-415.

Burney, C.F. *Notes on the Hebrew Text of the Books of Kings*. Oxford: Clarendon, 1903.

Burns, Dan E. 'Dream Form in Genesis 2.4b–3.24: Asleep in the Garden', *JSOT* 37 (1987): 3-14.

Calvin, John. *A Commentary on Genesis*. 2 vols. Trans. J. King, London: Banner of Truth Trust, 1965.

Cassuto, U. *A Commentary on the Book of Genesis*. 2 vols. Trans. I. Abrahams, Jerusalem: Magnes, 1964.

—'The Episode of the Sons of God and the Daughters of Man. (Genesis vi 1-4)', in *Biblical and Oriental Studies*. Trans. I. Abrahams, Jerusalem: Magnes, 1973, 1:17-28.

Cazelles, Henri. 'Connexions et structure de Gen., XV', *RB* 69 (1962): 321-49.

Chatman, Seymour. *Story and Discourse: Narrative Structure in Fiction and Film*. Ithaca/London: Cornell University Press, 1978.

Chauvin, Jacques. 'Une série pour l'année Luther', *EThR* 58 (1983): 221-31.

Chertok, Haim. 'The Life and Death of Abram the Doubter', *Judaism* 33 (1984): 458-64.

Chew, Hiang Chea. *The Theme of 'Blessing for the Nations' in the Patriarchal Narratives of Genesis*. Unpublished Ph.D. Thesis, University of Sheffield, 1982.

Childs, Brevard S. *Introduction to the Old Testament as Scripture*. Philadelphia: Fortress, 1979.

—*Myth and Reality in the Old Testament*. 2nd edn. London: SCM, 1962.

Clark, W.M. 'The Flood and the Structure of the Pre-Patriarchal History', *ZAW* 83 (1971): 184-211.

Clements, R.E. *Abraham and David: Genesis XV and its Meaning for Israelite Tradition*. London: SCM, 1967.

—' יֹג, gôy', *TDOT* 2:426-33.

Clines, David J.A. 'The Ancestor in Danger: But Not the Same Danger', in *What Does Eve Do to Help? and other Readerly Questions to the Old Testament*. JSOTS 94, Sheffield: JSOT Press, 1990, pp. 67-84.

—The Significance of the "Sons of God" Episode (Genesis 6:1-4) in the Context of the "Primeval History" (Genesis 1–11)', *JSOT* 13 (1979): 33-46.

—*The Theme of the Pentateuch*. JSOTS 10, Sheffield: JSOT, 1978.

—'The Theology of the Flood Narrative', *Faith and Thought* 100 (1972-73): 128-42.

—'What does Eve do to Help? and Other Irredeemably Androcentric Orientations in Genesis 1–3', in *What Does Eve Do to Help? and other Readerly Questions to the Old Testament*. JSOTS 94, Sheffield: JSOT Press, 1990, pp. 25-48.

—'What Happens in Genesis', in *What Does Eve Do to Help? and other Readerly Questions to the Old Testament*. JSOTS 94, Sheffield: JSOT Press, 1990, pp. 49-66.

Coats, George W. 'Abraham's Sacrifice of Faith. A Form-Critical Study of Genesis 22', *Interpretation* 27 (1973): 389-400.

—'The Curse in God's Blessing: Gen 12,1-4a in the Structure and Theology of the Yahwist', in J. Jeremias, and L. Perlitt (eds.), *Die Botschaft und die Boten*. Neukirchen-Vluyn: Neukirchener Verlag, 1981, pp. 31-41.

—*From Canaan to Egypt: Structural and Theological Context for the Joseph Story*. CBQMS 4, Washington, D.C.: The Catholic Biblical Association of America, 1976.

—*Genesis: With an Introduction to Narrative Literature*. Grand Rapids: Eerdmans, 1983.

—'The God of Death: Power and Obedience in the Primeval History', *Interpretation* 29 (1975): 227-39.

—'The Joseph Story and Ancient Wisdom', *CBQ* 35 (1973): 285-97.

—'Lot: A Foil in the Abraham Saga', in J.T. Butler, et al. (eds.), *Understanding the Word: Essays in Honor of Bernhard W. Anderson*. JSOTS 37, Sheffield: JSOT Press, 1985, pp. 113-32.

—'Redactional Unity in Genesis 37-50', *JBL* 93 (1974): 15-21.

—'Strife and Reconciliation: Themes of a Biblical Theology in the Book of Genesis', *HorBibTh* 2 (1980): 15-37.

—'Strife Without Reconciliation: A Theme in the Jacob Traditions', in Rainer Albertz et al. (eds.), *Werden und Wirken des Alten Testaments*. Göttingen: Vandenhoeck & Ruprecht, 1980, pp. 82-106.

Cohen, Norman, J. 'Two that are One—Sibling Rivalry in Genesis', *Judaism* 32 (1983): 331-42.

Cohn, Robert L. 'Narrative Structure and Canonical Perspective in Genesis', *JSOT* 25 (1983): 3-16.

Combs, Eugene. 'The Political Teaching of Genesis I–XI', in E.A. Livingstone (ed.), *Studia Biblica 1978: I. Papers on Old Testament and Related Themes*. JSOTS 11, Sheffield: JSOT Press, 1979, pp. 105-10.

Couffignal, Robert. 'La tour de Babel. Approches nouvelles de Genèse xi, 1-9', *RevTh* 83 (1983): 59-70.

Crenshaw, J.L. 'Method in Determining Wisdom Influence upon "Historical" Literature', *JBL* 88 (1969): 129-42.

—'Journey into Oblivion: A Structural Analysis of Gen. 22:1-19', *Soundings* 58 (1975): 243-56.

—'Popular Questioning of the Justice of God in Ancient Israel', *ZAW* 82 (1970): 380-95.

Dahlberg, Bruce T. 'On Recognizing the Unity of Genesis', *ThD* 24 (1976): 360-67.

Davidson, A.B. *An Introductory Hebrew Grammar*. Revised by John Mauchline. 26th edn. Edinburgh: T. & T. Clark, 1966.

Davies, G. Henton. 'Vows', *IDB* 4:792-93.

Dequeker, L. '"Green Herbage and Trees Bearing Fruit" (Gen. 1:28-30; 9:1-3)', *Bijdragen* 38 (1977): 118-27.

—'Noah and Israel. The Everlasting Divine Covenant with Mankind', in C. Brekelmans (ed.), *Questions disputées d'Ancien Testament: Méthode et théologie*. Bibliotheca Ephemeridum Theologicarum Lovaniensum 33, Gembloux: Leuven University Press, 1974, pp. 115-29.

—'La vocation d'Abraham', in P.M. Bogaert, et al. (eds.), *Abraham dans la Bible et dans la tradition juive*. Brussels: Institutum Iudaicum, 1977, pp. 1-32.

Driver, S.R. *The Book of Genesis*. 10th edn. London: Methuen, 1916.

—*A Treatise on the Use of the Tenses in Hebrew*. Oxford: Clarendon, 1892.

Dumbrell, W.J. 'The Covenant with Abraham', *RefThR* 38 (1982): 42-50.

Duncan, Roger. 'Adam and the Ark', *Encounter* 37 (1976): 189-97.

Eslinger, Lyle. 'A Contextual Identification of the *bene ha'elohim* and *benoth ha'adam* in Genesis 6:1-4', *JSOT* 13 (1979): 65-73.

Fishbane, Michael. 'Composition and Structure in the Jacob Cycle (Gen. 25:19–35:22)', *JJS* 26 (1975): 15-38.

—'Genesis 2:4b–11:32: The Primeval Cycle', in *Text and Texture: Close Readings of Selected Biblical Texts*. New York: Schocken, 1979, pp. 17-39.

Foh, Susan T. 'What is the Woman's Desire?', *WestThJ* 37 (1975): 376-83.

Fokkelman, J.P. *Narrative Art in Genesis: Specimens of Stylistic and Structural Analysis*. Assen/Amsterdam: Van Gorcum, 1975.

Forster, E.M. *Aspects of the Novel*. Harmondsworth: Penguin, 1962.

Fretheim, Terence E. *Creation, Fall, and Flood*. Minneapolis: Augsburg, 1969.

—'The Jacob Traditions: Theology and Hermeneutic', *Interpretation* 26 (1972): 419-36.

Fritsch, Charles T. '"God was with him": A Theological Study of the Joseph Narrative', *Interpretation* 9 (1955): 21-34.

Fritz, Volkmar. '"Solange die Erde steht"—Vom Sinn der jahwistischen Fluterzählung in Gen 6–8', *ZAW* 94 (1982): 599-614.

Gammie, John G. 'Theological Interpretation by Way of Literary and Tradition Analysis: Genesis 25–36', in Martin J. Buss (ed.), *Encounter with the Text: Form and History in the Hebrew Bible*. Philadelphia/ Missoula, Montana: Fortress/Scholars, 1979, pp. 117-34.

Gaston, Lloyd. 'Abraham and the Righteousness of God', *HorBibTh* 2 (1980): 39-68.

Genesis Rabbah. Trans. H. Freedman, London: Soncino, 1939.

Gibson, John C.L. *Genesis*. 2 vols. The Daily Study Bible, Edinburgh: Saint Andrew Press, 1981, 1982.

Gilbert, Maurice. ' "Soyez féconds et multipliez (Gen 1, 28)" ', *NRTh* 96 (1974): 729-42.

Ginzberg, Louis. *The Legends of the Jews*. Trans. Henrietta Szold, Philadelphia: The Jewish Publication Society of America, 1910.

Gnuse, Robert. 'Dreams and their Theological Significance in the Biblical Tradition', *CTM* 8 (1981): 166-71.

Goldingay, John. 'The Patriarchs in Scripture and History', in A.R. Millard, and D.J. Wiseman (eds.), *Essays on the Patriarchal Narratives*. Winona Lake, Indiana: Eisenbrauns, 1983.

Golka, Friedemann W. 'Die theologischen Erzählungen im Abraham-Kreis', *ZAW* 90 (1978): 186-95.

Gordis, Daniel H. 'Lies, Wives and Sisters: The Wife-Sister Motif Revisited', *Judaism* 34 (1985): 344-59.

Gordon, Cynthia. 'Hagar: A Throw-Away Character Among the Matriarchs?', in K.H. Richards (ed.), *Society of Biblical Literature 1985 Seminar Papers*. Atlanta: Scholars, 1985, pp. 271-77.

Gowan, Donald E. *When Man Becomes God. Humanism and Hybris in the Old Testament*. PTMS 6, Pittsburgh: Pickwick, 1975.

Green, Samuel G. *A Handbook to Old Testament Hebrew*. 2nd edn. London: The Religious Tract Society, 1908.

Greenberg, Moshe. *Introduction to Hebrew*. Englewood Cliffs: Prentice Hall, 1965.

Greenstein, Edward L. 'An Equivocal Reading of the Sale of Joseph', *LIBN* 2:114-25.

—'Reading Strategies and the Meaning of the Story of Joseph and his Brothers', Unpublished Paper, SBL International Meeting, Jerusalem, August 1986.

Gros Louis, Kenneth R.R. 'Abraham: I', *LIBN* 2:53-70.

—'Abraham: II', *LIBN* 2:71-84.

—'Genesis 3–11', *LIBN* 2:37-52.

Gross, Heinrich. 'Glaube und Bund—theologische Bemerkungen zu Genesis 15', in G. Braulik (ed.), *Studien zum Pentateuch. Walter Kornfeld zum 60. Geburtstag*. Vienna: Herder, 1977, pp. 25-35.

Gunkel, Hermann. *Genesis: übersetzt und erklärt*. 6th edn. Göttingen: Vandenhoeck & Ruprecht, 1964.

Gunn, David M. *The Fate of King Saul. An Interpretation of a Biblical Story*. JSOTS 14, Sheffield: JSOT Press, 1980.

Habel, Norman C. 'The Gospel Promise to Abraham', *CTM* 40 (1969): 346-55.

Harrisville, Ray A. 'God's Mercy—Tested, Promised, Done!', *Interpretation* 31 (1977): 165-78.

Hasel, Gerhard F. 'The Meaning of the Animal Rite in Genesis 15', *JSOT* 19 (1981): 61-78.

—*The Remnant: The History and Theology of the Remnant Idea from Genesis to Isaiah.* Berrien Springs, Michigan: Andrews University Press, 1974.

Hauge, Martin Ravndal. 'The Struggles of the Blessed in Estrangement. I', *StTh* 29 (1975): 1-30.

—'The Struggles of the Blessed in Estrangement. II', *StTh* 29 (1975): 113-46.

Hauser, Alan J. 'Linguistic and Thematic Links Between Genesis 4:1-16 and Genesis 2–3', *JETS* 23 (1980): 297-305.

Heaton, E.W. 'The Joseph Saga', *ExpT* 59 (1947): 134-36.

Helyer, Larry R. 'The Separation of Abram and Lot: Its Significance in the Patriarchal Narratives', *JSOT* 26 (1983): 77-88.

Hershon, Paul Isaac. *A Rabbinical Commentary on Genesis: Translated from the Judaeo-Polish, with Notes and Indices.* London: Hodder & Stoughton, 1885.

Hertz, J.H. (ed.). *The Pentateuch and Haftorahs. Hebrew Text, English Translation, with Commentary.* London: Oxford University Press, 1929.

Hopkins, David C. 'Between Promise and Fulfillment: Von Rad and the "Sacrifice of Abraham"', *BZ* 24 (1980): 180-93.

Houston, Walter. '"And let them have dominion . . .": Biblical Views of Man in Relation to the Environmental Crisis', in E.A. Livingstone (ed.), *Studia Biblica. I. Papers on Old Testament and Related Themes.* JSOTS 11, Sheffield: JSOT Press, 1979, pp. 161-84.

Humphreys, W. Lee. *Joseph and his Family: A Literary Study.* Columbia, South Carolina: University of South Carolina Press, 1988.

Hunter, Alistair G. 'Father Abraham: A Structural and Theological Study of the Yahwist's Presentation of the Abraham Material', *JSOT* 35 (1986): 3-27.

Hyman, Ronald T. 'Questions in the Joseph Story: The Effects and their Implications for Teaching', *RelEd* 79 (1984): 437-55.

Jeyaraj, B. *Land Ownership in the Pentateuch: A Thematic Study of Genesis 12 to Deuteronomy 34.* Unpublished Ph.D. Thesis, University of Sheffield, 1989.

Jobling, David. 'Myth and its Limits in Genesis 2.4b–3.24', in *The Sense of Biblical Narrative: Structural Analyses in the Hebrew Bible.* Vol. II. JSOTS 39, Sheffield: JSOT Press, 1986, pp. 17-43.

Josephus, Flavius. *Jewish Antiquities. Books I-IV.* Trans. H.St.J. Thackeray, London/Cambridge, Mass.: William Heinemann/Harvard University Press, 1930.

Joüon, Paul. *Grammaire de l'hébreu biblique.* 2nd edn. Rome: Institut Biblique Pontifical, 1947.

Kautzsch, E. (ed.). *Gesenius' Hebrew Grammar.* Trans. A.E. Cowley, Oxford: Clarendon, 1910.

Keukens, Karlheinz H. 'Der irreguläre Sterbesegen Isaaks: Bemerkungen zur Interpretation von Genesis 27, 1-45', *BN* 19 (1982): 43-56.

Kidner, Derek. *Genesis: An Introduction and Commentary.* London: Tyndale Press, 1967.

Kikawada, Isaac M. 'The Shape of Genesis 11:1-9', in J.J. Jackson and M. Kessler (eds.), *Rhetorical Criticism: Essays in Honor of James Muilenburg.* PTMS 1, Pittsburgh: Pickwick, 1974, pp. 18-32.

—'Two Notes on Eve', *JBL* 91 (1972): 33-37.

—'The Unity of Genesis 12:1-9', in A. Shinan (ed.), *Proceedings of the Sixth World Congress of Jewish Studies.* Jerusalem: Hebrew University Press, 1973, pp. 229-35.

King, J. Robin. 'The Joseph Story and Divine Politics: A Comparative Study of a Biographic Formula from the Ancient Near East', *JBL* 106 (1987): 577-94.

Klein, Jean-Paul. 'Que se passe-t-il en Genèse 18?', *PTh* 24 (1977): 75-98.

Klein, Ralph W. 'The Yahwist Looks at Abraham', *CTM* 45 (1974): 43-49.

Kline, Meredith G. 'Divine Kingship and Genesis 6:1-4', *WestThJ* 24 (1962): 187-204.

Knight, George A.F. *A Christian Theology of the Old Testament.* London: SCM, 1959.

Koch, Klaus. *The Growth of the Biblical Tradition: The Form Critical Method.* Trans. S. M. Cupitt, London: Adam & Charles Black, 1969.

—'Die Hebräer vom Auszug aus Ägypten bis zum Großreich Davids', *VT* 19 (1969): 37-81.

Kodell, Jerome. 'Jacob Wrestles with Esau (Gen 32:23-32)', *BibThBull* 10 (1980): 65-70.

Koehler, Ludwig and Walter Baumgartner. *Lexicon in Veteris Testamenti Libros.* Leiden: E.J. Brill, 1953.

Kraeling, Emil G. 'The Significance and Origin of Gen. 6:1-4', *JNES* 6 (1947): 193-208.

Kuntzmann, Raymond. 'Le symbole des jumeaux et le cycle du patriarche Jacob', *SémBib* 19 (1980): 32-39.

Lambdin, T.O. *Introduction to Biblical Hebrew.* London: Darton, Longman and Todd, 1973.

Lawlor, John I. 'The Test of Abraham: Genesis 22:1-19', *GThJ* 1 (1980): 19-35.

Lewis, Jack P. *A Study of the Interpretation of Noah and the Flood in Jewish and Christian Literature.* Leiden: E.J. Brill, 1968.

Limburg, James. 'What Does it Mean to "Have Dominion over the Earth?"', *Dialog* 10 (1971): 221-23.

Lohfink, Norbert. '"Seid fruchtbar und füllt die Erde an"', *BibKir* 30 (1975): 77-82.

Lowe, James H. (ed.). *'Rashi' on the Pentateuch: Genesis.* London: Hebrew Compendium, 1928.

Lowenthal, Eric I. *The Joseph Narrative in Genesis.* New York: Ktav Publishing House, 1973.

—Letter, *Commentary* (February, 1981): 17-18.

Luke, K. 'Isaac's Blessing: Genesis 27', *Scripture* 20 (1968): 33-41.

Lundbom, Jack R. 'Abraham and David in the Theology of the Yahwist', in C.L. Meyers (ed.), *The Word of the Lord Shall Go Forth: Essays in Honor of David Noel Freedman*. Winona Lake, Indiana: Eisenbrauns, 1983, pp. 203-209.

Maag, Viktor. 'Jakob—Esau—Edom', *ThZ* 13 (1957): 418-29.

McEvenue, Sean E. 'A Comparison of Narrative Styles in the Hagar Stories', *Semeia* 3 (1975): 64-80.

—'The Elohist at Work', *ZAW* 96 (1984): 315-32.

McGuire, Errol M. 'The Joseph Story: A Tale of Son and Father', in Burke O. Long (ed.), *Images of Man and God: Old Testament Short Stories in Literary Focus*. Sheffield: Almond Press, 1981, pp. 9-25.

Magonet, Jonathan. 'Die Söhne Abrahams', *BibLeb* 14 (1973): 204-10.

Marrs, Rick. 'The Sons of God (Genesis 6:1-4)', *RestQ* 23 (1980): 218-24.

Martin-Achard, Robert. *Actualité d'Abraham*. Neuchâtel: Delachaux et Niestlé, 1969.

Martens, E.A. *Plot and Purpose in the Old Testament*. Leicester: Inter-Varsity Press, 1981.

Matthews, Victor H. and Frances Mims. 'Jacob the Trickster and Heir of the Covenant: A Literary Interpretation', *PerRelSt* 12 (1985): 185-95.

Mauldin, F. Louis. 'Singularity and a Pattern of Sin, Punishment, and Forgiveness', *PerRelSt* 10 (1983): 41-50.

Mazor, Yair. 'Genesis 22: The Ideological Rhetoric and the Psychological Composition', *Biblica* 67 (1986): 81-88.

Meinhold, Arndt. 'Die Gattung der Josephsgeschichte und des Estherbuches: Diasporanovelle I', *ZAW* 87 (1975): 306-24.

Mendelsohn, I. 'Dream; Dreamer', *IDB* 1:868-69.

Miller, Patrick D. *Genesis 1–11: Studies in Structure and Theme*. JSOTS 8, Sheffield: JSOT Press, 1978.

Miscall, Peter D. 'The Jacob and Joseph Stories as Analogies', *JSOT* 6 (1978): 28-40.

—*The Workings of Old Testament Narrative*. Philadelphia/Chico: Fortress/Scholars, 1983.

Mitchell, John J. 'Abram's Understanding of the Lord's Covenant', *WestThJ* 32 (1969): 24-48.

Moberly, R.W.L. 'The Earliest Commentary on the Akedah', *VT* 38 (1988): 302-23.

Molina, Jean-Pierre. 'Noé et le déluge', *EThR* 55 (1980): 256-64.

Muilenburg, James. 'Abraham and the Nations: Blessing and World History', *Interpretation* 19 (1965): 387-98.

Müller, Hans-Peter. 'Imperativ und Verheißung im Alten Testament: Drei Beispiele', *EvTh* 28 (1968): 557-71.

Naidoff, Bruce D. 'A Man to Work the Soil: A New Interpretation of Genesis 2–3', *JSOT* 5 (1978): 2-14.

Neff, Robert Wilbur. 'The Birth and Election of Isaac in the Priestly Tradition', *BR* 15 (1970): 5-18.

Newman, Robert C. 'The Ancient Exegesis of Genesis 6:2, 4', *GThJ* 5 (1984): 13-36.

Ogden, Graham S. 'A Fresh Look at the "Curses" of Genesis 3:14-19', *TaiwJTh* 7 (1985): 129-40.

Patte, Daniel and Judson F. Parker. 'A Structural Exegesis of Genesis 2 and 3', *Semeia* 18 (1980): 55-75.

Peck, John. 'Note on Genesis 37:2 and Joseph's Character', *ExpT* 82 (1971): 342-43.

Peck, William Jay. 'Murder, Timing and the Ram in the Sacrifice of Isaac', *AnglThR* 58 (1976): 23-43.

Pedersen, Johannes. *Israel: Its Life and Culture*. London: Oxford University Press, 1926.

Petersen, David L. 'Genesis 6:1-4, Yahweh and the Organization of the Cosmos', *JSOT* 13 (1979): 47-64.

—'A Thrice-Told Tale: Genre, Theme, and Motif', *BR* 18 (1973): 30-43.

—'The Yahwist on the Flood', *VT* 26 (1976): 438-46.

Plöger, J.G. '*ᵃdhāmāh*', *TDOT* 1:88-98.

Polzin, Robert. ' "The Ancestress of Israel in Danger" in Danger', *Semeia* 3 (1975): 81-98.

Porter, J.R. 'The Daughters of Lot', *Folklore* 89 (1978): 127-41.

—'The Legal Aspects of the Concept of "Corporate Personality" in the Old Testament', *VT* 15 (1965): 361-80.

de Pury, Albert. *Promesse divine et légende cultuelle dans le cycle de Jacob: Genèse 28 et les traditions patriarcales*. 2 vols. Paris: Gabalda, 1975.

—'La tour de Babel et la vocation d'Abraham: Notes exégétiques', *EThR* 53 (1978): 80-97.

Rabinowitz, Isaac. 'Sarah's Wish (Gen. XXI 6-7)', *VT* 29 (1979): 362-63.

von Rad, Gerhard. 'The Form-Critical Problem of the Hexateuch', *Hexateuch*, pp. 1-78.

—*Genesis: A Commentary*. Revised edn. Trans. J.H. Marks, Philadelphia: Westminster, 1972.

—'The Joseph Narrative and Ancient Wisdom', *Hexateuch*, pp. 292-300.

—'The Promised Land and Yahweh's Land in the Hexateuch', *Hexateuch*, pp. 79-93.

Rahlfs, Alfred (ed.). *Septuaginta: Id est Vetus Testamentum graece iuxta LXX interpretes*. 2 vols. Stuttgart: Deutsche Bibelstiftung, 1935.

Ramsey, George W. 'Is Name-Giving an Act of Domination in Genesis 2:23 and Elsewhere?', *CBQ* 50 (1988): 24-35.

Redford, Donald B. *A Study of the Biblical Story of Joseph*. VTS 20, Leiden: E.J. Brill, 1970.

Rendtorff, Rolf. *Das Alte Testament: Eine Einführung*. Neukirchen: Neukirchener Verlag, 1983.

—'Genesis 8,21 und die Urgeschichte des Jahwisten', *KD* 7 (1961): 69-78.

—'Genesis 15 im Rahmen der theologischen Bearbeitung der Vätergeschichten', in R. Albertz, et al. (eds.), *Werden und Wirken des Alten Testaments: Festschrift für Claus Westermann zum 70. Geburtstag*. Göttingen/Neukirchen-Vluyn: Vandenhoeck & Ruprecht/Neukirchener Verlag, 1980, pp. 74-81.

—' "Subdue the earth": Man and Nature in the Old Testament', *ThD* 27 (1979): 213-16.

—*Das überlieferungsgeschichtliche Problem des Pentateuch.* BZAW 147, Berlin/New York: Walter de Gruyter, 1977.

Richardson, Alan. *Genesis 1–11: The Creation Stories and the Modern World View.* London: SCM, 1953.

Richter, Wolfgang. 'Das Gelübde als theologische Rahmung der Jakobsüberlieferungen', *BZ* 11 (1967): 21-52.

—'Traum und Traumdeutung im AT: Ihre Form und Verwendung', *BZ* 7 (1963): 202-20.

Rimmon-Kenan, S. *Narrative Fiction: Contemporary Poetics.* London: Methuen, 1983.

Robinson, Robert D. 'Literary Functions of the Genealogies of Genesis', *CBQ* 48 (1986): 595-608.

Rodd, C.S. ' "Shall not the judge of all the earth do what is just?" (Gen 18 25)', *ExpT* 83 (1972): 137-39.

Rogerson, J.W. *Anthropology and the Old Testament.* Oxford: Basil Blackwell, 1978.

—'Can a Doctrine of Providence be based on the Old Testament?', in Lyle Eslinger and Glen Taylor (eds.), *Ascribe to the Lord: Biblical and Other Studies in Memory of Peter C. Craigie.* JSOTS 67, Sheffield: JSOT Press, 1988, pp. 529-43.

—'The Hebrew Conception of Corporate Personality: A Re-Examination', *JTS* n.s. 21 (1970): 1-16.

Rosenbaum, M. and A.M. Silbermann (eds.). *Pentateuch with Targum Onkelos, Haphtorah and Rashi's Commentary.* New York: Hebrew Publishing Company, no date.

Rosenberg, Joel W. 'The Garden Story Forward and Backward: The Non-Narrative Dimension of Gen. 2–3', *Prooftexts* 1 (1981): 1-27.

Rowley, H.H. *The Biblical Doctrine of Election.* London: Lutterworth, 1950.

—*The Faith of Israel: Aspects of Old Testament Thought.* London: SCM, 1956.

Ruprecht, Eberhard. 'Vorgegebene Tradition und theologische Gestaltung in Genesis XII 1-3', *VT* 29 (1979): 171-88.

Sarna, Nahum M. *Understanding Genesis.* New York: Schocken, 1970.

Sasson, Jack M. ' "The Tower of Babel" as a Clue to the Redactional Structuring of the Primeval History [Gen. 1–11:9]', in G. Rendsburg et al. (eds.), *The Bible World: Essays in Honor of Cyrus H. Gordon.* New York: Ktav, 1980, pp. 211-19.

Savage, Mary. 'Literary Criticism and Biblical Studies: A Rhetorical Analysis of the Joseph Narrative', in Carl D. Evans, et al. (eds.), *Scripture in Context: Essays on the Comparative Method.* Pittsburgh: Pickwick, 1980, pp. 79-100.

Scharbert, Josef. *'brk; bᵉrākhāh', TDOT* 2:279-308.

Schiltknecht, Hans R. 'Konflikt und Versöhnung in der biblischen Erzählung von Jakob und Esau', *Reformatio* 22 (1973): 522-31.

Schmid, Hans H. *Der sogenannte Jahwist: Beobachtungen und Fragen zur Pentateuchforschung.* Zurich: Theologischer Verlag, 1976.

Scholes, Robert and Robert Kellogg. *The Nature of Narrative.* New York: Oxford University Press, 1966.

Schreiner, J. 'Segen für die Völker in der Verheißung an die Väter', *BZ* 6 (1962): 1-31.

Schwartz, Regina. 'Free Will and Character Autonomy in the Bible', *NotDEnglJ* 15 (1983): 51-74.

Seebass, Horst. 'Gen 15 2b', *ZAW* 75 (1963): 317-19.

Seybold, Donald A. 'Paradox and Symmetry in the Joseph Narrative', *LIBN* 1:159-73.

Skinner, John. *A Critical and Exegetical Commentary on Genesis*. 2nd edn. ICC, Edinburgh: T. & T. Clark, 1930.

Smith, Gary V. 'Structure and Purpose in Genesis 1–11', *JETS* 20 (1977): 307-319.

Snijders, L.A. 'Genesis XV. The Covenant with Abram', *OTS* 12 (1958): 261-79.

Speiser, E.A. *Genesis*. AB, Garden City, New York: Doubleday, 1983.

Starobinski-Safran, Esther. 'Sur le sens de l'épreuve: (Interpretations juives de Genèse 22)', *RevThPh* 114 (1982): 23-35.

Steck, Odil Hannes. 'Genesis 12 1-3 und die Urgeschichte des Jahwisten', in H.W. Wolff (ed.), *Probleme biblischer Theologie: Gerhard von Rad zum 70. Geburtstag*. München: Chr. Kaiser, 1971, pp. 525-54.

Stek, J.H. 'Dream', *ISBE* 1: 991-92.

Sternberg, Meir. *The Poetics of Biblical Narrative: Ideological Literature and the Drama of Reading*. Bloomington, Indiana: Indiana University Press, 1985.

Swindell, Anthony C. 'Abraham and Isaac: An Essay in Biblical Appropriation', *ExpT* 87 (1975): 50-53.

Terrien, Samuel. *The Elusive Presence: Toward a New Biblical Theology*. San Francisco: Harper & Row, 1978.

Thiselton, Anthony C. 'The Supposed Power of Words in the Biblical Writings', *JTS* n.s. 24 (1974): 283-99.

Thompson, Thomas L. 'Conflict Themes in the Jacob Narratives', *Semeia* 15 (1979): 15-26.

—*The Origin Tradition of Ancient Israel: I. The Literary Formation of Genesis and Exodus 1–23*. JSOTS 55, Sheffield: JSOT Press, 1987.

Trible, Phyllis. 'Eve and Adam: Genesis 2–3 Reread', in C.P. Christ and J. Plaskow (eds.), *Womanspirit Rising: A Feminist Reader in Religion*. San Francisco: Harper & Row, 1979, pp. 74-83.

Tsevat, Matitiahu. 'Hagar and the Birth of Ishmael', in *The Meaning of the Book of Job and Other Biblical Studies: Essays on the Literature and Religion of the Hebrew Bible*. New York: Ktav, 1980, pp. 53-76.

Turner, Mary Donovan. 'Rebekah: Ancestor of Faith', *LexThQ* 20 (1985): 42-49.

Unger, Merrill F. 'Some Comments on the Text of Genesis 15 2, 3', *JBL* 72 (1953): 49-50.

Van Gemeren, Willem A. 'The Sons of God in Genesis 6:1-4: An Example of Evangelical Demythologization?', *WestThJ* 43 (1981): 320-48.

Van Seters, John. *Abraham in History and Tradition*. New Haven: Yale University Press, 1975.

Victor, Peddi. *The Theme of Promise in the Patriarchal Narratives*. Unpublished Ph.D. Thesis, University of St. Andrews, 1972.

Vischer, Wilhelm. 'La réconciliation de Jacob et d'Esaü', *VC* 11 (1957): 41-51.

Vogels, Walter. 'Abraham et l'offrande de la terre', *StRel* 4 (1974-75): 51-57.

—'L'être humain appartient au sol: Gn 2,4b–3,24', *NRTh* 105 (1983): 515-34.

—*God's Universal Covenant: A Biblical Study*. Ottawa: University of Ottawa Press, 1979.

—'Lot, père des incroyants', *EglTh* 6 (1975): 139-51.

Vriezen, Th. C. 'Bemerkungen zu Genesis 12:1-7', in M.A. Beek et al. (eds.), *Symbolae F.M.T. De Liagre Böhl dedicatae*. Leiden: E.J. Brill, 1973, pp. 380-92.

Walsh, Jerome T. 'Genesis 2:4b–3:24: A Synchronic Approach', *JBL* 96 (1977): 161-77.

Waltke, Bruce K. 'Cain and His Offering', *WestThJ* 48 (1986): 363-72.

Webb, Barry G. *The Book of the Judges: An Integrated Reading*. JSOTS 46, Sheffield: JSOT Press, 1987.

Wehmeier, Gerhard. 'The Theme "Blessing for the Nations" in the Promises to the Patriarchs and in Prophetical Literature', *BangThF* 6 (1974): 1-13.

Weippert, M. 'Canaan, Conquest and Settlement of', *IDBS*: 125-30.

Wenham, Gordon J. 'The Coherence of the Flood Narrative', *VT* 28 (1978): 336-48.

—*Genesis 1–15*. WBC, Waco, Texas: Word Books, 1987.

—'The Symbolism of the Animal Rite in Genesis 15: A Response to G.F. Hasel', *JSOT* 22 (1982): 134-37.

Westermann, Claus. *Creation*. Trans. J.J. Scullion, Philadelphia: Fortress, 1974.

—*Genesis 1–11: A Commentary*. Trans. J.J. Scullion, Minneapolis: Augsburg, 1984.

—*Genesis 12–36: A Commentary*. Trans. J.J. Scullion, Minneapolis: Augsbur, 1985.

—*Genesis 37–50: A Commentary*. Trans. J.J. Scullion, Minneapolis: Augsburg, 1986.

—*The Promises to the Fathers: Studies on the Patriarchal Narratives*. Trans. D.E. Green, Philadelphia: Fortress, 1980.

White, Hugh C. 'The Initiation Legend of Isaac', *ZAW* 91 (1974): 1-30.

—'The Joseph Story: A Narrative Which "Consumes" its Content', *Semeia* 31 (1985): 49-69.

—'Word Reception as the Matrix of the Structure of the Genesis Narrative', in R. Polzin and E. Rothman (eds.), *The Biblical Mosaic: Changing Perspectives*. Philadelphia/Chico: Fortress/Scholars, 1982, pp. 61-83.

Whybray, R.N. *The Making of the Pentateuch: A Methodological Study*. JSOTS 53, Sheffield: JSOT Press, 1987.

Wifall, Walter. 'Gen 6:1-4—A Royal Davidic Myth?', *BibThBull* 5 (1975): 294-301.

Wilson, Robert R. *Genealogy and History in the Biblical World*. New Haven/London: Yale University Press, 1977.

Wolff, Hans Walter. 'The Kerygma of the Yahwist', *Interpretation* 20 (1966): 131-58.

Wyatt, Nicolas. 'When Adam Delved: The Meaning of Genesis III 23', *VT* 38 (1988): 117-22.

Yarchin, William. 'Imperative and Promise in Genesis 12:1-3', *SBTh* 10 (1980): 164-78.

Zeitlin, Solomon. 'Dreams and their Interpretation from the Biblical Period to the Tannaitic Time: An Historical Study', *JQR* 66 (1975): 1-18.

Zenger, Erich. *Die Sinaitheophanie: Untersuchungen zum jahwistischen und elohistischen Geschichtswerk*. Forschung zur Bibel, Würzburg: Echter Verlag, 1971.

Zimmerli, Walther. 'Promise and Fulfillment', trans. J. Wharton, in C. Westermann (ed.), *Essays on Old Testament Interpretation*. London: SCM, 1964, pp. 89-122.

Zucker, David Jeremy. 'Jacob in Darkness (and Light): A Study in Contrasts', *Judaism* 35 (1986): 402-13.

INDEXES

INDEX OF BIBLICAL REFERENCES

INDEX OF AUTHORS

JOURNAL FOR THE STUDY OF THE OLD TESTAMENT

Supplement Series